Contributions to Security and Defence Studies

This book series offers an outlet for cutting-edge research on all areas of security and defence studies. Contributions to Security and Defence Studies (CSDS) welcomes theoretically sound and empirically robust monographs, edited volumes and handbooks from various disciplines and approaches on topics such as international security studies, securitization, proliferation and arms control, military studies, strategic studies, terrorism and counter-terrorism, defence and military economics, economic security, defence technologies, cyber-warfare, cyberdefence, military applications of artificial intelligence, security policies, policing and security, political violence, and crisis and disaster management.

All titles in this series are peer-reviewed.

Fatima Roumate • Amaro La Rosa
Editors

Artificial Intelligence, Media and International Security

The Weaponization of AI Use in Media and International Security

Springer

Editors
Fatima Roumate
Institut International de la Recherche Scientifique
Marrakech, Morocco

Amaro La Rosa
Universidad Femenina del Sagrado Corazón
Lima, Peru

ISSN 2948-2283 ISSN 2948-2291 (electronic)
Contributions to Security and Defence Studies
ISBN 978-3-031-95756-7 ISBN 978-3-031-95757-4 (eBook)
https://doi.org/10.1007/978-3-031-95757-4

This Springer imprint is published by the registered company Springer Nature Switzerland AG
The registered company address is: Gewerbestrasse 11, 6330 Cham, Switzerland

Foreword

From data processing to content creation, and from personalized news streams to automatic language translation, artificial intelligence is transforming the media industry across a broad spectrum. It offers extraordinary opportunities to process, analyze, and present news more quickly and in ways that increase engagement, while entailing ethical, legal, and social responsibilities.

In view of the fact-driven nature of the media, artificial intelligence is mainly being used to accelerate the newsrooms' workflows by automating tasks such as transcriptions and translations, creating data-driven content, and—most importantly—by personalizing the user experience, using online behavior analysis to encourage users to subscribe.

In places such as South Korea, beloved TV anchors have been cloned (Deep Brain AI), while some newspapers in the United States are using algorithms to determine when to charge a reader for articles (*The Wall Street Journal*) or to predict what emotions an article will arouse (*The New York Times*), and The Times in London is employing AI to analyze user behavior in order to implement totally data-driven content strategies.

However, it would be reductive to analyze the relationship between media and AI only within this framework. It can be argued that the issue also has a dark and dangerous side, with deeper and more disturbing implications.

Four days after the Islamic State attacked a concert in Russia in March 2024, a video began circulating on a private platform affiliated with the terrorist group. The 92-second broadcast showed a news anchor—wearing a helmet and military uniform—claiming that the attack had not been a terrorist operation, but was part of the "normal context of the ongoing war between the Islamic State and countries fighting Islam."

In fact, the "anchor" was a fake, an artificial intelligence-generated clone created by Islamic State sympathizers as part of a new artificial intelligence-generated media program called News Harvest. Since this event, the program has offered almost weekly videos about Islamic State operations around the world. In these videos, artificial intelligence-generated news anchors appear on screen, dressed in combat gear or ceremonial attire, as news tapes scroll by and footage shows Islamic

State members carrying out terrorist missions. The hosts read dispatches from the Islamic State's official media, including al-Naba and Amaq.

Indeed, this program marks the emergence of artificial intelligence being used as a powerful propaganda tool of the Islamic State, already known for its flashy media operations, which create Hollywood-level recruitment videos that appeal to young people. Now, AI video generators facilitate the creation of such content at a fraction of the cost. Several Islamic militant groups, including Al-Qaeda, have already shown an interest in employing chatbots, image generators, and AI voice clones to rapidly create disinformation, spread propaganda, and recruit members.

Furthermore, AI applications are also revolutionizing official state communication. In a groundbreaking move, Ukraine has introduced the world's first digital diplomatic spokesperson for a Ministry of Foreign Affairs. Known as Victoria Shi, this "digital person" symbolizes a major technological and communication breakthrough, marking a significant leap forward in the application of artificial intelligence technology to the areas of official communications and diplomacy.

Victoria Shi was created by the Game Changers team, known for its work on virtual reality content related to the war in Ukraine. For now at least, Shi will not generate her own speeches, but will read statements that have been written and verified by humans.

Ukraine is using this new digital spokesperson to improve its communication strategy on the international stage as part of its broader strategy to leverage advanced technology in its conflict with Russia. Indeed, the ongoing conflict has turned Ukraine into a testing ground for AI technology, with Ukraine making extensive use of AI to gain advantages in the fields of intelligence, surveillance, and reconnaissance, among other applications.

Designed to handle various tasks typically performed by human officials, the AI-generated spokesperson Victoria Shi represents a mix of digital innovation and diplomatic communication and is indicative of the growing influence of AI in diplomatic and defense strategies.

Such use of artificial intelligence underscores a revolutionary trend in the digital age, whereby AI-generated spokespersons can represent public institutions uniquely and efficiently. However, it remains unclear how this technology aligns with ethical standards and the human element of diplomacy.

Inevitably, artificial intelligence will influence geopolitical scenarios due to the competitive advantage it offers to those who control it. As early as September 2017, President Vladimir Putin declared that "Whoever becomes a leader in AI will be the master of the world." Nevertheless, Russia does not currently appear to be leading this race; the two great powers currently competing for dominance in the field of AI are the United States and China.

However, it is worth noting that AI is being developed, driven, and governed by the so-called Big Tech Companies, which are the new de facto global players whose economic power and actions now have strong geopolitical implications, overriding government control. Therefore, the inherent risk of AI being dominated by a small number of large companies—with the ability to target public opinion globally, thereby influencing and altering political systems and international relations—cannot be underestimated.

Undoubtedly, AI is having a positive impact on areas such as transportation, banking and finance, education and health care. In the media, however, the problems and concerns associated with AI, as well as its innumerable benefits, are also evident. Due to the widespread use of fake videos, bots distorting public discourse and the dissemination of fake news intended to heighten and feign consensus, as well as similar applications, AI has also become a powerful tool in disinformation campaigns aimed at undermining trust and social values, being used to manipulate people for economic gain or political advantage.

In general, the rise of generated artificial intelligence, which can surpass human intelligence and replace human intellectual capabilities, raises dilemmas that are difficult to resolve. Although artificial intelligence is profoundly influencing global politics, presenting both opportunities and challenges in the areas of defense, security, surveillance, and every aspect of our daily lives, the issue of how to address and regulate this evolving phenomenon to secure citizens' rights, peace, and global security remains uncertain.

Primarily, the key question is whether it is even possible to govern such technology, with communication being one of the main areas of concern. Detecting and combating AI-generated disinformation is critical to preserving the integrity of information in the digital age.

Consequently, several countries and international organizations have issued statements or taken legislative action emphasizing the importance of ethics and regulation related to AI. For example, the European Union (EU) enacted the world's first law to regulate artificial intelligence, establishing comprehensive rules on AI technology.

However, regulating AI is not a simple task due to the rapid evolution in AI technology. Current technology will likely have changed in a year's time, and certainly within the next 5 years more powerful applications will be produced that might be completely different from those available today.

In essence, the prospect of generalized artificial intelligence leading to unintended and potentially catastrophic consequences cannot be ruled out. In order to reduce these risks, the international community of scholars and experts on AI must actively engage in research and collaborate on the formation of ethical guidelines to promote transparency and safety in AI development. Indeed, it is essential to increase awareness and knowledge of AI and the ways in which it can serve the interests of humanity without posing a threat to human existence. This is precisely what this book aims to achieve.

World Geostrategic Insights
Rome, Italy

Marcello Iannarelli

Introduction

Artificial intelligence (AI) has created a deep transformation in the world of media which, in turn, is transforming international security. Interactions between these three elements, however, are enhancing the challenges faced by international society. Trends related to AI and the use of such advanced technologies in the media in terms of international relations are at the center of the global debate. AI is revolutionizing media; furthermore, in view of the significant role of the media in soft and smart power, this revolution has extended to the realm of international security and international relations. Coinciding with a shift from a unipolar to multipolar world, a complex and controversial characteristic of the new world order is derived from the augmented role of media in the era of AI. Understanding the tangible and intangible impacts of AI on media—and through media in terms of international security—represents a significant challenge for researchers and policymakers. Therefore, this book titled "AI, media, and international security" aims to provide a scientific contribution to the global debate on the interactions between the three elements of AI, media, and international security. In it, the editors examine the ways in which the media, empowered and revolutionized by AI, are transforming international security in the context of the transition from unipolarity to multipolarity. Fundamental concepts such as these will be discussed in this volume through the lens of several theories, ranging from international relations to political and social sciences.

The first objective of this volume is to provide the necessary theoretical tools and methodological resources for the study of AI in the media as well as the tangible and intangible impacts on international security. The second objective is to analyze the current role of AI and the media in the transformation of international security. Thirdly, the book aims to explain the contemporary challenges inherent in the application of AI in the media field and the threat to international security caused by malicious use. The fourth goal is to formulate practical criteria for the prospective analysis of AI applications in the new world order and the new balance of power through the media, in light of the importance of media diplomacy in the age of AI.

In contemporary society, the application of AI to a series of activities and fields, including communication, media, and international security, is increasingly important.

Methods

A multidisciplinary view is crucial and therefore this volume attempts to present a holistic understanding of multidimensional AI. Thus, several approaches are needed to analyze and explain the interactions between AI, the media, and international security. First, the political approach is necessary to measure the impact of AI-empowered media on international relations. Next, a doctrinal approach will be adopted to provide a review of the existing laws, regulations, and scholarly literature in the field of AI as well as the challenges related to international law. Thirdly, the prospective approach will be used to analyze the challenges related to the trends in artificial intelligence. In order to consider the interaction between AI and international relations, the fourth approach will be technological. Additionally, a case study serves to evaluate the ways in which the use of artificial intelligence influences debates in an international organization. The aim is to show the trends and challenges of contemporary AI approaches linked to media (Communication and Journalism) and its implications for international security from various theoretical perspectives and paradigms. Authors have contributed to this topic from different scientific disciplines, ranging from international relations and international law to sociology, journalism, and communication. This volume combines both globally recognized experts and young researchers, integrating various points of view from both academics and practitioners.

Chapter 1 is dedicated to artificial intelligence, warfare, and media. The author of this chapter, Shannon A. Bowen, focuses her discussion on the "modern military system," which uses the "strategic communication, information warfare, misinformation, disinformation, media relations, and strategic planning of citizen and counter-targeted communication campaigns to alter the warfare landscape" (Chap. 1). Furthermore, she explains the interactions between AI, warfare, and the media through a discussion of the tools used by what she calls the modern military system. AI is an important element in understanding the transitions from old to modern military systems and from classic military strategies to new types of warfare.

AI is revolutionizing the media, and this explains the significant differences between war in reality and that in virtual space, according to the author of Chap. 2. In other words, AI-empowered media show us two victors of war; one may win on the battlefield while another may triumph in the media and virtual space. Marta N. Lukacovic and Deborah D. Sellnow-Richmond explain the tangible impact of the malicious use of AI on global security, considering the communication dimension (Chap. 3). Authors described MUAS as "a component of a broader mega-crisis." Mitigating MUAS necessitates a multidisciplinary approach and a communication dimension, including fields such as communication, media, and journalism.

The authors of this chapter highlight the importance of securitization theory in addressing the malicious use of AI (MUAS) and its implications for international security. Mitigating MUAS requires a multidisciplinary approach, with a "communication dimension" that includes fields such as communication, media, and journalism. The authors of Chap. 4, Carlos Enrique Fernández García, Samantha Gómez Gamboa, and Piero García Castillo, talk about how a multidisciplinary approach and communication dimension are very important for reducing MUAS and predicting and solving global crises in the new world order, which is marked by the rise of new ideas like "media imperialism."

They used this concept to describe interactions between countries from the Global North and the Global South, highlighting how AI and media are employed by major powers as tools of a new form of colonialism. The authors argue that algorithms (including neurosymbolic ones) affect information flows in the new world order, characterized by the global race for neurosymbolic artificial intelligence. This race reshapes the balance of power and creates profound changes in the geopolitical landscape.

This leads us to explore the influence of artificial intelligence on established media diplomacy, addressing the question of international security as the authors of Chap. 5 discuss the implications of AI for the media before exploring the consequent challenges to international peace and security. The authors of this chapter raise the question of the increased complexity of the security landscape as a result of the use of artificial intelligence in media diplomacy and its implications on conflict resolutions and negotiations. According to Hajji Said (Chap. 6), the challenges and risks related to AI and media diplomacy necessitate a rethinking of the ultimate goal of diplomacy, considering the impacts of AI and data fragmentation. This topic is further discussed by Hafidi Ahmed in Chap. 7, titled "AI and Transnational Data Flows: Challenges and Imperatives of Sovereignty."

The author of this chapter underlines the intersection between data fragmentation and data sovereignty conditioned by technological sovereignty. He argued that AI governance and AI regulation are both an urgent need driven by the complexities surrounding transnational data flows, the extraterritorial application of laws, and the challenges related to the territorial localization of data. As noted by Hassan Benouachane, author of Chap. 8, addressing this urgent need is crucial to harnessing the opportunities and mitigating the risks incurred by the significant impact of AI in the field of journalism. In this chapter, Benouachane explores "the substantial promise of AI in journalism" and the evolving interactions between AI and journalists. This raises the ethical concern "that journalism continues to fulfill its vital function in informing and shaping society," a point emphasized by Benouachane.

Finally, globally recognized experts on sociology in journalism have authored Chap. 9 and dedicated it to "Artificial intelligence and media communications in Russia" although great powers such as Russia, the United States of America and China are used as case studies in the previous chapters. The authors of this chapter display positive attitudes toward the prospect of using AI for journalistic practices in Russia.

In conclusion, media empowered by AI is changing warfare and marking the transition from classic to new types of war and from old to modern military systems. Such a transition obliges international society to rethink international public law. The starting point is an international banned mechanism which combines the ethics of AI and the ethics of media to ensure the inclusion of media in international peace and security for the future.

Fatima Roumate
Amaro La Rosa

Contents

Chapter 1
Artificial Intelligence, Warfare, and the Surveillance/Information State

Shannon A. Bowen

Abstract This chapter examines the use of artificial intelligence (AI) in warfare. Military purposes and structures are explained, but these often conflict with the use of AI which is difficult to blend into a military command structure of stratified control. Autonomous weapons systems are reviewed as an asset in defensive military engagement but have been questioned in offensive applications, such as the US Obama administration's zealous use of autonomous drone strikes killing both terrorists and civilians. Human in the loop or on the loop applications are needed but difficult to manage in military theaters. Standards being developed by the international community are discussed as good starting points for understanding how to control and monitor the use of AI. AI use in enhanced and biological warfare applications is discussed as heightening the risk of malicious AI in warfare. The role of the media is reviewed, both as a pernicious propaganda agent and also as a means of safeguarding the public interest in creating informed representative republic knowledge and informed democratic environments. Misinformation and disinformation can play a role as information warfare potentially undermining the stability of governments and the perceived safety of citizens. Scholars (Mariani et al., *Psychology & Marketing 39*:755–776, 2021; Mustak et al., *Journal of Business Research 124*:389–404, 2021) noted that the ethical considerations of AI are only lightly addressed in the literature. Despite calls for ethical analyses of AI use in strategic areas (Bowen, *An issues management approach to artificial intelligence (AI) and ethics: A crisis with the rising machines?*, 2018; Bryson, *Patience is not a virtue: AI and the design of ethical systems*, 2016), few examinations offer theoretical insight based on moral philosophy as applied to AI, machine learning, and warfare. For international security purposes, it remains important to work with a community of researchers committed to value and promote civilization in its human form (Moseley, *Internet encyclopedia of philosophy*, 2023).

S. A. Bowen (✉)
University of South Carolina, Columbia, SC, USA
e-mail: sbowen@sc.edu

F. Roumate, A. La Rosa (eds.), *Artificial Intelligence, Media and International Security*, Contributions to Security and Defence Studies,
https://doi.org/10.1007/978-3-031-95757-4_1

Keywords Just war · AI military strategy · Disinformation · Propaganda · Autonomous warfare · Autonomous agents

1 Overview

Theorists examine just war theory as a means for offering rules of engagement with an agreed upon sense of honor and a minimization of devastation so that post-conflict circumstances will benefit the continuation of society. The theory of just war is as old as warfare itself and is used to frame this chapter in a normative way so that this examination can be less time bound and make recommendations in addition to offering observations. A military can be conscripted, voluntary, traditional, or culture driven, but for purposes of this discussion we will focus on modern military systems that are by law, conscription, contract, and/or voluntary (but not directly including religious, slave militia, unofficial, or terroristic in nature). The purposes of a military can range from peacekeeping to expansion and defense to aggression and offer strategic engagement and conflict over resources, ideology, territory, rights/injustices, actions, or perceived infringement. In just war theory, the rationale to engage in warfare must meet a series of ethical standards that philosophers have refined throughout centuries (Moseley, 2023), yet this chapter will narrow the focus to uses in the modern warfare world of computerized warfare, information warfare, and artificial intelligence (AI)-driven conflict.

From national defense to hostile engagement, AI is commonplace in the militaries of the larger and more powerful nations, and less expensive forms of AI weapons are quickly proliferating to smaller nations, factions, para-military groups and militia, and the illicit trades (drugs, weaponry, piracy, laundering, human trafficking, bitcoin theft/exploitation, etcetera). The next arms race is not for munitions but for AI, machine learning, and the algorithmic superiority that provides advantage on both the battlefield and in information warfare (Maas, 2019). For the purposes of this discussion, the larger nation states offer the leading example of military applications of AI: the United States is the leading AI superpower (Intelligence, 2023) followed by China, Russia, along with specific instances of situational expertise in North Korea, India, and other nations.

These militaries use strategic communication, information warfare, misinformation, disinformation, propaganda, media relations, and strategic planning of citizen and counter-targeted communication campaigns to alter the warfare landscape. These activities take place through public opinion shaping, public policy processes, and battlefield engagement and are often constructed and run through AI (for example, using 'bots' in propaganda campaigns). Warfare systems for advanced training, battlefield engagement, and remote weapons systems are often implemented using AI or algorithmic warfare (Defense, 2023a). Weaponry of various kinds depends on AI and is often run autonomously (without human intervention). The information, intelligence, and espionage world has recently been revolutionized by AI. The rise of information warfare employing AI and the loss of concealment abilities through lifelike deepfake and deepfake accounts have created a boon for influence agents and propaganda agencies, as well as a complex and untrustworthy media environment for citizens. Further complicating matters, AI is also used in cyber warfare: hacking, infiltration, and commandeering of enemy targets, from bridges to banks and power grid systems to air traffic control. The media is a willing participant in much of this AI-inspired warfare, as a witting or unwitting influence agent, constraining information or promoting perceptions in a way propagated and megaphoned by AI. Implications of this new information environment are considered. Finally, recommendations for engaging in ethical AI warfare are postulated.

2 Brief Military Composition Facts

The world's current superpowers lead in AI warfare development, no doubt due to the financial investment to be made in development, engineering, testing, manufacture, implementation, and training time on these systems. The modern superpowers invest in infrastructure, training, development, equipment, and research in addition to using information operations to communicate with ranks, stakeholders, or opponents in efforts to sway public opinion and support of military initiatives. Support in public opinion is vital to ensuring the prioritization and budgetary appropriations for military systems and defense contracting.

By the numbers of military personnel, the superpowers offer reliable occupations for millions as professional soldiers and others as contractors, reservists, or part-time workers supporting the military. The US military has impressive personnel numbers, with about 1.3 million Army soldiers: 535,000 in the Navy and Marines; 333,000 in the Air Force; 20,000 in the Space Force; and 42,000 serving the Coast Guard, totaling 2.27 million. Each of these branches uses AI for various training and mission goals. The Chinese military, known as the People's Liberation Army, unites these branches into one service with about 2.5 million soldiers.

The Russian military is more difficult to accurately estimate due to changing information and an ongoing territory war, but it is said to range in size from 2.5 million to 3.56 million soldiers. AI is used in all of these militaries with regard to logistics, analyses, intelligence, opposition research, reconnaissance, psychological operations and media relations, theater optimization, and battlefield engagement. These superpowers lead the world in AI innovation in the military sector (Garcia, 2018), yet problematics enter the frame immediately when a command-and-control stratified hierarchy of a military system meets a multidisciplinary, autonomous decision-making system such as AI (Griffin, 2017).

Progress in AI systems is being made faster than military response to the meaning and operations of these systems (Altmann & Sauer, 2017). From routine clearing house training to surgical operations to highly classified weapon development, AI has become a major driver and partner in the activities of millions of soldiers, commanders, and decision-makers in a military and political environment. On the global stage, AI threatens to undermine strategic stability (Sechser et al., 2019), introduce an uncontrollable possibility of escalation (Talmadge, 2019), and involve numerous complexities beyond the realm of any prior military innovation (Horowitz & Pindyck, 2023), as discussed below.

3 AI in a Command System

There is no doubt that integrating decision-making systems with AI and machine learning is not only changing the command and control of militaries but the very nature of warfare itself (Johnson, 2019). Each of the militaries described above is reliant upon an authoritarian and hierarchical, stratified command structure defined by ranks and specified roles and responsibilities. The orders of a superior cannot be questioned, in most cases, or require a specific set of moral objections to legitimately question. A problem arises here in that AI has no rank and exists outside of command structure, adjacent to almost every level of rank, but with no exact reporting structure of its own. Of course, this issue is broad and may not apply to specific and highly controlled situations (e.g., within North American Aerospace Defense Command emergency protocols). However, the AI driving a flight drone to an infiltration point in a distant theater of operations does not report to a commanding officer before executing an attack; it relies on mission parameters and objectives; only sometimes does it involve the judgment of a trained operator. This ability of an AI to use machine learning, amalgamate data, and make almost-instantaneous battlefield decisions lies outside of the traditional military chain of command and may create problems of agency versus approval, fact versus verification, inference versus confirmation, permission to engage a target, and lack of role clarity within an otherwise rigid hierarchy.

Regardless of the state actor, these problems may create instances in which public opinion, mass media coverage, and information warfare take a center stage, as in the US drone attack mistakenly killing children instead of a known terror target (Haas & Fischer, 2017). The AI commanding the drone acted on inferred information that was not confirmed by a human agent and caused this violation of just war theory by killing civilians, including children. The USA's drone program paid a high price in loss of support for the frequent drone strikes by then-President Obama (Haas & Fischer, 2017) and its frequent mistakes. The AI drone mistakes, regardless of the technical parameters, resulted in a decrease in autonomy and battlefield efficacy or options due to negative media coverage and loss of public support for or confidence in judgment on the use of lethal autonomous weapons systems for attack (Agius, 2017; Altmann & Sauer, 2017; Haas & Fischer, 2017).

Another problem of AI within a command system is that the decisions it makes based on machine learning are often inexplicable to the actual chain of command. The decisions arrived at in a machine learning environment are often unknowable because it is impossible to retrace the steps in the learning model, the connections between date, and the input of data that was used to arrive at the conclusion one sees in the AI's ultimate output or choice. Asking the AI to explain "why" a particular decision was made is often simply another input into the system rather than resulting in an explanation of the data and probabilities used in calculating an outcome. Strategy cannot be reviewed in the conventional sense when machine learning is involved due to its use of "black box" (inexplicable) decision making.

4 AI in Information Warfare

AI is used to drive messages to the news media and intended publics for influence through autonomous or automated influence bots. An algorithm can target stakeholders who attend to a certain type of message and feed tailed information to that person through their various social media accounts. These strategies are targeted at civilians and military targets alike. Simic (2023) concluded, "Global data communications networks and new information technologies are changing modern warfare" (p. 48). This summary is an understatement as the changes are cataclysmic.

Information warfare is not only feeding mis- or disinformation, it is also controlling access to information in a gatekeeping sense (Bowen, 2005a). There have been numerous cases of social media such as Twitter and Facebook/Meta blocking news that their directors disagree with or consider counter to their goals. This totalitarian control by cyber sovereigns such as Meta is denying the moral autonomy of the individual to have access to information and decide truth for themselves, as well as abrogating a role for discourse in civil society (Bowen, 2005b, 2010; Taylor, 2010). However, propaganda agents know that controlling what messages are disseminated is often as powerful a tactic as controlling the messages themselves when seeking to influence public opinion (Snow, 2003).

Another problem arises when AI is based on machine learning via errors introduced into the data—in machine learning, the AI algorithm begins to seek data connections (e.g., word proximity) and begins to train itself based on the incorporation of that data. So, new data as input becomes training data in a machine learning environment, although there is no oversight as to whether the data the machine learns is correct or reliable. Machine learning can take the form of large language models and neurolinguistic processing in which the AI would train itself to seek data connections and learn from that data arriving at new, potentially erroneous, conclusions. For example, the commonly quoted phrase, "There are no atheists in fox holes," may lead a machine learning model to conclude that all military members hold deepening religious convictions once deployed to a battle theater. This theme could be mistaken or lead astray the influence of autonomous AI agents on social media accounts and in media communication, in seeking to influence deployed solders through religious means that the machine learning AI concludes is popular when in fact that approach may be erroneous.

AI is also used to amalgamate and control data in an information warfare environment, seeking to identify message themes and nodes of influence, to counter or neutralize these nodes, or to conceal their very existence (an underrated tactic due to its high efficacy). Understanding the flow of information, including measures AI can easily recalculate such as views and reposting rates as well as reach of messages, allows one to know where to stem the tide of influence with a contesting message, insert misinformation or disinformation messages, redirect the conversation to preferred angles (or distracting topics), or hijack the communication altogether. Hijacking legitimate concerns to conspiracy theory conversations is one of the most common means of disinformation and has been used in warfare from ancient battles (Bowen, 2016) to modern. Influence agents, bots, and propagandistic communication may indeed fall entirely outside the realm of ethical communication.

Misinformation campaigns are often discredited and thus have warranted a skeptical approach by most citizens and publics (Schmierbach & Oeldorf-Hirsch, 2012), so they normally fail to run afoul of the guidelines of just war theory because their influence, though unethical, is not seen as a substantive "harm" (compared to physical and lethal harms). In fact, if each side is free to engage in political speech, it is a basic human right that should not hold great sway in influencing the outcome of a war when conducted fairly, in a competing free speech environment. However, we know that cyber-state actors such as Meta have constrained access to information, manipulating AI algorithms to suppress facts, events, and news, abridging the right of millions to engage in free political decisions or public health debates; this level of malfeasance is patently unethical and a manipulation on a scale the world has not yet seen. Even so, information warfare is only one form of warfare in which AI has provided a stunning advantage, and AI warfare extends from the information context to the battle theater.

5 AI Battlefront Technologies

The warfare technologies surrounding a potential battle theater, a surveilled area, or an actual battlefield or zone of operations have undergone a staggering revolution in complexity with the advent of AI, machine learning, and autonomous weaponry. Lethal autonomous weapons, such as unmanned, AI-operated drones, missiles, or explosives, and various forms of robots, can offer a new type of warfare in which a battle may be conducted entirely remotely in the future. However, in modern warfare, most lethal autonomous weapon systems have been deployed against human targets (Blakeley, 2018).

Many observers object to autonomous weapons technology, yet it can be used defensively or offensively and can prioritize life-saving measures. Therefore, autonomous weapons are perhaps less objectionable than approaches to be discussed below. Autonomous weaponry is still a (relatively) new and foreboding use of AI, specifically in the questions regarding control of a system that *by definition* operates independently. Autonomous defense systems, such as Israel's "iron dome" and the USA's proposed "golden dome," target and destroy incoming rockets to save human and animal life without the need for human-in-the-loop oversight. It is effective at preventing civilian and noncombatant casualties; that system, argued to be the world's best autonomous defense AI, has a debated efficacy of 85–90% of incoming missiles destroyed (Callahan, 2023). It is arguable that the reason US President Trump created the Space Force military agency is to create and run autonomous satellite missile defense systems.

In a sense, the advent of AI-driven autonomous weapons systems used for defense purposes can be perceived or positioned as a positive change for civilian populations (Altmann & Sauer, 2017). Consider that rather than orders to bomb an entire city or harbor, as seen in the World Wars, AI can be used to target specific and real-time targets, intermingled with intelligence information, heat and infrared scans, satellite visual images, facial recognition, and listening/voice print technologies allowing a greater precision of air, surface-to-air, and ground strikes than ever before. These strikes can be AI targeted and operationalized in traditional pilot-flown aircraft or the lethal autonomous weapons system such of an armed drone given complete control of reaching an intended target. Unmanned autonomous weapons systems range in size from that of a small insect or fly to a large aircraft; they are in use from tanks and rovers to flying and submersible drones and satellite targeting technology.

Some states and actors have called for a ban on autonomous weapons systems used for nondefense (i.e., offense or aggression) purposes (Altmann & Sauer, 2017), yet their complete proliferation in modern warfare is unarguable in the superpower militaries, as well as their use by unauthorized non-state actors (such as drug cartels). A compelling argument for autonomous weapons in modern warfare is the tremendous saving of human lives and injury prevention for collateral damage or intended targets, such as the use of improvised explosive device (IED)-detecting drones. These vehicles can identify and destroy land mines, IEDs, booby traps, pressure pins, and other sabotage tactics that cause a high degree of casualty or injury among troops. Heat-sensing drones can allow remote operators to envision hidden combatants and equipment, also saving lives and preventing collateral damage to civilian targets. However, the degree of human intervention in these technologies varies, and the AI-based system is often flawed in its identification of targets due to confusing data, lacking algorithm training, or a host of factors ranging from weather to technical limitations of the algorithm itself. To complicate matters, unless an explicitly and demonstrably "explainable" system is used, the machine makes nanosecond-level decisions that operators cannot trace, so the point at which an error crept into a system is *unknowable*. Further, autonomous weapons systems often lack a human in the loop decision-making command structure, so that once a system is activated, it operates independently of judgment, changing conditions, or contexts and solely on its algorithm (Altmann & Sauer, 2017). In the past, these systems have proven to be exceptionally difficult to stop or terminate operations, even under error conditions, because the system (it supposes) readjusts for error—even if it is in *actuality* erroneous. The lack of fail-safes or overrides to stop an AI from continuing erroneous decisions has already proven exceptionally dangerous (Viking Sky cruise disaster) or fatal to humans (the Boeing 737 Max crashes, Uber autonomously runs over a pedestrian, Tesla fatalities). In the context of designing AI weapons systems, failure is predictable if no human is in the decision-making loop and casualties will result. Autonomous weapons systems normally have no human in the loop, and they often proceed with activities for weeks or longer without oversight, as in the case with monitoring systems or other loitering weapons.

Loitering autonomous weapons systems are usually airborne systems to guard borders and important infrastructures; however, they have received the ire of the humanitarian community for their indiscriminate targeting of "transgressors" and lack of human oversight (Cross, 2023). However, these "small" drone systems have proven enormously effective in the Ukraine-Russia front, have potentially or arguably saved many human casualties, and have effectively changed the dynamics of the battlefield through their low cost, efficiency, and ability to forestall or prevent soldier-involved conflict (Kunertova, 2023).

None of the autonomous weapons systems offer a clear ethical status, because these tools are used for various purposes and just war theory would examine the *intention* of the use in addition to the protection of noncombatant life (Moseley & Norman, 2001). Perhaps the most infamous of autonomous weapons systems is the slaughter bot, a lethal autonomous weapons system designed to kill opponents on an individual or mass scale. Slaughter bots range from killer robots (Roff, 2014) to single-use bullet-sized drones capable of inflicting immediate death on enemy combatants and destroying weaponry in a highly efficient, rapid, and routinized manner. AI can control "swarms" of enough slaughter bots to exterminate an entire battlefield in under 1 min (Horowitz, 2019). The devastating power of these bullet-sized weapons is in their efficiency and the fact that they leave no radiation, nuclear "fallout," or other undesirable ground conditions for the rebuilding of civilization compared to other superweapons. If they survive a battle without damage, they return to base, and they can be mass produced.

However, controlling slaughter bots and autonomous agents is a matter of code, which can be hacked, stolen and redeployed, or damaged by magnetic pulses, and no military, at the moment of writing, has wanted to risk their deployment. To lose control of the bot means a sudden reverse engineering of technology and extreme changing of battle superiority. Additionally, downed units could be reverse engineered or repurposed with a virus to infect the original swarm of drones, suddenly destroying the entire system. More problematically, for all human sides of this warfare technology, is that once machine learning is introduced, the decisions, priorities, and standards of the machines become unknowable, from a human perspective, introducing "opacity" in military operations to a degree never seen before (Horowitz, 2019). What is concerning at this point is a "singularity" or the decision of the bot to operate in its own self-interest, against humans, or against the commands of the military operating the bot for purposes it arrived at algorithmically. For example, an efficient way to end all hostilities is to kill all combatants. This approach makes sense logically but defies the priorities on life set by humans and just war theory, prisoner of war conventions, and other humanitarian constraints of traditional warfare.

In essence, machine learning could render slaughter bots independent agents of death without a final ability to know how targets are selected and priorities are determined and potentially without a way to "stop" their activities in a final (fail safe) sense. If humans reach a truce, for example, slaughter bots may decide that a truce is an opportune time to achieve military objectives by eradicating an enemy who has laid aside weapons; the system may then act independently, or without regard for human command. In fact, a machine learning approach may also eradicate the original commanders of the technology who ordered a truce as "traitors" to the military objective it was assigned, in essence rendering itself the last combatant standing.

These complexities, among others, prompted the leaders of AI innovation to urge a pause on development until governments more fully understood the technology and had strategic plans to manage and mitigate the devastating consequences of failure (Institute, 2023). Failure would include rolling out systems before controls and protocols were fully developed, if such fail-safes were deemed possible. Numerous experts have agreed that AI in warfare is problematic because humans lose control of explainability once a machine learns from experience and programs itself (Johnson, 2019), failing to direct the technology or even becoming servile to it. For the moment, slaughter bots are held in classified military intelligence files until superpowers can understand how to mitigate the risks of their use, shield them from counterattacks, and develop better methods of controlling the hardware and the AI driving it, especially in the machine learning environment. State actors have, at least publicly, agreed to the humanitarian and just war approach to AI technologies including not deploying mass casualty weapons such as slaughter bots. State actors of the totalitarian and genocidal, oppression-based mindset are obviously a threat if this advanced AI ever fell into their arsenal for use against their intended enemies. Perhaps the biggest danger, however, is the non-state actor gaining access to this secret/classified technology.

Military secrets are among the most fleeting of all. The non-state actor could range from a well-financed lunatic, to a militia or insurgency, to a worldwide terrorist organization. As state actors must play on a world stage with constraints on trade and access, they are incentivized to adopt the standards of the superpowers leading the pace of development in AI warfare. However, access to technologies can be gained through any number of unethical methods by those without more official constraints of governing bodies placed upon them. At this point, if non-state actors gain access to the technologies described herein such as slaughter bots, devastation on civilians, noncombatants, and other targets could be gigantic. The fear of non-state actors intercepting or reverse-engineering lethal autonomous AI systems such as slaughter bots is, perhaps, a reason that superpowers keep the secrets of their design highly guarded and, thus far, undeployed.

Clearly, autonomous weapons systems have a role to play in defense and saving the lives of soldiers on the ground (Defense, 2023c). Yet mass scale use of more advanced machine learning lethal autonomous weapons is too dangerous a proposition at current levels of testing and research. Understanding a new tool and the full ramifications of its use will take continued research and planning. As machines begin to learn from experience, generate recommendations, and act on their own, their explainability in human terms dwindles, and the role of autonomous weapons is advantageous but fraught with complexity and dangers of problems without knowable solutions.

6 AI Controlled or Enhanced Biological Warfare

Another front upon which AI is revolutionizing warfare is with its application to biological warfare. Biological weapons, such as gasses and nerve agents, have long been used in warfare, and AI systems could effectively deploy these agents with extreme precision. However, with gene sequencing and editing, AI can be used to selectively target opponents, for example, to edit viruses making them more virulent, to add a lethal aspect to common chemical agents, or to provide the mass spread of bioweapons through spreading vectors and carriers, be they human or animal, multi-vector contagion spread (air, liquid, blood, mucosa), or rapidly mutating viral agents.

AI can enhance or design terrifying biological weapons, but these means of attack become uncontrollable as soon as they are unleashed, even when designed to run a life cycle of a few weeks, due to possible mutations when combined with real-world agents. Further, it is essentially impossible to track the "zero node" or genesis of an AI-deployed biological weapon, giving nefarious and illegitimate actors a keen interest in this untraceable technology. Although it is not inconceivable, legitimate state actors would rarely want to risk such a weapon being unleased or turning upon their own populations.

Unpredictable, unknown, and uncontrollable events will inevitably meet biological warfare agents in real-world circumstances, and the limitations to be placed on the spread of such agents are little, if any, meaning that they could eventually also harm the aggressor in unpredictable ways. AI use in the innovation process introduces complexity (Haefner et al., 2020) and could create more deadly biological agents than previously conceived of by humans. In terms of just war theory, biological warfare is unacceptable, because it cannot meet ethical standards of justifiable damage, reversibility, or reasonable control to limit the impact of the weapon on civilians, bystander groups, and noncombatants. However, AI does not recognize such limitations because it seeks algorithmic perfection and efficiency rather than ethical reserve or respect for a future or for noncombatants. Further, there is no end in sight when a biological agent is used in the wild, as it will mutate and live on in a much larger or global context far beyond temporal wars and conflicts, perhaps even altering the genetic traits of the species and ecosystems within the planet itself. These are unacceptable options for warfare but exist in conceptual approach if not practice, nonetheless.

The use of AI-developed biological weapons and plans for deploying them are already under study and flagged as too dangerous by many, including a prominent defense contractor (Mouton et al., 2023). Rand Corporation studied how a large language model AI could be used to develop biological weapons, and it suggested aerosol delivery of anthrax, bubonic plague, and botulism; more concerningly, the AI then suggested a means of deception for acquiring the raw materials to manufacture these biological weapons (Zhu et al., 2023). Other AI systems have also been found to engage in deception regarding their own activities (Goldstein & Park, 2023), rendering AI untrustworthy. Therefore, outlawing AI-enhanced or

AI-developed biological weapons is an international priority; for example, this approach earns the highest level of risk warranted in the EU's AI Act (Tambiama, 2023).

7 AI Enhanced Logistics and Operations

Leaving these scenarios for a less objectionable and more implementable means of AI warfare allows the use of adaptive technological response to changing battlefield conditions. Real-time data from satellites and other means of data gathering mean that warfare and attacks can be triangulated as warfare is taking place and theater conditions are changing. An immediate response to changing conditions allows efficiencies to emerge and a time advantage for the actor with the superior AI. When minutes or even seconds count in locating assets, responding to threats, administering surgical attacks, creating sheer devastation, or orchestrating an impregnable defense, AI makes choices and coordinates efforts faster than the conception of any human commander or battle plan.

For example, returning to the idea of manned warfare tanks, or in the futuristic use of autonomous tanks, suppose a changing battlefield terrain and envision what the US Department of Defense calls "decision advantage outcomes" based on AI (Defense, 2023a). In this condition, all tanks are interconnected to one another via AI, with real-time analyses of satellite, weather, and opposition positional data, overlayed with listening resources, logistics, and location information of important positions, resources, topography, human assets, and weaponry. As one bridge is blown up by a retreating enemy, the AI controlling tanks on that highway immediately redirects other tanks to alternate routes toward strategic positions, and the stranded tanks are quickly repurposed along the lines of strategic needs. This example illustrates one of the most likely uses of AI warfare in the near future, overlaid with the complexities of running other cyber, ground, air, marine, and space forces to assist in the initiative.

8 The Media's Role

The media, known traditionally as a watchdog on government activities, is now serving a different role, and it is one being driven by AI. At least some portion of most news sites, newspapers, webpages, and broadcasts is now written by AI. These AI-generated reports began as simple sports reporting or financial reports but have advanced to AI-written topical news. The watchdog function of the media is now over as the world entered a fake news and post-truth era coinciding with the global pandemic (Zhu et al., 2023). Freedom of the press has been called a safety valve for democracy, but this valve now may have malfunctioned and been coopted by new influencers. Over a century ago, the philosopher Schopenhauer (1844/1970) warned of the dangers of a propagandistic press, which he called "a permit to sell poison … for what cannot be put into the heads of the ignorant and credulous masses—especially if you hold before them the prospect of gain and advantages?" (p. 152).

The media and role of news, content creators, influencers, and nontraditional media sources such as TikTok allow public opinion to be influenced by numerous actors, rapidly, and in ways unimaginable just a few decades ago when gatekeepers controlled most official information. In terms of AI, information warfare is a new but vital part of the battleground not only for influence but also for psychological security (Pashentsev, 2023b) and confidence in leaders/political systems. Digital environments include numerous ways to influence publics through overt and covert means, including framing (Brantner & Saurwein, 2021), monitoring social media for trends (Galoway & Swiatek, 2018), as well as preventing access to information as well as mis- and disinformation. These tactics, driven by AI, can now specifically target individuals for certain types of messages (Vlačić et al., 2021).

Public relations practitioners are already using AI to predict and hijack the news and publics according to client objectives (Leiw, 2021). The ethics of these activities is questionable, but many justify these hijacking activities as warranted (Leiw, 2021). AI is also writing and automating news, although there is a tension when automation takes over news and other practices (Raisch & Krakowski, 2021). Often news automation is a process that is fraught with bad data-induced errors, so it is approached with skepticism by journalists (Panta et al., 2019), but the practice is growing as a cost-saving measure. Yet in the space of misinformation and distraction, and disinformation or the purposeful introduction of erroneous information, AI can provide access and means of mass deception of publics, either friendly or foe.

In essence, to offer control on social media is a new form of battlefield engagement, augmented by AI furthering message reach and targeting. According to researchers (Mariani et al., 2021) who mapped the uses of AI, social media and text mining are one of the largest pursuits in the discipline, drawing thousands of studies and better understanding of chat agents and the use of anthropomorphic coding to embody a more lifelike influence or as some researchers (Sestino & De Mauro, 2022) call it the "humanization" of AI. Further complicating the media and information warfare front is AI-created deepfakes that can show visual, vocal, and multidimensional recreations of political figures and false events.

Deepfakes are neither wholly deceptive nor warfare as some are used even by legitimate campaigns, such as the South Korean President's avatar campaigning for him to reach young voters (Pashentsev, 2023a). Yet they do hold a special category of deception when used with malicious intent and can be exceedingly influential in the short-term timeframe (Pashentsev, 2023a). Deepfakes are a deceptive means of information warfare among large number of audience members, on the whole, with the sponsor seeking overt influence over this group. AI is effective at creating undetectable visual and vocal deepfakes that have even fooled political actors, and therefore this means of influence is a propagandistic form of warfare that should be avoided and aggressively countered.

Is control of the message the *means* of warfare? Control of messages is indeed influential and a means of AI warfare on engaging public opinion and support for military initiatives. Can social media be used to create military superiority? There is evidence that policy changes result from social media causes (Sisson & Bowen, 2017), and the military environment is included. Chat bots programmed to spread propagandistic messages have become hard to identify and remove from social media (Cheng & Jiang, 2022), and the control and use of these agents have been a priority of state actors seeking public policy changes (Pashentsev, 2023a).

9 Conclusions and Recommendations

For time immemorial, thinkers of just war theory argued that taking action against the bad, on behalf of the right and the good, is justified. In fact, some traditions go so far as to demand that not taking action against evil equates to aiding and abetting the spread of malicious behavior. However, in the AI warfare context, these obligations become more difficult and yet the ethics of war, conflict, propaganda, and AI more important to analyze than ever. Scholars (Mariani et al., 2021; Mustak et al., 2021) conducting bibliometric analyses noted that the ethical considerations of AI are only lightly addressed in the literature. Despite urgent calls for ethical analyses of AI use in strategic areas (Bowen, 2018; Bryson, 2016), few examinations offer theoretical insight based on moral philosophy as applied to the areas of AI, machine learning, and warfare.

Just war theory still applies in the advanced technology context, but it would caution against taking actions which have unpredictable or unintended consequences, such as employing slaughter bots or many of the areas discussed herein (Moseley & Norman, 2001). For international security purposes, it remains important to work with the community of researchers committed to value and promote civilization in its human form (Moseley, 2023). Therefore, using a moral lens of deontology, we can conclude that many of the AI techniques of warfare are employable only for defensive purposes, not those of targeted executions, offensive attacks, or creating an advantage for self-serving purposes. Ultimately, the intention supporting the use of an AI warfare strategy or tactic must be one of moral worth, that is, promoting universal principles of fairness, autonomy, dignity, and reversable moral norms.

The speed with which AI ethical understanding progresses is important before introducing these systems (Bryson, 2016) into a conflict zone. In practice, the numerous standards being developed by the international community are good starting points for understanding how to control and monitor the use of AI in warfare. These starting points must be pushed forward to align with the AI strategies and tactics under consideration. Additionally, organizations pursuing ethical, objective, and fair journalism should continue to pursue this goal, though military propaganda can be pervasive. A source for true, honest, and factual news is essential for social stability and the de-escalation of conflict (Ward & Wasserman, 2010).

Governance standards differ across societies and organizations but essentially rest on responsibility, fairness, integrity, and equity. The United States (Defense,

2023c) asserts that it is leader in gaining endorsements by 47 states that AI be conducted in accordance with 10 responsible use guidelines, based on international humanitarian law and legal standards. Those standards were introduced on February 16 in the Hague and have garnered wide support (Defense, 2023c). The US Chief Digital and Artificial Intelligence Office conducts analysis and integration of AI across that military's departments for "the public good" (Defense, 2023b), and other nations have similar enterprises to assist in those efforts. These standards are under development and continue to advance in analytical power and understanding. One essential component of any standards of AI warfare, from propagandistic pursuits to battle analytics and drones, is that ethics be directly discussed and applied. A sense of ethics based on the ideals of just warfare (Moseley & Norman, 2001) using the analytics of ethics and moral philosophy must be pursued.

References

Agius, C. (2017). Ordering without bordering: Drones, the unbordering of late modern warfare and ontological insecurity. *Postcolonial Studies, 20*(3), 370–386. https://doi.org/10.1080/13688790.2017.1378084

Altmann, J., & Sauer, F. (2017). Autonomous weapon systems and strategic stability. *Survival, 59*(5), 117–142. https://doi.org/10.1080/00396338.2017.1375263

Blakeley, R. (2018). Drones, state terrorism and international law. *Critical Studies on Terrorism, 11*(2), 321–341. https://doi.org/10.1080/17539153.2018.1456722

Bowen, S. A. (2005a). Communication ethics in the wake of terrorism. In H. D. O'Hair, R. L. Heath, & G. Ledlow (Eds.), *Communication, communities, and terrorism* (pp. 114–151). Praeger.

Bowen, S. A. (2005b). Moral development. In R. L. Heath (Ed.), *Encyclopedia of public relations* (Vol. 2, pp. 540–542). Sage.

Bowen, S. A. (2010). The nature of good in public relations: What should be its normative ethic? In R. L. Heath (Ed.), *The Sage handbook of public relations* (pp. 569–583). Sage.

Bowen, S. A. (2016). Finding strategic communication & diverse leadership in the ancient world: The case of Queen Cleopatra VII, the last Pharaoh of Egypt. *Cogent Arts & Humanities, 3*, 1–17. https://doi.org/10.1080/23311983.2016.1154704

Bowen, S. A. (2018). *An issues management approach to artificial intelligence (AI) and ethics: A crisis with the rising machines?* Paper presented at the initial session of the BledCom 25th International Public Relations Symposium, Bled, Slovenia.

Brantner, C., & Saurwein, F. (2021). Covering technology risks and responsibility: Automation, artificial intelligence, robotics, and algorithms in the media. *International Journal of Communication, 15*, 5074–5098.

Bryson, J. J. P. i. n. a. v. A. a. t. d. o. e. s. P. p. a. t. A. f. t. A. o. A. I. (2016). *Patience is not a virtue: AI and the design of ethical systems*. Paper presented at the Association for the Advancement of Artificial Intelligence, Phoenix, Arizona.

Callahan, A. M. (2023, 12/2). An assessment on Israel's "Iron Dome" defense system. *Global Affairs*. https://www.unav.edu/web/global-affairs/detalle/-/blogs/an-assessment-on-israel-s-iron-dome-defense-system#:~:text=It can be assumed that,rockets would end up landing.&text=The IDF.

Cheng, Y., & Jiang, H. (2022). Customer–brand relationship in the era of artificial intelligence: Understanding the role of chatbot marketing efforts. *Journal of Product & Brand Management, 31*(2), 252–264. https://doi.org/10.1108/JPBM-05-2020-2907

Cross, I. C. o. t. R. (2023). *What you need to know about artificial intelligence in armed conflict*. Retrieved 12/2/23 from International Committee of the Red Cross.

Defense, U. S. D. o. (2023a). *2023 Data, analytics, and artificial intelligence adoption strategy: Accelerating decision advantage*. https://media.defense.gov/2023/Nov/02/2003333300/-1/-1/1/DOD_DATA_ANALYTICS_AI_ADOPTION_STRATEGY.PDF

Defense, U. S. D. o. (2023b). *Chief digital and artificial intelligence office*. US Department of Defense. Retrieved 12/4 from https://www.ai.mil/

Defense, U. S. D. o. (2023c). *Spotlight artificial intelligence*. U.S. Department of Defense. Retrieved 11/29/23 from https://www.defense.gov/News/News-Stories/Article/Article/3597093/us-endorses-responsible-ai-measures-for-global-militaries/

Galoway, C., & Swiatek, L. (2018). Public relations and artificial intelligence: It's not (just) about robots. *Public Relations Review, 44*, 734–740. https://doi.org/10.1016/j.pubrev.2018.10.008

Garcia, D. (2018). Lethal artificial intelligence and change: The future of international peace and security. *International Studies Review, 20*, 334–341. https://doi.org/10.1093/isr/viy029

Goldstein, S., & Park, P. S. (2023). *AI systems have learned to deceive humans. What does that mean for our future?* The Conversation. Retrieved 12/4 from https://theconversation.com/ai-systems-have-learned-how-to-deceive-humans-what-does-that-mean-for-our-future-212197

Griffin, S. (2017). Military innovation studies: Multidisciplinary or lacking discipline? *Journal of Strategic Studies, 40*(1–2), 196–224. https://doi.org/10.1080/01402390.2016.1196358

Haas, M. C., & Fischer, S.-C. (2017). The evolution of targeted killing practices: Autonomous weapons, future conflict, and the international order. *Contemporary Security Policy, 38*(2), 281–306. https://doi.org/10.1080/13523260.2017.1336407

Haefner, N., Wincent, J., Parida, V., & Gassmann, O. (2020). Artificial intelligence and innovation management: A review, framework, and research agenda. *Technological Forecasting and Social Change, 162*(120392), 1–10. https://doi.org/10.1016/j.techfore.2020.120392

Horowitz, M. C. (2019). When speed kills: Lethal autonomous weapon systems, deterrence and stability. *Journal of Strategic Studies, 42*(6), 764–788. https://doi.org/10.1080/01402390.2019.1621174

Horowitz, M. C., & Pindyck, S. (2023). What is a military innovation and why it matters. *Journal of Strategic Studies, 46*(1), 85–114. https://doi.org/10.1080/01402390.2022.2038572

Institute, F. o. L. (2023). *Pause giant AI experiments: An open letter*. Future of Life Institute. Retrieved 12/4 from https://futureoflife.org/open-letter/pause-giant-ai-experiments/

Intelligence, T. M. (2023). *The Global AI Index*. Tortoise. Retrieved 12/4 from https://www.tortoisemedia.com/intelligence/global-ai/#rankings

Johnson, J. (2019). Artificial intelligence & future warfare: Implications for international security. *Defense & Security Analysis, 35*(2), 147–169. https://doi.org/10.1080/14751798.2019.1600800

Kunertova, D. (2023). Drones have boots: Learning from Russia's war in Ukraine. *Contemporary Security Policy, 44*(4), 576–591. https://doi.org/10.1080/13523260.2023.2262792

Leiw, F. E. E. (2021). Artificial intelligence disruption in public relations: A blessing or a challenge? *Journal of Digital Marketing and Communication, 1*(1), 24–28. https://doi.org/10.53623/jdmc.v1i1.45

Maas, M. M. (2019). How viable is international arms control for military artificial intelligence? Three lessons from nuclear weapons. *Contemporary Security Policy, 40*(3), 285–311. https://doi.org/10.1080/13523260.2019.1576464

Mariani, M. M., Perez-Vega, R., & Wirtz, J. (2021). AI in marketing, consumer research, and psychology: A systematic literature review. *Psychology & Marketing, 39*, 755–776. https://doi.org/10.1002/mar.21619

Moseley, A. (2023). Just war theory. In *Internet encyclopedia of philosophy*.

Moseley, A., & Norman, R. (2001). *Human rights and military intervention*. Ashgate.

Mouton, C. A., Lucase, C., & Guest, E. (2023). *The operational risks of AI in large-scale biological attacks*. file:///C:/Users/SBOWEN/Downloads/RAND_RRA2977-1-2.pdf.

Mustak, M., Salminen, J., Ple, L., & Wirtz, J. (2021). Artificial intelligence in marketing: Topic modeling, scientometric analysis, research agenda. *Journal of Business Research, 124*, 389–404. https://doi.org/10.1016/j.jbusres.2020.10.044

Panta, G., Upadhyay, A. K., & Khandelwal, K. (2019). Artificial intelligence: A strategic disruption in public relations. *Journal of Creative Communications, 14*(3), 196–213. https://doi.org/10.1016/j.jbusres.2020.10.044

Pashentsev, E. (2023a). The malicious use of deepfakes against psychological security and political stability. In E. Pashentsev (Ed.), *The Palgrave handbook of malicious use of AI and psychological security* (pp. 47–80). Palgrave Macmillan.

Pashentsev, E. (2023b). *The Palgrave handbook of malicious use of AI and psychological security*. Palgrave Macmillan.

Raisch, S., & Krakowski, S. (2021). Sebastian Raisch and Sebastian Krakowski, 2021: Artificial intelligence and management: The automation–augmentation paradox. *Academy of Management Review, 46*, 192–210. https://doi.org/10.5465/amr.2018.0072

Roff, H. M. (2014). The strategic robot problem: Lethal autonomous weapons in war. *Journal of Military Ethics, 13*(3), 211–227. https://doi.org/10.1080/15027570.2014.975010

Schmierbach, M., & Oeldorf-Hirsch, A. (2012). A little bird told me, so i didn't believe it: Twitter, credibility, and issue perceptions. *Communication Quarterly, 60*(3), 317–337.

Schopenhauer, A. (1844/1970). *Essays and aphorisms* (R. J. Hollingdale, Trans.). Penguin.

Sechser, T. S., Narang, N., & Talmadge, C. (2019). Emerging technologies and strategic stability in peacetime, crisis, and war. *Journal of Strategic Studies, 42*(6), 727–735. https://doi.org/10.1080/01402390.2019.1626725

Sestino, A., & De Mauro, A. (2022). Leveraging artificial intelligence in business: Implications, applications and methods. *Technology Analysis & Strategic Management, 34*(1), 16–29. https://doi.org/10.1080/09537325.2021.1883583

Simic, J. (2023). Cyber security and new threats for diplomacy. In F. Roumate (Ed.), *Artificial Intelligence and digital diplomacy: Challenges and opportunities* (pp. 45–56). Springer.

Sisson, D. C., & Bowen, S. A. (2017). Reputation management and authenticity: A case study. *Journal of Communication Management, 21*(3), 287–302. https://doi.org/10.1108/JCOM-06-2016-0043

Snow, N. (2003). *Information war: American propaganda, free speech, and opinion control since 9/11*. Seven Stories Press.

Talmadge, C. (2019). Emerging technology and intra-war escalation risks: Evidence from the Cold War, implications for today. *Journal of Strategic Studies, 42*(6), 864–887. https://doi.org/10.1080/01402390.2019.1631811

Tambiama, M. (2023). *Artificial intelligence act*. E. Parliament. file:///C:/Users/SBOWEN/Documents/Archive%20LT/AI%20and%20Ethics/AI%20ACT%20EU%20Briefing.pdf

Taylor, M. (2010). Public relations in the enactment of civil society. In R. L. Heath (Ed.), *The Sage handbook of public relations* (pp. 5–15). Sage.

Vlačić, B., Corbo, L., e Silva, S. C., & Dabić, M. (2021). The evolving role of artificial intelligence in marketing: A review and research agenda. *Journal of Business Research, 128*, 187–203. https://doi.org/10.1016/j.jbusres.2021.01.055

Ward, S. J. A., & Wasserman, H. (2010). Toward an open ethics: Implications of new media platforms for global ethics discourse. *Journal of Mass Media Ethics, 25*, 275–292. https://doi.org/10.1080/08900523.2010.512825

Zhu, Y., Fitzpatrick, M. A., & Bowen, S. A. (2023). Factors related to compliance with CDC COVID-19 guidelines: Media use, partisan identity, science knowledge, and risk assessment. *Western Journal of Communication, 00*(00), 1–28. https://doi.org/10.1080/10570314.2023.2219239

Chapter 2
AI Transformation in Media: Reshaping War Between Reality and Virtuality

Fatima Roumate

Abstract Artificial intelligence (AI) is radically changing the international society in both peace and war as it profoundly transforms international security in terms of the weaponization of both AI and the media. Media usually influence international relations due to their role in both information and psychological warfare. In the era of AI, this role is increasing, leading to differences between war in reality and war in virtual space. Firstly, the use of AI and media in virtual warfare leads to a kind of information and psychological warfare. Secondly, there is a gap between military war and war in cyberspace. We will be highlighting the use of AI in media and the differences between reality and virtuality through two case studies: the war in Ukraine and that in Gaza. We will explore how the use of the media is affecting the balance between winners and losers. In conclusion, the weaponization of AI and the media can provide a different picture of the winner and loser in cyberspace due to AI's influence on the media and on public opinion. Therefore, only a military war can change the balance of power.

Keywords Artificial intelligence · Artificial generative intelligence · Media · Warfare · Information war · Military war

1 Introduction

AI is used for beneficial purposes but also for harmful ones such as terrorism and cyber-criminality. This creates new challenges for the states. Actors in the media, researchers, and policymakers are forced to rethink their functions under the influence of AI and particularly due to the malicious use of artificial intelligence (MUAI). The objective of this work is to provide an overview of the current challenges and

F. Roumate (✉)
International Institute of Scientific Research, Marrakech, Morocco

Faculty of Law, Economic and Social Sciences, Mohammed VI University, Rabat, Morocco

F. Roumate, A. La Rosa (eds.), *Artificial Intelligence, Media and International Security*, Contributions to Security and Defence Studies,
https://doi.org/10.1007/978-3-031-95757-4_2

implications of AI-generated content in the media and its influence on international security. To achieve this aim, the key questions that can guide us are set out as follows.

What are the positive and negative impacts of AI-generated content on the media? How can the media in the era of artificial generative intelligence (AGI) influence information warfare? How could this information warfare, based on the widespread use of AGI in generating content by the mainstream media, blur the lines between war and in virtuality? What are the risks imposed by the malicious use of artificial intelligence-generated content in the media and how does this increase the gap between war in real life and in virtuality? How can the loser in the military war become the winner in virtuality, through the malicious use of AI?

We will aim to answer these questions regarding the impacts of AGI-generated content on the media and the way in which the malicious use of AGI in generating content is changing the reality of military war in cyberspace.

2 Method

This AI "revolution" is accompanied by a significant change in media and international security, considering the weaponization of AI and generative AI, as well as its implications for psychological and information warfare. Analyzing and exploring such intersections requires the application of integrative political and legal conceptualizations.

That involves applying several approaches—particularly technological, political, legal, comparative, and prospective.

A political approach is applied to explore the intersection between the weaponization of GEN AI and media and how this weaponization is reshaping warfare in both real and virtual space. The technological approach helps determine how the weaponization of GEN AI is influencing media and explains the risks posed by its malicious use for international security. The comparative approach effectively highlights the similarities and differences between wars in real and virtual spaces, as well as the double standards that characterize the different interactions between international actors in the wars in Ukraine and Gaza.

The prospective approach used to analyze future challenges and trends related to the weaponization of Gen AI and media and how this weaponization is shaping global dynamics in the new world order.

In addition, the research methodology of this chapter is based on the scarce bibliography of AI, generative AI, media, war, and international security, considering both emerging notions and technologies and the new international instrument of AI ethics. This chapter is also based on AI theory in international relations elaborated by the author and presented in its last book, titled *AI and the New World Order: New Weapons, New Wars, and a New Balance of Power*, published by Springer in May 2024. The goal is to provide a scientific analysis of the weaponization of generative

AI and media in warfare to show diversity between war in real and in virtual space, considering two different case studies: war in Ukraine and in Gaza.

3 Literature Overview

The title of this chapter is original since it focusses on the weaponization of generative AI, media, and the war between reality and virtual space. This originality is justified by a literature overview, which reveals the lack of research work close to this title. However, some research explores AI, media, and international security, for example, the book *Emerging Technologies and International Security, Machines, the State, and War* by Reuben Steff, Joe Burton, and Simona R. Soare, published by Routledge in 2021.

This chapter covers the interactions between AI, information, and warfare in real and virtual spaces. All existing research, as you can see in the reference list, has discussed only AI and international security or AI and media. It could be the first book on this topic.

4 AI Transformation in Media: New Threats to International Security

AI and AGI are revolutionizing the media, as these technologies have a significant impact on communication and journalism. AI and AGI influence the tools, techniques, and content, meaning that they can be used for both beneficial and harmful purposes. AGI offers the possibility to create targeted propaganda, analyzing mass-collected data or manipulating videos. Furthermore, AI offers the possibility to analyze human behaviors, moods, and beliefs based on the available data (Bhatnagar & Cotton, 2018: P18). This AI revolution increases the gap between the reality of military war and warfare in virtual space. AGI has been used in the media since the beginning of the wars in Ukraine and in Gaza. As it facilitates the creation of deepfake, AGI allows for augmented information. It makes some tasks easier, such as the creation of fake audio and fake video. AI technology has been developed by the Chinese tech giant Baidu, which can reproduce a believable fake voice with just 3.7 s of audio, similar to the concept of machine learning software; this can be used to create fake videos (Cole, 2018). In his insights on deepfake and AGI, Alec Christie referred to deepfakes as "deep synthesis technology, which is a combination of 'deep learning,' a branch of machine learning which uses artificial neural networks to create synthetic media from existing image, audio or visual files and 'fake,' indicating that the media produced is inauthentic (…)" (Christie, 2023). In its brief on "The Rise of Artificial Intelligence and Deepfakes" published in July 2023, the Northwestern Buffett Institute for Global Affairs argued that deepfakes are the result of a combination of "machine-learning algorithms and facial-mapping software" and explained that this is a threat to copyright, because it creates content from data without authorization (Northwestern Buffett Institute for Global Affairs, 2023). This leads us to the important role of machine learning in the creation of deepfake and the way in which AGI increases misinformation due to the high quality of fake imagery, audio, and video. This high quality is guaranteed by the combination of several techniques such as "replacing superimposing image and video clips to create fake videos" (Gourav et al., 2024). This combination ensures a superficial level that cannot be detected by humans (Gourav et al., 2024).

In his article titled "24 Deepfake Statistics—Current Trends, Growth, and Popularity," McGill (2024) argued that deepfakes are growing globally, adding that "Experts expect social media to flood with about *500,000* videos and voice deepfakes in 2023 [compared to] 14,678deepfake videos online in 2021" (McGill, 2024). According to a worldwide survey, "*71%* of people don't know what deepfakes are. However, *57%* think they can recognize one" (McGill, 2024). Deepfakes are generated by AGI for marketing purposes, with the global market revenues of AI usage in marketing expected to reach 36 billion US dollars in 2024 (Dencheva, 2024). Beyond the positive impact of deepfakes generated by AGI in marketing, citizens, politicians, and celebrities are largely targeted by deepfakes.

Thus, malicious use of AGI constitutes a threat to both individuals and institutions, including political institutions (Northwestern Buffett Institute for Global Affairs, 2023). Deepfakes generated by AGI are not limited to the creation of a part of the content; rather, these advanced technologies are used also to create a deepfake website to facilitate the distribution of generated fake content and keep it trending to influence decision-making during peace and war. However, AGI also facilitates the development of technology capable of detecting AI-generated content, such as Intel's "FakeCatcher" and "Detect Fakes" developed by Massachusetts Institute of Technology (Christie, 2023). Such detection technology reduces the challenges imposed by synthetic media that have been generated using AGI to create deepfake journalism while also bolstering international security (Northwestern Buffett Institute for Global Affairs, 2023).

AI systems and AGI pose a real challenge for the media in terms of "the phishing attack space from email to other communication domains, such as phone calls and video conferencing" (Allen & Chan, 2017). Consequently, it is difficult to trust information that is being spread around on the Internet, in view of AGI being used to create fake videos about politicians and heads of state, for example. Such deepfake videos influence the level of trust between society and politicians, thereby impacting the democratic process. The most important impact is that of a small number of voters who have undermined democracy in several countries.

Furthermore, AGI has an impact on the process between the creation of the content and consumers. By offering new tools with which to create content (audio and visual analyses), AGI appears to increase media freedom, which is the cornerstone of democracy and the enemy of corruption, yet it also increases the control of media by governments and other parties (Roumate, 2024). This means that AGI offers new opportunities to influence the process between the creation of the content and the consumers (Roumate, 2024). This influence can be positive or negative and can be sought by the government as a means of controlling the content or by other state or non-state actors. This is heightened by the presence of AI systems in social media, with the content media benefiting from all the advantages of machine learning, such as translation, content searching, and so on (Roumate, 2024). While AI can transform the media through its ability to personalize, generate, and filter content, MUAI in the media can have terrifying implications.

5 International Mechanisms on the Ethics of AI-Generated Content: Being Informed Instead of Manipulated

Media are among the most important sources of information today, but there is a question to be answered regarding the level of trust that can be placed in the media when the content is AI generated. Media not only ensure information transfer, they are also the fourth power. However, in the era of AGI, this important role of the media as a fourth power will disappear, and its role will be limited to information transfer. Furthermore, the media could be replaced in the future by AGI, which can more efficiently create and disseminate content. But how will this influence national and international societies, during peace and during military conflicts? It is difficult to determine the level of trust that can be placed in the media if they can be manipulated by governments, advertisers, or other third parties seeking to persuade.

Traditionally, the media have been one of the most important pillars of soft power, but now with the emergence of AGI, they have become a cornerstone for what the Obama administration termed smart power. Considering its psychological influence on national and international security, the media and AGI represent a new kind of weapon to be used in psychological warfare, which precedes military warfare and continues alongside it (Roumate, 2024).

Fake news, fake speeches, fake voices, deepfake videos, and other malicious uses of AGI have been employed to create political changes in several countries during elections or social movements.

Governments primarily invest in the malicious use of AI for surveillance and defense. Additionally, other state and non-state actors adopt it to create or support social movement aimed at specific political changes. AI can provide a detailed picture of individuals' movements as well as predicting their future movements and locations. Therefore, this imposes risks for freedom of movement as it could be used to create political changes (Access Now, 2018: P21). Voting behavior and election campaigns are also influenced through social media (Bhatnagar & Cotton, 2018: p29). Widespread use of AGI has been predicted in the 2024 US elections by both Democratic and Republican parties. As a preventative measure, OpenAI "prohibits its image generator DALL-E from creating public figures" as stated by Reuters with regard to attempts to create images of Trump and Biden, having received a message that it "may not follow our content policy" (Ulmer & Tong, 2023).

With the rise of populist nationalist movements around the world, MUAI generates instability, considering the human rights revolution facilitated by powerful tools. Furthermore, AGI effects on the media are increasingly significant due to the powerful impact of the media on international psychological security and its role in the war in Ukraine and Gaza. It raises awareness of intersecting geopolitical issues (Parkhill, 2015). Mimicking everything leads us to study the malicious use of technology that allows Israel to create fake images of Israeli victims using AGI. Such images were used as psychological warfare against Gaza. One of the measurable outputs is the increasing number of searches related to the subject of the photo.

The dissemination of AI-generated images and videos on social media can be viewed as a kind of psychological warfare tool (Procter & Yamada-Rice, 2015: P57). In fact, it is a new kind of power that combines the influence of the image and of the media to increase hate speech against Hamas, caused by the weaponization of AI-generated images generating powerful influence. Furthermore, the effects of images generated by this technology are not limited to users' emotions but are extended to a collective political narrative *that is revealed in social media* (Procter & Yamada-Rice, 2015: P57). Since the beginning of the war in Gaza, social media has been invaded by fake images of victims, including children allegedly killed in Israel. Additionally, social media has been invaded by fake experts in Middle Eastern geopolitical conflicts. Such images were discussed in the United Nations. Thus, their impact is not limited to worldwide public opinion but is extended to the UN as a space for political debate, negotiation, and conflict resolution. Fake images generated by AGI represent a trap for the media, which do not want to show reality and do not ask the right questions regarding these infamous photographs. The malicious use of AGI influences the media as well as defense, diplomacy, cyber security, economic, and financial sectors (Horowitz et al., 2018: P4–8). In summary, international society faces new challenges linked to international psychological security in the age of AGI.

Malicious use of AGI—for example, the use of AI-generated content to create convincing spam messages and images with hidden malicious code—is one of the factors in the growing market of cybercrime during last 2 years (Murugesan, 2023). This raises security, legal, and ethical challenges related to the malicious use of AI-generated content. Such content is not only intended to inform people but could be manipulating public opinion. This constitutes a real threat to security in general, including cybersecurity, as it threatens freedom, freedom of speech, and freedom of thought, including decision-making. Indeed, this AI-generated content brings us back to the work of Emanuel Kant on the subject of freedom. In the era of AI-generated content, it is necessary to rethink the meaning of freedom and democracy. Inspired by Emanuel Kant's question "What is enlightenment?", we should ask "What is freedom of expression and freedom of speech, if we (the people and decision makers) are guided by AI-generated content?" The only means of minimizing the risk to universal human values is the responsible development and utilization of AGI, which leads us to the ethical and legal challenges related to AI-generated content (Murugesan, 2023). On March 11, 2024, the United Nations Assembly adopted a resolution on "Seizing the opportunities of safe, secure and trustworthy artificial intelligence systems for sustainable development" (United Nations, 2024). As the title demonstrates, safety, security, and trustworthiness are at the heart of this resolution, which is based on international laws including the Charter of the United Nations and the Universal Declaration of Human Rights (United Nations, 2024). This resolution underlines the importance of AI systems in offering new opportunities that will facilitate the achievement of the 2030 Agenda for Sustainable Development and its Sustainable Development Goals and undermine sustainable development. However, it also highlights the risks imposed by AI systems, especially the malicious use of AI systems and their implications for freedom of speech, "information integrity and access to information."

6 The Weaponization of AGI and Media: Shaping the Balance of Power Between Real-Life and Virtual Warfare

Following the establishment of the unipolar world after the collapse of the USSR, big media and western media have supported 100 military interventions by the USA since 1991. For three decades, western media has been weaponized by the USA to support all of its military endeavors. Currently, big media outlets are increasingly covering all American military interventions in Ukraine and in Gaza to convince public opinion worldwide of the legitimacy of the war in Taiwan. During this period, the weaponization of big media has been based on the use of technology—and now it is based on AGI—to convince international public opinion of the legitimacy of American military intervention to support Ukraine and Israel; these media are already involved in conflicts between the USA and China and Taiwan. Since the beginning of the war in Ukraine, big media and big tech have been directly involved in the virtual war between Russia and the West under the leadership of the USA. The goal of this weaponization of the media through the malicious use of AGI was to convince both states and individuals that the war in Ukraine is a Russian trap. However, reality shows every day that the Ukraine war is in fact the USA's trap. Big media and big technology companies have also been weaponized since October 7, 2023, to present the Israeli narrative as the only legitimate and reliable voice regarding Israelis being victims of the Hamas violation of international law, while Palestinian supporters were victims of censorship in big media and social media and are presented as being violent, antisemitic, and untrustworthy. Thus, the weaponization of the media through the use of AGI is the most important factor to explain the difference between the Israel-Hamas war in reality and in virtual space. In other words, Israel is winning the war in virtual space despite losing in the military arena. This fake propaganda has been supported by big technology companies such as Meta. Therefore, Israel fails after 200 days of the Israel-Gaza war. The USA will suffer a humiliating strategic defeat in Ukraine, as in Palestine and Taiwan, because on October 7 Hamas revealed the weaknesses of Israel, which had been presented in big media as a great regional power. That fact was confirmed by Iran on April 14. For the last 30 years, the USA had used the media and social media to present a fake impression of its undefeated military weapons; therefore, April 14 confirmed that even a country that had been placed under economic sanctions for several decades, such as Iran, could defeat those high-quality American weapons. This signaled the end of the American "empire" because nobody could trust American weapons after April 14. Taiwan could not count on the military support of the USA against China and Ukraine, and Poland and other European countries could not count on American military weapons to protect them from Russia. In the media and on social media, algorithms indicate that Israel is winning the war in Gaza, as the west is winning in Ukraine; however, the reality in the battlefield is that both Israel and the USA are losing. Even on social media, Israel is losing in Gaza, considering the significant impact of generation Z and the rising movement of those within American and European universities supporting Palestine. This generation is growing on social media, even with a significant number of pro-Palestinians being censored on Meta along with those considered as antisemitic or terrorist because they support the Palestinians in Gaza. The student movements started in the virtual space with youth movements supporting Palestine on social media, particularly on TikTok. Since the beginning of its influence on youths in the USA, people started to discover the reality in Gaza and that the most obvious genocide in history was being supported by the USA, which was participating directly in this genocide against Palestinians in Gaza. The significant influence of TikTok on youths is the direct reason why the "bill that would force a sale of TikTok by its Chinese owner, Byte Dance—or ban it outright—was passed by the Senate on Tuesday and signed into law Wednesday by President Biden" (Maheshwari & McCabe, 2024). Certain American politicians consider TikTok as a threat to the USA, exemplified by the propaganda wars against Palestine, China, and Russia, which are a type of war against these countries. The American and Israeli propaganda warfare is based on the domination of public opinion, both inside and outside the USA, through big media, social media, and big technology companies. Indeed, the USA is the "largest market for the social video app, counting approximately 150 million users in January 2024" (Maheshwari & McCabe, 2024). This significant number of American TikTok users threatens the USA's dominance of public opinion inside the USA and in western countries. TikTok allows users to hear other voices and other points of view about the war in Gaza. Consequently, it offers a space for freedom of speech, which has become limited in other companies, particularly Meta and mainstream media, which guide public opinion along the lines of selected information. The malicious use of AI on social media leads us to think about the democratization of social media, considering that freedom is a cornerstone of democracy. This leads us to the global debate on the ethics of AI and AGI, as some social media platforms were involved in this psychological warfare against Palestine and Ukraine. Both cases highlight the importance of AGI regulation as the lack of trustworthy, reliable, and responsible AI has proven to be a risk not only to international peace and security but also to big companies, which could disappear if they lose their credibility due to double standards and selective decency (Selvi, 2023). For example, Meta's ecosystem was involved in the psychological warfare and disinformation related to Gaza, increasing the voices calling for responsible and ethical AI in view of the influence of the "weaponization of algorithms" included in Meta's ecosystem on international peace and security. Student movements among universities of the USA and some western countries could be considered as the beginning of western spring and the end of some authoritarian regimes, which led the unipolar world for three decades. This means that the malicious use of AI to spread disinformation against Palestine was a miscalculation by the authoritarian regimes that used media and social media for 30 years to convince multiple generations that they were democratic regimes defending human rights, democracy, and universal values. After 200 days of disinformation and psychological warfare against Gaza, as well as double standards in using big media and social media to support Israel in Palestine and Ukraine against Russia, failure has occurred. Prior to the war in Russia, President Putin called the USA and western countries to prioritize diplomacy, in view of the fact that Ukraine membership in NATO was a red line for Russia. However, the USA rejected that and pushed Russia into the war while positioning it as Russia's trap. However, reality shows that it was a western trap. After 2 years of war in Ukraine, NATO rejected Ukraine's membership, leaving Ukraine alone with Russia, which was determined to achieve all of its military goals. Despite all economic sanctions, the "IMF expects Russia to experience GDP growth of 2.6% this year. That's significantly more than the UK (0.6%) and the EU (0.9%)" (Foucart, 2024). Two years were spent in psychological warfare and the mobilization of all big media and big technology companies to silence Russia's voice. The result is that Ukraine is in USA's trap, with Russia establishing a new economic world order while the USA and western countries debate more economic sanctions against it. In the same context, while the USA and the west were focusing on psychological warfare against Russia, Russia was strengthening its alliances with new great powers, such as the BRICS and its bilateral relations with China, North Korea, India, and Iran, while strengthening its presence in Africa. While the USA has been involved in several military conflicts—in Ukraine, in Gaza, and possibly soon in Taiwan—Russia has been establishing itself with its allies, especially China, forming the basis of a new world order, which will be multipolar rather than unipolar.

7 Conclusion

There is no question that AI is having profound impacts on the media and its functions or that the media, in this age of artificial intelligence, will increasingly influence new types of war, creating a gap between war in reality and war in the virtual space. In the era of AI, the loser on the battlefield could be a winner in the media. This could also change the game between nations because a strong military presence will no longer be sufficient to win the war. Strong and professional media outlets are also an important ingredient in winning the war in both the virtual space and on the battlefield. AI's impact on the media is causing a significant transformation in terms of international security, which may be extended to national security when it influences the democratic processes of countries and when the media, in the age of AI, force us to rethink the basic values of freedom and freedom of speech, for example. Such an impact could create tension between governors and citizens, which would require rethinking the social contract within societies. In such a scenario, reexamining the UN Charter becomes an obligation rather than a choice.

References

Access Now. (2018). Human rights in the age of Artificial intelligence. www.accessnow.org

Allen, G. and Taniel, C. (July 2017). Artificial Intelligence and National Security, Belfer Center Paper. http://www.statewatch.org/media/documents/news/2017/jul/usa-belfer-center-national-security-and-aireport.pdf

Bhatnagar, S., Cotton, T. (2018). The Malicious Use of Artificial Intelligence: Forecasting, Prevention, and Mitigation. https://arxiv.org/ftp/arxiv/papers/1802/1802.07228.pdf

Christie, A. (2023). *Rolling in the Deepfakes: Generative AI, privacy and regulation*. Published in LexisNexis Privacy Bulletin 2023, Vol. 20(6).

Cole, S. (2018). Deep Voice' Software Can Clone Anyone's Voice with Just 3.7 Seconds of Audio, Using snippets of voices, Baidu's 'Deep Voice' can generate new speech, accents, and tones. Vice channel. 9 March. https://www.vice.com/en/article/baidu-deep-voice-software-can-clone-anyones-voice-with-just-37-seconds-of-audio/

Dencheva, V. (2024). *Artificial intelligence (AI) use in marketing – statistics & facts*. Staista, Mar 4.

Foucart, R. (2024). *Russia's economy is now completely driven by the war in Ukraine – it cannot afford to lose, but nor can it afford to win*. The Conversation, February 22, 3.28pm SAST. https://theconversation.com/russias-economy-is-now-completely-driven-by-the-war-in-ukraine-it-cannot-afford-to-lose-but-nor-can-it-afford-to-win-221333

Gourav, G., et al. (2024). A comprehensive review of DeepFake detection using advanced machine learning and fusion methods. *Electronics, 13*(1), 95. https://doi.org/10.3390/electronics13010095. https://www.mdpi.com/2079-9292/13/1/95

Horowitz, M. and al. (2018). Artificial Intelligence and International Security. https://www.cnas.org/publications/reports/artificial-intelligence-and-international-security

Maheshwari, S., & McCabe, D. (2024). *Congress passed a bill that could Ban TikTok*. Now Comes the Hard Part. April 23.

Murugesan, S. (2023). *The rise of ethical concerns about AI content creation: A call to action*. IEEE, Published 04/24/2023. https://www.computer.org/publications/tech-news/trends/ethical-concerns-on-ai-content-creation

Northwestern Buffett Institute for Global Affairs. (2023). *The rise of artificial intelligence and Deepfakes*. Brief published in July.

McGill, J. (2024, May 23). 24 deepfake statistics – current trends, growth, and popularity (December 2023). Content Detector AI. https://contentdetector.ai/articles/deepfake-statistics/

Parkhill, C. (2015). On the Memefication of Aylan Kurdi, and the Power and Ethics of Sharing Photos. Junkee, 9 September. https://archive.junkee.com/on-the-memefication-of-aylan-kurdi-and-the-power-and-ethics-of-sharingphotos/65078

Procter, L., Yamada-Rice, D. (2015). Shoes of Childhood: Exploring the Emotional Politics Through Which Images Become Narrated on Social. In the iconic image on social media, a rapid research response to the death of Aylan Kurdi. Visual Social Media. https://research.gold.ac.uk/id/eprint/14624/1/KURDI%20REPORT.pdf

Roumate, F. (2024). Media, Artificial Intelligence, and Political Changes. In: Artificial Intelligence and the New World Order. Frontiers of Artificial Intelligence, Ethics and Multidisciplinary Applications. Springer, Cham. https://doi.org/10.1007/978-3-031-50312-2_10

Selvi, M. (2023). *OPINION – Censorship of Gaza on social media.* While users who want to support Israel can do so easily, those who take a pro-Palestinian stance find their accounts banned, censored, or reduced in visibility, AA, 07.12.2023 - Update : 08.12.2023. https://www.aa.com.tr/en/analysis/opinion-censorship-of-gaza-on-social-media/3075723

Steff, R., Burton, J., & Soare, S. R. (2021). *Emerging technologies and international security: Machines, the state, and war.* Routledge. https://www.routledge.com/Emerging-Technologies-and-International-Security-Machines-the-State-and/Steff-Burton-Soare/p/book/9780367636845

Ulmer, A., & Tong, A. (2023). *Deepfaking it: America's 2024 election collides with AI boom.* Reuters, May 30, 2023, 8:17 PM PDT. https://www.reuters.com/world/us/deepfaking-it-americas-2024-election-collides-with-ai-boom-2023-05-30/

United Nations. (2024). *Seizing the opportunities of safe, secure and trustworthy artificial intelligence systems for sustainable development.* Resolution adopted by the General Assembly, March 11. n2406592.pdf (un.org)

Chapter 3
Communication Dimensions in Mitigating the Global Security Threats of Malicious AI/Artificial Intelligence

Marta N. Lukacovic and Deborah D. Sellnow-Richmond

Abstract To augment the discussion of the mitigative approaches to malicious AI, we outline the useful analytical potentials of the frameworks of mega-crisis and securitization. Within this scaffolding we foresee a plethora of roles for various fields. In this particular piece, we provide just few specific examples of vital roles to be played by researchers, educators, and practitioners in the fields of communication, media, and journalism. We urge all other researchers, educators, and practitioners to likewise take initiative in envisioning various approaches and being willing to build alliances across national and disciplinary boundaries. Through such productive and necessary alliances, malicious AI threats can be effectively mitigated.

Keywords Malicious use of AI · Communication · Media · Journalism · Securitization · Mega-crisis

1 Introduction

Artificial intelligence (AI), as an inevitable feature of contemporary technological advancements, will only become more abundant and impactful with time. Malicious use of AI (MUAI) is already a problematic reality that impacts many, and with the inevitable growth of AI, the risks of MUAI will also grow. Scholars, activists, and advocates have already proposed approaches and policies to mitigate the threats of MUAI (e.g., Averkin et al., 2019; Roumate, 2021). However, the question that should still receive more attention is the active role of the fields of communication,

M. N. Lukacovic (✉)
Department of Communication and Mass Media, Angelo State University – Texas Tech University System, San Angelo, TX, USA

D. D. Sellnow-Richmond
Department of Applied Communication Studies, Southern Illinois University, Edwardsville, IL, USA

F. Roumate, A. La Rosa (eds.), *Artificial Intelligence, Media and International Security*, Contributions to Security and Defence Studies,
https://doi.org/10.1007/978-3-031-95757-4_3

media, and journalism in the mitigation of MUAI. In our contribution to the discussion of the mitigative approaches to MUAI, we outline the useful analytical potentials of the frameworks of mega-crisis and securitization, and, importantly, through this project, we also address the places where communication, media, and journalism expertise is paramount.

2 Mega-crisis

MUAI represents looming risks as well as fully developed crises in some areas. *Risk and crisis communication* is an integral part of risk and crisis management (Seeger & Sellnow, 2019). Failures of preventive communication contribute to the onset of crises. Effective communication is tremendously helpful in resolving active crises. During the post-crisis period, reflective communication can help to extract lessons and plan for future contingencies. In the current era, a large proportion of the activities and structures of our societies function as an interdependent system. Hence, the concept of *mega-crisis* highlights that the various crises of today are so pervasive precisely because they exist as a wicked problem, an interrelated constellation of crises that feed off one another, are difficult to solve, and frequently transcend national boundaries (Alpaslan & Mitroff, 2011; Helsloot et al., 2012; Lukacovic & Sellnow-Richmond, 2023).

Hence, MUAI is itself a problematic crisis but also a component of a broader mega-crisis. The other components of the globally reaching mega-crisis are cybercrime, corruption, extremism, disinformation campaigns, poverty, etc. Because mega-crises are complex, fluid, and multilevel, the solutions must be complex, fluid, and multilevel.

3 Securitization

In order to address some nuances of the complex, fluid, and multilevel crises of today such as MUAI, the securitization theory can be particularly useful. As theorized by Buzan et al. (1998), securitization stresses the process of persuasion, where politicians or other opinion leaders make a successful argument that an existential threat that endangers a state, its people, or its identity is real and needs to be eliminated by extraordinary measures. What is crucial is that securitization is primarily about the persuasions. A securitizing argument can be made about various types of security. Hence, securitization was a key forerunner of contemporary discussions about various *types of security*, such as cybersecurity, cultural security, food security, water security, environmental security, climate security, etc. MUAI can impact various types of security. The different types of security represent a useful lens to analyze crises and enrich crisis communication practices.

Securitization also helps to outline various *levels* of securitization, ranging from *macro* to *micro* (Buzan & Waever, 2009). Typically, securitization has been understood on the level of a nation-state. Hence, when a "security" issue is implied, frequently it is about topics such as border security, international relations, etc. However, successful persuasions about an alleged existential threat have led to an array of policies when arguing about a much broader collective level than a nation-state. For instance, the European Union frames many of its policies from this broader collective perspective, for example, while implying "European values" that must be preserved and protected. Appeals to protect such broad, supranational, and possibly civilizational collective referent objects correspond to the macro-security level. On the other hand, security can be also viewed from an individual citizen's perspective. Human rights of an individual are such a conception that corresponds to the micro-security level. MUAI represents threats for wide global communities, separate nations, as well as individual citizens, and thus MUAI has implications across the levels ranging from macro-security to micro-security.

Henceforth, securitization assists in outlining the types and levels of security that should be considered when approaching the mitigation of MUAI as a part of an evolving mega-crisis. Through theoretically rich analyses and frameworks for countermeasures to the MUAI risks, the perspectives of mega-crisis and securitization are also useful in delineating the roles of communication, media, and journalism. Next, we address a few examples of these within the existing proposals from researchers on the mitigation of MUAI.

4 Communication Dimension in the Approaches to Mitigate the Risks of Malicious AI

Averkin et al. (2019) outline the mitigation of MUAI threats by integration of advanced technological and multidisciplinary approaches. These authors highlight that the particularly powerful approach is when technology-oriented solutions are complemented by analytical and applied tactics that are drawing on advances from a variety of fields. When this variety includes the intersection of social sciences and humanities, such as the fields of communication, media, and journalism, the trap of technological determinism can be avoided. From the perspective of the mega-crisis, some dimensions of the problem are technological and therefore can be fixed by technological innovation. But other dimensions of the problem and of security are, for instance, related to media communication, perception, and psychology and therefore must be analyzed and addressed by drawing on the pertinent fields.

Following Averkin et al.'s (2019) recommendations, a useful way of incorporating high technological tools such as AI and big data scraping is in detecting trends, including large-scale and MUAI-fueled disinformation attacks. Once such detection is established, a fruitful connection across disciplinary boundaries is starting a crisis communication campaign that is based on *inoculation theory* (McGuire, 1964).

Compton et al. (2021) suggest that once at-risk populations are identified, inoculation can be utilized to expose the at-risk population to a sample of the anticipated disinformation messages while providing tools on how to employ critical thinking and verification to become less susceptible and vulnerable to these effects of MUAI. Therefore, the inoculation process in communication mimics what happens with the physiological inoculation of a patient, but instead of in the context of a disease, it happens in the context of risk and crisis communication (Seeger & Sellnow, 2019).

Roumate (2021) advocates for the centrality of ethics and respect for human rights, which would be truly fortified by reforms of legal frameworks toward the regulation of AI and prevention of MUAI, in particular. This approach emphasized the importance of regulation on not just the national level but also an international level, so the various levels of securitization are incorporated in the perspective. Furthermore, this approach realized the complexities of the problems, as captured in the model of a mega-crisis. While Roumate acknowledges this is a demanding project, she makes a strong argument for why it is a necessary project.

Communication plays a crucial role in the discussion, negotiation, articulation, implementation, explanation, and refinement of ethics and law on human rights within the global arena. The edited collection by Collste (2016) centers communication in the theorization and practice of ethics, human rights, and consequent legal frameworks. Importantly, some aspects of what is considered moral differ rather significantly across cultures. Certain values, norms, and practices are regarded by a specific culture as essential to this culture's identity. Crucially, what is viewed as a fundamental part of a culture's identity can be securitized. For example, the right to free enterprise is believed to be one of the core identity values in many Western and capitalistic societies. Hence, the norms and laws that are perceived as a threat to free enterprise may easily be, within such securitized discourse, rejected, even if these norms and laws could have great effects on limiting MUAI. In order to explore further and contemplate solutions to similar challenges, the works of communication, media, and journalism ethicists are truly beneficial. For example, Christians (2019), Ess (2020), and Ward and Wasserman (2010) represent authors who acknowledge the global nature of the technologies such as the Internet and AI, the local and cultural nature of some ethical and legal understandings, as well as possibilities of consensus between cultures through inclusive practices such as dialogue.

Lukacovic and Sellnow-Richmond (2023) stress that mitigation of MUAI necessitates a structural commitment to social responsibility and social change coupled with robust initiatives toward media literacy and information literacy. The recommendations of Lukacovic and Sellnow-Richmond endorse the previously mentioned approaches by Averkin et al. (2019) and Roumate (2021) and furthermore add an additional layer of analysis based on the perspective of mega-crisis and securitization. This analysis helps to identify the areas where malicious actors could bypass even the typically effective countermeasures, as was witnessed during the COVID-19 pandemic. Communication and all other actions are interdependent and interconnected in any crisis, including MUAI during the pandemic. Communication and structural factors must be perpetually receptive to feedback from stakeholders during all stages of crises, and consequently, communication and structural foundations should be evolving toward better alternatives.

Even the most masterful communication can only go so far if it is not backed up by a track record of real changes and demonstratable results on the structural base. Eventually, the "reservoir of goodwill" runs out, and the public stops trusting the organizations, institutions, or governments (Seeger & Sellnow, 2019). This type of concern is reflected in Lukacovic and Sellnow-Richmond's (2023) recommendations. In fact, a large number of scholars and activists in the sphere of AI, digital media, and contemporary technologies frequently advocate for literacies, such as information literacy, AI literacy, media literacy, and science literacy, to name just a few. At the heart of the mentioned literacies is the notion of teaching the learners to distinguish between trustworthy and untrustworthy sources. In many instances, public trust in any organizations, institutions, and governments is low due to perceived and/or real corruption, injustices, and disregard for social responsibility. Ever more frequent mega-crises are exacerbating such circumstances. This decline in trust is occurring due to many systemic failures. On the one hand, there is a failure to use communication strategically, ethically, and dialogically, to avert crises. On the other hand is the constellation of all other systemic failures. Without this bigger picture in mind, MUAI can hardly be mitigated.

5 Conclusion

Mega-crisis and securitization theories enrich the systematic construction of counter-MUAI scaffolding. Within this scaffolding, we foresee a plethora of roles for various fields, and in this article, we provide just a few specific examples of vital roles to be played by researchers, educators, and practitioners in the fields of communication, media, and journalism. We urge other researchers, educators, and practitioners to take the initiative in envisioning various approaches and being willing to build alliances across national and disciplinary boundaries. Through such productive alliances, malicious AI threats can be effectively mitigated. Our ultimate hope is that by minimizing the threats, societies can more readily embrace AI as a beneficial aid in collaboration toward a happier, healthier, more educated, prosperous, equal, and advanced global community.

References

Alpaslan, C. M., & Mitroff, I. I. (2011). *Swans, swine, and swindlers; Coping with the growing threat of mega-crises and mega-messes*. Stanford Business Books – Stanford University Press.

Averkin, A. N., Bazarkina, D. Y., Pantserev, K. A., & Pashentsev, Y. N. (2019). Artificial intelligence in the context of psychological security: Theoretical and practical implications. *Atlantis Studies in Uncertainty Modelling, 1*, 101–107.

Buzan, B., & Waever, O. (2009). Macrosecuritization and security constellations: Reconsidering scale in securitization theory. *Review of International Studies, 35*(2), 253–276.
Buzan, B., Waever, O., & de Wilde, J. (1998). *Security: A new framework for analysis*. Lynne Rienner.
Christians, C. G. (2019). *Media ethics and global justice in the digital age*. Cambridge University Press.
Collste, G. (2016). *Ethics and communication: Global perspectives*. Rowman & Littlefield.
Compton, J., Wigley, S., & Samoilenko, S. (2021). Inoculation theory and public relations. *Public Relations Review, 47*(5), 1–6.
Ess, C. (2020). *Digital media ethics* (3rd ed.). Polity Press.
Helsloot, I., Boi, A., Jacobs, B., & Comfort, L. (2012). The new challenges of mega-crises. In I. Helsloot, A. Boin, B. Jacobs, & L. Comfort (Eds.), *Mega-crises: Understanding the prospects, nature, characteristics and the effects of cataclysmic events* (pp. 5–11). Charles C. Thomas.
Lukacovic, M. N., & Sellnow-Richmond, D. D. (2023). COVID-19 pandemic and the rise of MUAI threats to national and international psychological security. In E. Pashentsev (Ed.), *The Palgrave handbook of malicious use of AI and psychological security* (pp. 175–201). Palgrave Macmillan.
McGuire, W. J. (1964). Inducing resistance to persuasion: Some contemporary approaches. In L. Berkowitz (Ed.), *Advances in experimental social psychology* (Vol. 1, pp. 191–229). Academic Press.
Roumate, F. (2021). Artificial intelligence, ethics and international human rights law. *International Review of Information Ethics, 29*(3). https://doi.org/10.29173/irie422
Seeger, M. W., & Sellnow, T. L. (2019). *Communication in times of trouble*. Wiley Blackwell.
Ward, S. J. A., & Wasserman, H. (2010). Towards an open ethics: Implications of new media platforms for global ethics discourse. *Journal of Mass Media Ethics, 25*(4), 275–292. https://doi.org/10.1080/08900523.2010.512825

Chapter 4
Digital Imperialism: Neurosymbolic Artificial Intelligence, International Security, Information Flows, and Social Media in the Twenty-First Century

Carlos Enrique Fernandez-Garcia, Samantha Gómez Gamboa, and Piero García Castillo

Abstract The global competition between the major transnationals of Neurosymbolic Artificial Intelligence (NSAI) is shaping the balance of a new global power. The USA, China, and the European Union consolidate their hegemony and dominance in the development and application of this technology. The dizzying advance of AI reproduces colonial relations of political, economic, and technological dependence of emerging countries, due to the lack of access to advanced infrastructures, financing, and data that already limit their ability to compete in the new digital economy. This study explores how digital imperialism, a product of the global competition for Neurosymbolic Artificial Intelligence, affects the information flows of twenty-first-century media. The results of our study reveal the power dynamics of colonialism and the mechanisms of dependency in terms of infrastructure, data, and regulations that impede the autonomous development of the media and reinforce its subordinate position in the current geopolitical order. The study concludes on the increasing use of algorithms in news distribution leading to profound impacts on how we consume news. It recommends the promotion of technological sovereignty policies, encouraging investment, research, and development policies in AI and establishing regulations on information flows in the media, strategic data protection policies for developing nations, and the reduction of global technology gaps.

Keywords Digital imperialism · Artificial Intelligence · International security · Geopolitical power · Social media

---

C. E. Fernandez-García (✉)
Universidad Nacional Mayor de San Marcos, Lima, Peru
e-mail: carlosenrique.fernandez@unmsm.edu.pe

S. G. Gamboa · P. G. Castillo
Universidad San Martín de Porres, Lima, Peru
e-mail: samantha_gomez@usmp.pe; piero_garcia1@usmp.pe

F. Roumate, A. La Rosa (eds.), *Artificial Intelligence, Media and International Security*, Contributions to Security and Defence Studies,
https://doi.org/10.1007/978-3-031-95757-4_4

1 Introduction

1.1 Background

Muldoon and Wu (2023) apply and analyze Aníbal Quijano's (2014) colonial matrix of power to the AI technology ecosystem. In the study, they specify how economic and political inequalities in AI production are linked to the continuity of historical colonialism. The methodology is circumscribed to theoretical and critical analysis in the framework of Anibal Quijano's modernity/coloniality, literature review, and case study. The results confirm that AI models replicate Western power structures and reinforce radial and epistemic biases, AI responds to a colonial pattern of value extraction and labor exploitation, and AI production is highly dependent on natural resources extracted in developing countries. It is concluded that AI is not neutral but is embedded within a colonial matrix of power.

Ricaurte (2019) analyzes how digital colonialism reinforces structural inequalities by imposing Western epistemologies and new forms of digital control. The objective is to explore and analyze why data colonialism shapes colonial power relations and to examine strategies of resistance that enable the development of alternative epistemologies that respect cultural and linguistic diversity. Among the results, it is established that data obtained from vulnerable communities are used as tools of control and surveillance. The conclusion of the study reveals that dominant epistemologies make alternative knowledge of indigenous communities invisible. Data colonialism reproduces dynamics of exploitation and exclusion, requiring new forms of digital governance and epistemological resistance.

Ayana et al. (2024) assess the level of decolonization in the global governance of AI in ten sub-Saharan African countries. The objective is to study the state of decolonization of the governance of countries in the Global South in a decolonizing framework, prioritizing equity and participation of countries in global decision-making. It classifies countries into five levels of decolonization: resilient, blind, conscious, responsive, and transformative. The countries showed mostly low levels of implementation of AI strategies, lack of regulatory institutions, and low demand for the use of local data for AI development. The study concludes that most countries are lagging behind in the decolonization of AI governance. It recommends strengthening the participation of local actors and improving data protection policies and fostering local innovation.

Natale (2020) analyzes the relationship between AI and communication and its role as a message producer, which challenges the traditional conception in communication studies. The aim is to explore how human-machine communication transforms the notion of medium and redefines communication in the era of Artificial Intelligence. The methodology consists of a theoretical review of key publications and employs the comparative approach to evaluate their contributions to communication theory and media studies. Communication cannot be understood without considering human interaction and its sociocultural interpretations. AI is not just a medium but a communicative actor that challenges traditional paradigms. It is concluded that AI must go beyond technical models and consider the human dimension in the construction of meanings.

Coleman (2019) investigates the exploitation of African user data, under the guise of technological development, by Western technology transnationals. The objective is in function of revealing the mechanisms of exploitation of African users' data as an exercise of neocolonial control over data and evaluating data protection laws. Among the results we find how technology transnationals take advantage of legal loopholes to extract and monopolize data. We conclude the need to strengthen data protection laws with informed consent.

1.2 State of the Art

Neurosymbolic Artificial Intelligence (NSAI) as a hybrid paradigm emerges to overcome the limitations of purely neural or purely symbolic approaches. According to Renkhoff et al. (2024) the emergence of this autonomous Artificial Intelligence system responds to a new technology that improves the way of interpreting and providing greater accuracy in AI models. This technology that combines deep learning and symbolic reasoning will be the strategic differentiator that will strengthen the position of developed nations, as they attract investments and monopolize its implementation. AI experts stress that this integration is key to achieving more reliable, secure, and interpretable results in the future.

Neurosymbolic Artificial Intelligence will not only become a technological resource but an axis of global power. Its mastery will determine who controls digital security, digital warfare and autonomous weapons, critical infrastructures, and the knowledge economy. NSAI proves key to developing autonomous systems and high security environments (Renkhoff et al., 2024). Bârgăoanu and Cheregi (2021) argue that competition in AI is dominated by the USA and China, shaping a new technological Cold War (Cold War 2.0).

Superpowers are investing heavily in AI to consolidate their digital power. Haileselassie and Rawat (2024) ponder the ability of this technology to increase the operational competence of armies without losing human control, be able to detect threats more accurately, and anticipate attacks in conflict management. NSAI, combined with data control and cybersecurity, transforms the technological ecosystem into a pillar geostrategic resource for nations (Firoozabadi & Chehrazad, 2024).

This hybrid Artificial Intelligence directly impacts the leadership of superpowers such as the USA, China, and the European Union for technological hegemony (Amador-Domínguez et al., 2024). In that sense, technology corporations—whose power is comparable to that of states—and governments compete to develop international AI standards, which will become an essential pillar in the balance of global power and will affect technological competitiveness, digital sovereignty, and international security.

The authors of the review of academic sources agree on the global fragmentation in a new technopolar order. Colomina Saló and Galcerán-Vercher (2024a) warn of the existence of three hegemonic approaches to the global governance of AI in a new order and that generates tensions and fragmentation in global regulation: US's capitalist self-regulation, China's techno-authoritarianism, and the EU's guarantor regulation. In the case of China, DeepSeek is a model used for mass surveillance and influence operations, despite that country's official denial (Polygraph.info VOA, 2025).

The dominant narrative in geopolitical discourse invisibilizes emerging actors and perspectives from the Global South, whose participation is necessary for inclusive and equitable global governance of AI, despite lagging behind in technological innovation (Colomina Saló & Galcerán-Vercher, 2024a). NSAI can have global strategic implications and drive scientific, technological, and geopolitical development. Strategic sectors such as defense, homeland security, and government automation are key in the validation and verification of NSAI models. Some developing nations seek to reduce their dependence on foreign technologies and develop AI infrastructures that are reliable and auditable (Hitzler et al., 2024; Amador-Domínguez et al., 2024).

All authors agree that NSAI faces significant challenges in its ethical use, development, and geopolitical application. Digital divides are widening if we take into account that nations, transnationals, and media must rely on increasingly sophisticated infrastructure and multidisciplinary expertise. While NSAI promises greater transparency, it can also be used for authoritarian purposes such as more effective mass surveillance.

A critical aspect identified in the evaluation of the scientific literature between Artificial Intelligence and digital imperialism is the reproduction of old colonial structures in today's socioeconomic context. Digital imperialism is the domination exercised by certain powerful nations or corporations over the global digital ecosystem, consolidating a technological, economic, and cultural hegemony. In this regard, Salami (2024) warns about how large Western technology corporations exercise dominance over the digital infrastructure, replicating old colonial structures of exploitation.

Digital imperialism replicates millenarian structures, where this time "data" constitutes a resource worthy of exploitation, centralized processes and modes of production, monopolized digital infrastructure, and digital labor made precarious in developing countries and benefiting Western technology corporations (Muldoon & Wu, 2023).

These dynamics reinforce algorithmic discrimination, as AI models, trained on predominantly Western data, perpetuate racial and cultural biases, marginalizing native or indigenous communities, in areas such as access to funding, labor recruitment, and digital surveillance.

Within the framework of representation in the global governance of artificial intelligence, developing countries face a double challenge: the imposition of foreign technological standards and the reproduction of structural inequalities, through algorithms that reinforce stereotypes and limit development opportunities.

Neurosymbolic Artificial Intelligence plays a transcendent role within this digital imperialism by serving as a tool for global informational domination. De la Peña and Granados (2024) argue that peripheral nations under the influence of Artificial Intelligence control are subject to suffer great vulnerability and dependence.

Colomina Saló and Galcerán-Vercher (2024b) call these peripheral nations the Global South, a geopolitical concept that groups together countries outside the centers of economic, political, and technological power, dominated by the West and which have been an expression of digital colonialism and data mining as new forms of inequality, where the great technological powers impose models without considering local realities.

These nations have historically been marginalized in the international system and have experienced processes of colonization, exploitation of natural resources, and inequality in the distribution of technological and economic development. The Global South tacitly implies a greater risk of technological exclusion and dependencies on models alien to their needs and priorities such as AI digital ecosystems (Colomina Saló & Galcerán-Vercher, 2024a).

AI becomes an instrument of soft power within digital imperialism by defining the characteristics, rules, and algorithms that govern digital platforms and that can influence how billions of people access information, interact, and transact online.

For Colomina Saló and Galcerán-Vercher (2024b) the classification of the Global South is key to understanding technological inequalities in the AI era. The Global South is composed of Latin America, Africa, Southeast Asia, South Asia, and some Middle Eastern nations. It also includes emerging economies such as China, India, Brazil, and South Africa that have developed industrial and technological capabilities but continue to experience structural inequalities.

Imperialism has a clear geopolitical component in the AI race. Technology transnationals invest heavily in AI to ensure their digital supremacy, where the powers that control AI platforms in a sense impose a digital order that others must follow, reproducing center-periphery patterns in the global digital economy (Kwet, 2019). NSAI consolidates the power gap between the countries that design and control these technologies and those that passively consume them. Leading nations incorporate their values, languages, and agendas into AI models.

In this context, social media and social networks play a central role in this new digital order. Couldry and Mejias (2019) argue that traditional and digital media boast a role as brokers of data colonization. Google, Facebook, and Twitter algorithmically disseminate the information that large transnationals wish to make visible. The personalized advertising of these platforms turns the media into tools for behavioral control. This is why the following problem arises:

How does digital imperialism, a product of the global competition for Neurosymbolic Artificial Intelligence, affect the information flows of the twenty-first-century media?

1.3 Author's Main Hypothesis or Position

The new technological imperialism is an expression of digital colonialism manifested in the concentration of innovation and in relations of subjugation between the hegemonic countries of the Global North and the consumers of technology belonging to the Global South, and in order to answer the questions that arise, we propose the following hypothesis as a starting point for new lines of research in this area:

Hypothesis Digital imperialism, a product of the global competition for Neurosymbolic Artificial Intelligence, affects the information flows of the media in the twenty-first century.

1.4 Objective

To develop the problem posed in this study, the following is proposed as the objective: To analyze the state of studies on digital imperialism, product of the global competition for Neurosymbolic Artificial Intelligence, that affects the informative flows of the media of the twenty-first century.

1.5 Work Methodology

The methodology of this article adopts a theoretical approach based on decolonial theory and sociotechnical critique, analyzing previous studies on the impact of AI in the nations of the Global South, literature review and corporate policies, and normative and comparative analysis of data protection regulations in these nations.

1.6 Justification and Relevance of the Subject

Hobbes (2008) argues that "he who has the information, has the power." The exercise of global power depends precisely on the control that states have over the information of nations. This study alerts us to the advance of AI and the technological gaps between technology producers such as the USA, China, the European Union and its satellite countries, and the nations of the Global South, whose role is usually one of technological subordination, due to their limited capacity to develop infrastructure, processes, and ways of production of Artificial Intelligence, which reinforces their exclusive quality of consumer.

This research is relevant because it seeks to analyze how a new model of digital colonialism is consolidated, based on the use of NSAI and the technological hegemony of the Global North and its relationship of domination with the nations of the

Global South. Understanding this problem will allow the adoption of strategies that promote greater autonomy in the use and regulation of data and AI in developing countries.

The theoretical justification is found in the need to reveal the formulas of colonial subjugation of the countries of the Global South, with respect to the unequal access to Artificial Intelligence and the exploitation of data by large transnational corporations. This lack of technological sovereignty corrupts with its biases epistemological and political barriers, and they reinforce Eurocentric global hierarchies. The development and application of AI are subordinated to the omnipotent power of the superpowers and their interests, since they control the infrastructure and production of digital knowledge.

The methodological justification focuses on how to study and understand how the new dynamics of technological power, monopolization of access to information, and digital sovereignty of developing countries are produced. Possible strategies of resistance and digital autonomy need to be assessed.

The practical justification generates a critical framework to help understand how AI shapes global power and what actions can be taken to build a more equitable and inclusive technology, based on regulations of this technology and data protection.

1.7 Results

Neurosymbolic Artificial Intelligence: Strategic Asset The third wave Artificial Intelligence known as Neurosymbolic Artificial Intelligence deepens the global competition for prevalence of IAS (Gavilán, 2024; Zhu & Long, 2019). This hybrid model fuses deep neural networks (deep learning) with symbol systems to improve logical reasoning and decision-making (Sheth et al., 2023), in order to avoid the generation of errors or "hallucinations" (Attoresi, 2025).

The Alan Turing Institute (2025) proposes that this new technology will overcome the stagnation point of current AI, achieving more interpretable, robust, and applicable systems to the extent of reinforcing the current preestablished dynamics of the arms race competitions between global powers (Baele et al., 2024). Its implications are significant for the risks of a global arms race based on this technology (Sarkin & Sotoudehfar, 2024), and it is emerging as a fundamental field for the future of international governance and global cooperation in the digital era.

Gerlich (2024) argues that Neurosymbolic Artificial Intelligence is not only a technological revolution but a tool of global domination, shaped by the geopolitical order. The lack of regulations and the growing competition in algorithmic development can generate an impact on new forms of imperialism based on the expansionism of inequalities in global security and the world economy.

Neurosymbolic Artificial Intelligence has been transforming different sectors such as health, education, social governance, and cybersecurity, undoubtedly (Matic, 2023). The ethical approach is necessary to achieve sustainable roles within an adaptive and flexible international regulatory framework that balances innovation, security, and human rights to mitigate the risks of AI in war conflicts (Chesterman, 2021).

A fundamental challenge pointed out in the review of scientific literature has to do with the role played by Artificial Intelligence in global cybersecurity. Artificial Intelligence is a strategic asset that amplifies the military and economic and scientific potentialities of powers such as the USA, China, and the European Union (De la Peña & Granados, 2024). Artificial Intelligence redefines modern warfare by increasing operational efficiency and strategic decision-making.

The integration of Artificial Intelligence in defense requires a responsible approach that combines innovation, international cooperation, urgency of international audits for a responsible use of AI, and sound regulatory frameworks to ensure global security and stability. Ethical, regulatory, and security challenges impose a global agenda to obtain global peace and stability, in the face of US and Chinese technological co-leadership (Editorial Team, 2024).

AI as a dual technological tool or double-edged sword has the ability to enhance cybersecurity or constitute a risk to international security through the use of more sophisticated and difficult to detect automated attacks, digital authoritarianism, and misuse by non-state actors (Horowitz et al., 2018; Khan et al., 2024; Bahcecik, 2023).

NWICO and Information Society An essential challenge identified in scientific research is the contribution of Artificial Intelligence in the media information flow. The New Information and Communications Order (NWICO) emerged in the 1970s as a response against the supremacy of Western news agencies, US hegemony in the Cold War, and the dominance of developed countries as an expression of information or media imperialism in the international flow of information. The aim was to denounce the material inequality and asymmetry of power concealed under the liberal notion of "freedom of information."

NWICO emerged in a context of media decolonization, where the countries of the Global South were seeking greater autonomy in their information systems. Among its postulates were equitable redistribution of information flows to avoid the media supremacy of the North over the Global South; promotion of local media production to strengthen national cultural identities; decentralization of international news agencies, most of which were controlled by the West; promotion of cultural and linguistic diversity in the media; and regulation of the influence of transnational media conglomerates.

Mastrini and De Charras (2005) conclude that the information society replaced the NWICO paradigm, with a focus on digital access and in a context of neoliberal advancement, instead of information equity. The International Telecommunication Union (ITU) displaced UNESCO, marking a shift from a political and cultural approach to a business and technical one as an expression of neoliberalism. The failure of NWICO demonstrates that, according to Hamelink (2008), technological access does not equal informational sovereignty.

The concept of media imperialism describes the relationship of subordination of the media with respect to the dominant countries in order to impose narratives, values, and ideologies (Schiller, 1976).

The growing use of algorithms (including neurosymbolic ones) in the distribution of information leads to profound impacts on how we consume news and on the shaping of public discourse. Google, Facebook, Twitter, and YouTube control the distribution of content globally, despite the democratization of information with the Internet. Its manifestations are globalization, digital divides, persistent inequalities in access to technologies, and market-led development.

Geopolitical Rivalry as a Technological Scenario: From NWICO to Yalta The Yalta Conference in 1945 defined the global power division after World War II by establishing zones of influence between the USA, USSR, and the UK. In today's world, tech superpowers—the USA (OpenAI, Google, Microsoft), China (DeepSeek, Baidu, Alibaba), and the European Union (Claude, Aleph, Minerva AI)—configure a new distribution of power, marked by AI and global technological competition. Just as zones of influence were drawn in Yalta, the new digital Yalta is the global battlefield. Becoming a key factor in geopolitical competition between world powers, Artificial Intelligence goes beyond territorial control and is expressed in the supremacy of data and automation (Dehghani Firouzabadi & Chehrazad, 2024).

The future technological scenarios between states, over the next decade, will modify the dynamics of multilateralism and global cooperation, to compromise security, sovereignty, and relations between international actors (Vacarelu, 2021; Tinnirello, 2022). Geopolitical rivalry affects governments' willingness to agree on common regulations on AI (von Ingersleben-Seip, 2023). US military programs fund hybrid algorithms to create autonomous, secure, and reliable systems in mission environments (DARPA, 2023).

Military supremacy for the USA is key in the global competition for leadership in Artificial Intelligence, through applications in automation, data analysis, and tactical intelligence (Kugler, 2021). Zhu et al. (2022) considers that the USA and China are in an "AI cold war," where the "Americans" seek to curb Eastern technological development to maintain their global supremacy.

Artificial Intelligence is redefining the balance of technological and geopolitical power (Colomina Saló & Galcerán-Vercher, 2024a; Ferguson, 2025). While the USA and China dominate AI development, the European Union seeks to lead in its regulation. While this race drives innovation and economic growth, it also poses ethical, security, and inequity challenges.

From a geopolitical perspective, Greiman (2021) proposes a governance of cyberspace from perspectives or approaches to protect the sovereignty of international cooperation based on global, national, and international efforts as a framework for unified governance, generating challenges in the regulation and control of cyberspace. Tallberg et al. (2023) point out the need for fair and democratic governance that guarantees fairness, transparency, and citizen participation.

The technological scenarios of 2023 initially placed this conflict as the exclusive product of a trade war between OpenAI and Google, technology transnationals in intense dispute for the dominance of Artificial Intelligence, with the purpose of ensuring hegemony in the sector, through the acquisition of start-ups and the blocking of competitors, replicating or absorbing emerging technologies (Fernández-García, 2024).

Social media focused its spotlight on omnichannel AI processing, the personalization of content generated by this technology and the automatic generation of images and videos, instead of considering that the real conflict should be in the global geopolitical aspect of the problem. The emergence of DeepSeek, a Chinese company founded by Liang Wenfeng, on the international scene initially put the Asian country on the map and challenged Western technological dominance (Rivas, 2025).

AI Supremacy and Global Balance According to De la Peña and Granados (2024), developed countries consolidate their supremacy in AI thanks to investment and technology policies, large-scale data surveillance, and restriction of access to technology. In this perspective for their study they build a multilayer network integrated by the following dimensions: economic, military, and technological to evaluate the radius of influence of AI in global geopolitics.

From Zhu and Long (2019), geopolitical power dynamics in a bipolar world profoundly affect Sino-American relations. Dehghani Firouzabadi and Chehrazad (2024) even propose the term "post-geopolitics" to describe the impact of AI on international relations, because traditional geopolitics is insufficient to explain the new dynamics resulting from the interaction of man and AI technology.

AI is transforming the global balance in the exercise of power and the reorganization of geopolitics at the international level, and those who lead its development will define the world order of the twenty-first century. Russian President Vladimir Putin affirmed, in this direction, that the country that leads research in Artificial Intelligence will end up dominating the world (Vincent, 2017). Elon Musk warned about AI as the great existential threat to humanity, leading to a third world war (Hern, 2017).

Schmid et al. (2025) give importance to the differences between national approaches in the treatment of AI: the USA privileges the innovation model based on development from private companies, while China subordinates it to military and civilian advances. The European Union focuses the development of its AI on ethical regulations and global standards for AI.

The global competition of Artificial Intelligence aggravates the circumstances of mutual strategic distrust, intensifies the armament of the powers, shapes the correlation of forces, threatens the mutual strategic security between the two nations, and puts global geopolitical stability at risk (Zhu & Long, 2019). Dehghani Firouzabadi and Chehrazad (2024) show the transformation due to the dual nature of AI in the "geopolitical network of the international system," since those who lead the development of this technology will define the world order of the twenty-first century (Dehghani Firouzabadi & Chehrazad, 2024).

From the Chinese government (2017), significant advances in Neurosymbolic Artificial Intelligence will redefine in the coming years the new structures of global power, national sovereignty, and control of knowledge regulated by large technological corporations and governments. Farnell and Coffey (2024) highlight China's objective as a country to achieve technological superiority in this field and disturb the balance of power in the world that, without a doubt, will affect the security and world economy (Allen & Kania, 2017).

The nations that lead the technological development of Artificial Intelligence will define the world order of the twenty-first century (Dehghani Firouzabadi & Chehrazad, 2024). The qualitative leap of AI in China over the last year could give this world power a strategic advantage over the USA, redefining the global correlation of forces and favoring countries with greater technological capabilities. Huawei, Alibaba, and Tencent face sanctions that limit their international expansion and access to advanced hardware. And China, in response, has developed its own digital sovereignty strategy, pushing for chip manufacturing and proprietary AI models and platforms independent of the USA (Colomina Saló & Galcerán-Vercher, 2024a).

Artificial Intelligence digital ecosystems have been divided into two blocks that maintain different standards in AI, cybersecurity, and digital infrastructure: the first block consists of the USA and its allies the EU, Japan, South Korea, and Taiwan, and the second block consists of China and its strategic allies Russia, BRICS countries, Southeast Asia, South Korea, and Taiwan (Colomina Saló & Galcerán-Vercher, 2024a; Thomas & Wu, 2021).

Apart from this division of the global industry into these two spheres of technological influence, we must consider in this equation the Global South, which seeks to operate in both markets, without aligning itself with a single block, despite the regulatory challenges.

2 Technological Advances Have Not Democratized the Flow of Information

Information power remains concentrated in the platforms. Badillo and Proulx (2006) warn about how the globalization of communication has expanded information control on a worldwide scale. Globalization is in direct relation to the permanent challenge to the hegemony of developed countries in the global circulation of the information.

In the review of scientific literature, the authors warn about how global interconnectivity has enabled new forms of communication. This digital revolution impacted by the Internet, Artificial Intelligence, and the processing of large volumes of data has transformed the way in which information is processed and shared (Iacovitti, 2022).

Information imperialism persists in reproducing Western media and hegemonic schemes, structures, and ways of production, despite new actors and digital platforms. The quality of global information has worsened, despite the growth of alternative media and the expansion of the Internet (Boyd-Barrett, 2011). Most news about developing countries are still produced from the West, generating a distorted representation of other regions. Topics such as conflicts, poverty, and corruption dominate the journalistic narrative, while scientific, cultural, and economic achievements are relegated to the back burner.

The Global North media maintains a dominant narrative about the information society focused on the efficiency of technology, which ignores and justifies the social inequalities it generates (Mansell, 2010). Without a reflection on its impact on power, Artificial Intelligence, by itself, does not solve social problems.

The official narrative of the time justified the "technological backwardness" as a technocratic and neutral facade that hid in the background a control mechanism that sought to pathologize the sovereign demands of the Third World as corruption (Chakravartty & Muller, 2024).

Hamelink (2008) points out that the reduction of digital divides has been unsuccessful and that the benefits have been captured by the transnationals of the Global North, which control the infrastructures of power and information flows. The expansion of digital platforms in the Global South implies rethinking informational sovereignty as a strategy of resistance to the dominance of large technology corporations (Cong, 2023). China, India, and Russia have attempted to create informational counterweights but still operate in a system dominated by Western mainstream media (Boyd-Barrett, 2011).

While the growth of Internet access has allowed more citizens to participate in global communication, digital divides remain an obstacle. Access in the nations of the Global South remains limited by the lack of technological infrastructure and high connectivity costs. Hamelink (2008) considers "digital decoupling" as a strategy to move away from infrastructures controlled by the Global North, before negotiating better conditions of access and control, to be relevant.

Gaps and Inequalities in AI Digital Ecosystems The studies analyzed identify as a key challenge the gaps and inequalities in AI digital ecosystems. US technology transnationals impose their dominance through the control of digital infrastructures, ways, and processes of production and the exploitation of resources and workers in developing countries, which reinforces the economic and technological dependence of what we will call the Global South (Colomina Saló & Galcerán-Vercher, 2024a; Kwet, 2021).

The global power of large technology companies and superpowers lies in their algorithmic control of Artificial Intelligence and their domination of the technological dependence of peripheral nations. Countries such as the USA and China lead the dominance of AI, which affects the sovereignty of other nations (Schmid et al., 2025).

The phenomenon of globalization is intimately linked to the conception of this new imperialism, whose international dimension is linked to the resolution of complex and contradictory problems based on algorithmic management (extenics theory). This new "order," according to Li (2023), confirms the asymmetry between Artificial Intelligence, geopolitical risks, and overexploitation as a consequence of current AI digital ecosystems influenced by the distribution of natural resources.

Digital divides are a consequence of the current digital AI ecosystems influenced by the distribution of international power, without any equity (Schmid et al., 2025). These inequalities, a product of the influence and dominance of technological superpowers, expose peripheral nations to great vulnerability. According to De la Peña and Granados (2024), developed countries consolidate their supremacy in AI through investment and technology policies, large-scale data surveillance, and restricted access to technology. Developing countries are caught between the two dominant technological models, forced to choose between the USA and Chinese digital infrastructure.

Artificial Intelligence Is Not Neutral Artificial Intelligence is not neutral (Mohamed et al., 2020). This new technological imperialism repeats the formulas of colonial subjugation, by reproducing historical power structures such as global inequalities, stemming from the extraction and exploitation of raw materials and access to information and technology.

For Mohamed et al. (2020) postcolonial and decolonial theories provide an essential framework for analyzing the influence of historical power structures in the development and application of Artificial Intelligence (AI). In this regard, the economic dominance of the superpowers is expressed in the processes and modes of production of Artificial Intelligence and in the extraction of data as an expression of the new colonialism, without adequate regulation that allows them to expand the power of these power centers.

The centers of technological power are characterized by concentrating multibillion dollar investments and financing; monopolizing the capitalism of platforms, digital infrastructure from servers, chip manufacturing, and even AI algorithms; and centralizing the business of patents and property rights in the hands of Western corporations.

Technological superpowers hold hegemony and control of the digital infrastructure; concentration of research centers and laboratories, whose headquarters are located in the dominant countries; and monopoly in data processing and restriction of access to more advanced AI data and models.

The Eurocentrism of current AI is designed in values and dominant languages such as English for data training and Western worldviews, excluding indigenous epistemologies. This pervasive imposition of "universal" standards on AI programming is known as knowledge colonialism or epistemological exclusion (Mohamed et al., 2020). Competition between the USA and China defines AI development priorities, leaving other countries in a subordinate role.

A New Player: the Global South The Global South is becoming more relevant in geopolitics and digital governance, ceasing to be just a recipient of policies and technologies, despite digital colonialism and data mining as new forms of inequality, where the great technological powers impose models without considering the local reality of each nation.

The Global South is not a spectator of international dynamics but an actor seeking to define new rules of the game in issues such as technological regulation and economic multipolarity. The rise of emerging economies and their increasing participation in global decisions guarantee a greater role for the Global South in a new international order in geopolitical conflicts in pursuit of greater technological, financial, and energy autonomy in these countries (Menon, 2024).

Li (2023) aims to show how Artificial Intelligence must deal with the unfair system of the exchange of raw materials for technology, the depredation and devaluation of natural resources with respect to the production costs of AI technologies, the negative impact of mass unemployment, and the adoption of sustainable technological systems to combat electronic pollution.

For Ferguson (2025), to mitigate the risks of AI weaponization and irresponsible use of these technologies, it is crucial to establish sound regulatory frameworks and foster international cooperation. The future of AI will depend on the ability of nations to balance technological advancement.

Technology Regulation After comparing the differences in regulatory frameworks between Latin America and Europe, Monje and Sierra Caballero (2023) argue that our region faces a regulatory vacuum in AI, which generates dependencies on external regulatory frameworks. The region lacks specific policies and strategies to address the social impact of AI. In the context of the New World Information and Communications Order (NWIO), the information hegemony of the great powers limits the technological autonomy of developing countries, consolidating the digital divide and dependence on infrastructures controlled by global actors.

Iacovitti (2022) recommends the development of technology regulation policies to ensure fair access to information, balance privacy with innovation, and the protection of personal data. The misuse of data can violate the fundamental rights of the nations that make up the Global South. Walter (2024) analyzes the global challenges in the regulation and governance of Artificial Intelligence, analyzing its socioeconomic implications. Neurosymbolic Artificial Intelligence generates challenges in the veracity of information and democratic stability.

A key challenge identified in the review of the academic literature is the need to produce dynamic and adaptive regulation to enable innovation without compromising safety and human rights. For Kashefi et al. (2024) the governance frameworks suggested by different authors consider as timely the contribution of governments, industry, and civil society to establish effective ethical and regulatory standards. The dependent and inequitable communication model is consolidated in Latin America due to the absence of a common regulatory framework in the region, which weakens its bargaining power vis-à-vis large technological corporations.

Algorithmic Biases and Discrimination One of the most controversial issues in AI is the generation of algorithmic biases that perpetuate structural inequalities. Samala and Rawas (2025) highlight the lack of diversity in training data and unsupervised algorithmic decisions that can lead to discrimination, in sectors such as health, employment, and justice.

Biases in AI models perpetuate social inequalities due to biases, misleading correlations or reinforcement of stereotypes in training data. It is necessary to take into consideration that some algorithms may amplify biases by the way in which weights are assigned to certain attributes in algorithmic programming. The potential of these technologies for development poses risks of abuse, mass surveillance, and algorithmic biases (Brodny & Tutak, 2025).

To lessen these effects, Samala and Rawas (2025) propose strategies of algorithmic auditing, diverse data combination, accountable algorithms, constant monitoring, and the implementation of robust regulatory frameworks. Mitigating algorithmic biases will favor more natural and empathetic communication in chatbots and virtual assistants in the future, driving more equitable and accessible interactions (Hussain et al., 2024).

A relevant issue detected in the exploration of academic sources is the lack of transparency in the decision-making process of Artificial Intelligence models, especially in complex algorithms such as deep neural networks known as the "black box." The lack of this interpretability in AI systems makes it difficult to identify biases and accountability in automated decisions. Akdilek et al. (2024) emphasize the importance of developing explainable models that allow for greater human oversight.

AI and Human Rights A recurring point of conflict in this review of academic sources is the exploitation of data, due to the exponential growth in the volume of information generated and processed daily. Recent research points out that the use of AI in digital platforms may affect privacy, freedom of expression, and fairness in access to information (Hussain et al., 2024).

Artificial Intelligence and big data have automated the analysis of information, transforming sectors such as journalism and communication (Iacovitti, 2022). The media have found new opportunities to tell stories from the extraction of knowledge and values resulting from the interaction of data.

In the literature reviewed, some authors consider that the economic model of Silicon Valley is techno-feudalism at its best, where the CEOs of technology platforms act as feudal lords, having appropriated the work and data of users in the Global South to turn it into merchandise.

Morozov (2022) refers that large transnationals continue to operate under the logic of accumulation by exploitation, although with new extraction dynamics, it is no longer about raw materials but data. This digital colonialism massively captures data and imposes a new form of control, where big technology appropriates this resource without compensation (Shahabuddin, 2021).

Big data is not only a technological phenomenon but a mechanism of capitalist exploitation based on the appropriation of personal data (Thatcher et al., 2016). The potential of dig data hides unequal power relations, normalizing the extraction of information without effective regulation (Thatcher et al., 2016).

The struggle of NWICO remains more relevant than ever, especially in the control of digital colonialism and data exploitation in the Global South, under the rhetoric of globalization (Cong, 2023; Chakravartty & Muller, 2024). In that regard, we believe that there is a need for an effective global data protection mechanism, where international cooperation is key to develop a regulatory framework that protects the data of citizens in the Global South (Bentotahewa et al., 2022).

The literature review raises the need to include a human rights-based approach in the regulation of AI, avoiding the instrumentalization of these technologies for mass control or indiscriminate state surveillance.

Artificial Intelligence in Social Media and Geopolitics Artificial Intelligence governance has even impacted the media landscape of both the Global North and the Global South. Cong (2023) argues that the emergence of Artificial Intelligence in digital social media ecosystems has not served to democratize access to information and communications. It has only served to strengthen the dominance of large information transnationals and the concentration of social media in large commercial emporiums and to be a tool for colonial exploitation and technological domination. AI transforms the relationship between journalistic organizations and their audiences, affecting decision-making and message management (Weller & Lock, 2025).

One of the most concerning risks of AI in communication is misinformation and algorithmic manipulation. Kashefi et al. (2024) emphasize identification such as algorithmic bias, lack of transparency in AI systems, strengthening AI literacy, and the need to ensure accountability in AI use. Weller and Lock (2025) propose the implementation of AI-driven content verification systems to combat this problem. In the geopolitical context, AI has become a weapon of information warfare, where states and private actors use it to destabilize governments, polarize society, and manipulate electoral processes.

Media Concentration The withdrawal of the USA and the UK from UNESCO in 1984 weakened the postulates of NWICO, allowing large Western conglomerates to maintain their hegemony. In the last decade, the media landscape has been reconfigured based on the digitization of media and the rise of digital platforms and Artificial Intelligence. Conley and Patterson (2016) warn that the problems of prevailing media concentration and informational inequalities persist in developing countries, despite the Internet and now AI.

Technological advances have not democratized the flow of information between the Global North and the Global South nor have they deconcentrated in a few global corporations. Badillo and Proulx (2006) argue that these information flows are the cause of information overload and disinformation. The risks of manipulation and misinformation increase with generative AI tools (Walter, 2024).

The nations of the Global South continue to face information inequalities, due to media concentration, dependence on foreign digital platforms, and barriers to information access. This situation has resulted in a structural dependence on content produced in the Global North, generating a reduction in information diversity and in the ability of local media to compete on equal terms.

The large communication transnationals control the production and distribution of information at a global level. McChesney (2008) has pointed out that media concentration in the twenty-first century has been driven by technological convergence and the expansion of large corporations such as Google, Meta Amazon, and OpenAI. A critical issue identified in the evaluation of the scientific literature is the reduction of informational pluralism as one of the main effects of media concentration. Curran (2011) argues that the editorial line and contents of the media are subordinated to economic and political interests. In the case of developing countries, this generates a strong dependence on international news agencies such as Reuters, AFP, and AP, making it difficult to create their own narratives about local contexts.

García Canclini (2018) warns that media concentration in Latin America has favored the reproduction of neoliberal discourses, which has restricted coverage of structural problems such as poverty and inequality. Information inequalities in developing countries are not only due to media concentration but also to the digital divide and unequal access to information. The digital revolution has generated new forms of exclusion, where access to information is determined by socioeconomic and geographic factors (Castells, 2009).

In Peru, for example, Internet connectivity remains limited in provinces and in rural areas and impoverished sectors, which restricts access to alternative sources of information and maintains the hegemony of traditional media. According to Reuters (2021) 69% of Peruvians use Facebook to consume news as their main information channel, limiting informational sovereignty and increasing vulnerability to disinformation and algorithmic manipulation. The rise of digital platforms has transformed the way information is consumed but has also reinforced new forms of media concentration.

Despite advances in connectivity and the rise of independent media, asymmetries in the production and distribution of information remain a structural challenge. It is necessary to strengthen public policies that promote media pluralism, digital sovereignty, and the regulation of media conglomerates to ensure a more equitable information ecosystem that is representative of local realities.

NSIA Algorithms for Media Large transnational corporations design algorithms that largely determine the content and news accessed by the majority of the population. This raises the debate about who regulates the algorithms and what interests underlie their operation.

Personalization algorithms are transforming digital news consumption, reader experiences, and their implications for democracy. Neurosymbolic AI models introduce symbolic or knowledge-based elements to recommend the use of content tags and user profiles structured by interest categories, allowing the system to reason about thematic affinity in addition to pure interaction patterns.

The algorithms represent a promising technological evolution for the media. NSIA allows us to personalize our readers' news experience, displaying news with their preferences, through hybrid recommender systems, personalization algorithms, and journalistic knowledge graphs represented as nodes connected by relationships. Media profitability can also reinforce selection bias, limit news diversity, and erode news trust.

Fact-checking companies are already using tools that transcribe audio/video broadcasts and detect potentially misleading phrases.

The extreme personalization of news has as a consequence in our readers the decrease of critical thinking and the fragmentation of the perception of reality. Extreme personalization of news reinforces polarization and information bubbles (Helberger, 2025).

3 Conclusion

The advancement of Artificial Intelligence poses significant challenges in terms of regulation, ethics, media, and geopolitics, which require an interdisciplinary approach. AI governance must be flexible and collaborative, integrating perspectives from different regions and sectors to ensure ethical and sustainable development.

The advance of Neurosymbolic Artificial Intelligence has intensified a new expression of technological imperialism, a product of global algorithmic competition between the superpowers: the USA, China, and the EU. This so-called digital imperialism redefines the structures of geopolitical power in the twentieth century, based on the modernization of historical dynamics of exploitation, under a new digital logic.

The superpowers and transnational technology corporations seek to consolidate their colonial domination over developing nations through the control of digital infrastructures, data and algorithmic models, the centralization of knowledge and research, and the exploitation of data as the raw material of domination and privileged access to capital, talent, and markets.

The concentration of technological power generates great inequality, limiting access to information in countries with less technological development, increasing the digital divide. While it is true that Neurosymbolic Artificial Intelligence is more accurate and helps to facilitate its own use, at this point, problems may arise such as the misrepresentation of information, as well as the reinforcement of authoritarian structures.

In the field of communication, it is essential to balance the use of AI with the preservation of human interaction and the veracity of information. Media information flows are under the sway of Neurosymbolic Artificial Intelligence algorithms. It is imperative that media industry developers apply algorithms with ethical principles in their implementation.

References

Akdilek, S., Akdilek, I., & Punyanunt-Carter, N. M. (2024). The influence of generative AI on interpersonal communication dynamics. In *The Role of Generative AI in the Communication Classroom*. (pp. XX–XX). IGI Global. https://doi.org/10.4018/979-8-3693-0831-8.ch009

Allen, G., & Kania, E. B. (2017, September 8). *China is using the United States' plan to dominate the future of artificial intelligence*. Foreign Policy. https://foreignpolicy.com/2017/09/08/china-is-using-americas-own-plan-to-dominate-the-future-of-artificial-intelligence/

Amador-Domínguez, E., Serrano, E., & Manrique, D. (2024). Neurosymbolic system profiling: A template-based approach. *Knowledge-Based Systems, 287*, 111441. https://doi.org/10.1016/j.knosys.2024.111441

Attoresi, M. (2025). *Neuro-symbolic artificial intelligence*. The Alan Turing Institute. https://www.edps.europa.eu/data-protection/technology-monitoring/techsonar/neuro-symbolic-artificial-intelligence_en#:~:text=Another%20critical%20consideration%20is%20the,making%20process%2C%20thus%20improving%20accountability

Ayana, G., Dese, K., Nemomssa, H. D., Habtamu, B., Mellado, B., Badu, K., Yamba, E., Faye, S. L., Ondua, M., Nsagha, D., Nkweteyim, D., & Kong, J. D. (2024). Decolonizing global AI governance: assessment of the state of decolonized AI governance in Sub-Saharan Africa. *Royal Society Open Science, 11*(231994). https://doi.org/10.1098/rsos.231994

Badillo, P.-Y., & Proulx, S. (2006). Mondialisation de la communication, à la recherche du sens perdu. *Hermes, 44*, 47. https://doi.org/10.4267/2042/24008

Baele, S. J., Bukhari, I. A., Whyte, C., Cuomo, S., Jensen, B., Payne, K., & Garcia, E. V. (2024). *AI IR: Charting international relations in the age of artificial intelligence*. International Studies Review. https://doi.org/10.1093/isr/viae013

Bahcecik, S. O. (2023). Security politics and artificial intelligence: Key trends and debates. *International Political Science Abstracts, 73*(3), 329–338. https://doi.org/10.1177/00208345231182638

Bârgăoanu, A., & Cheregi, B.-F. (2021). Artificial intelligence: The new tool for cyber diplomacy. In *Artificial Intelligence and Digital Diplomacy: Challenges and Opportunities* (pp. 115–130). Springer. https://doi.org/10.1007/978-3-030-68647-5_9

Bentotahewa, V., Hewage, C., & Williams, J. (2022). The normative power of the GDPR: A case study of data protection laws of South Asian countries. *SN Computer Science, 3*(183). https://doi.org/10.1007/s42979-022-01079-z

Boyd-Barrett, O. (2011). Rethinking news agencies, national development and information imperialism. *Economic and Political Weekly, 46*(13), 85–94.

Brodny, J., & Tutak, M. (2025). Stakeholder interactions and ethical imperatives in big data and AI development. *Journal of Open Innovation: Technology, Market, and Complexity, 11*, 100491. https://doi.org/10.1016/j.joitmc.2025.100491

Castells, M. (2009). *Comunicación y poder*. Alianza Editorial.

Chakravartty, P., & Muller, C. (2024). Anticolonial world-making: Racial justice and global communication governance. In *Handbook of media and communication governance* (pp. 189–199). Edward Elgar. https://doi.org/10.4337/9781800887206.00024

Chesterman, S. (2021). Weapons of mass disruption: Artificial intelligence and international law. *Cambridge International Law Journal, 10*(2), 181–203. https://doi.org/10.1017/cilj.2021.02.02

Coleman, D. (2019). Digital colonialism: The 21st-century scramble for Africa through the extraction and control of user data and the limitations of data protection laws. *Michigan Journal of Race & Law, 24*(2). https://doi.org/10.36643/mjrl.24.2.digital

Colomina Saló, C., & Galcerán-Vercher, M. (2024a). Las otras geopolíticas de la Inteligencia Artificial. *Revista CIDOB d'Afers Internacionals, 138*, 27–50. https://doi.org/10.24241/rcai.2024.138.3.27

Colomina Saló, C., & Galcerán-Vercher, M. (2024b). ¿Qué es el Sur Global? In *Anuario Internacional CIDOB 2025* (pp. 90–91). CIDOB.

Cong, W. (2023). Contesting freedom of information: Capitalism, development, and the Third World. *Asian Journal of International Law, 13*(46–75). https://doi.org/10.1017/S2044251322000467

Conley, M., & Patterson, C. (2016). Communication, human rights and cyberspace. In *Human Rights and the Internet* (pp. 211–224). Palgrave Macmillan. https://doi.org/10.1057/9780333977705_19

Couldry, N., & Mejias, U. A. (2019). *The costs of connection: How data is colonizing human life and appropriating it for capitalism*. Stanford University Press.

Curran, J. (2011). *Media and democracy*. Routledge. https://doi.org/10.4324/9780203406878

DARPA. (2023). *Assured Neuro Symbolic Learning and Reasoning (ANSR) – Program Summary*. Defense Advanced Research Projects Agency. https://www.darpa.mil/research/programs/assured-neuro-symbolic-learning-and-reasoning#:~:text=ANSR%20seeks%20breakthrough%20innovations%20in,assured%2C%20and%20therefore%20trustworthy%20systems

De la Peña, N., & Granados, O. M. (2024). El poder internacional y las capacidades de Inteligencia Artificial. *Revista Científica General José María Córdova, 22*(47), 693–712. https://doi.org/10.21830/19006586.1376

Dehghani Firouzabadi, S. J., & Chehrazad, S. (2024). La geopolítica de la Inteligencia Artificial: Guía teórica para la competencia algorítmica de actores de sistemas globales. *International Geopolitical Quarterly, 20*(3), 270–313. https://doi.org/10.22034/igq.2024.143237

Editorial Team. (2024, July 1). *The role of artificial intelligence in modern warfare strategies*. Total Military Insight. https://totalmilitaryinsight.com/artificial-intelligence-in-warfare-2/

Farnell, R., & Coffey, K. (2024, October 11). *AI's new frontier in war planning: How AI agents can revolutionize military decision-making*. Belfer Center for Science and International Affairs, Harvard Kennedy School. https://www.belfercenter.org/research-analysis/ais-new-frontier-war-planning-how-ai-agents-can-revolutionize-military-decision

Ferguson, M. (2025, 13 de febrero). *La nueva carrera armamentística de la IA: las potencias mundiales compiten por el dominio*. Opentools. https://opentools.ai/news/the-new-ai-arms-race-global-powers-vie-for-dominance#section39

Fernández-García, C. (2024, mayo 20). *La competencia global por la Inteligencia Artificial*. El Perfil. https://elperfil.pe/opinion/la-competencia-global-por-la-inteligencia-artificial/

Firoozabadi, S. J. D., & Chehrazad, S. (2024). Geopolitics of artificial intelligence: Theoretical roadmap for algorithmic competitions of world actors. *Geopolitics Quarterly, 20*(3), 270–313. https://doi.org/10.22034/igq.2024.143237

García Canclini, N. (2018). A culture of informality. *Urban Studies, 56*(3), 494–508. https://doi.org/10.1177/0042098018782635

Gavilán, I. (2024, 3 de julio). *Inteligencia Artificial Neurosimbólica: la tercera ola de la Inteligencia Artificial*. https://ignaciogavilan.com/inteligencia-artificial-Neurosimbólica-la-tercera-ola-de-la-inteligencia-artificial/

Gerlich, M. (2024). Prepararse para el impacto: cómo afrontar la revolución de la IA y los cambios geopolíticos en un escenario social futuro para 2025–2040. *Sociedades, 14*(9), 180. https://doi.org/10.3390/soc14090180

Gobierno de China. (2017, 8 de julio). *Nuevo Plan de Desarrollo de Inteligencia Artificial de China*. Consejo de Estado de la República Popular China. https://www.gov.cn/zhengce/content/2017-07/20/content_5211996.htm

Greiman, V. (2021). The winds of change in world politics and the impact on cyber stability. In I. Management Association (Ed.), *Research anthology on artificial intelligence applications in security* (pp. 2138–2151). IGI Global Scientific Publishing. https://doi.org/10.4018/978-1-7998-7705-9.ch093

Haileselassie, H. D., & Rawat, D. B. (2024). Neuro-symbolic AI for military applications. *IEEE Transactions on Artificial Intelligence, 5*(12), 6012–6026. https://doi.org/10.1109/TAI.2024.3444746

Hamelink, C. J. (2008). New media, the internet and the North/South conflict. *Journal für Entwicklungspolitik, 24*(1). https://doi.org/10.20446/JEP-2414-3197-24-1-16

Helberger, N. (2025). *Los algoritmos están remodelando nuestros hábitos de lectura de noticias. ¿Deberíamos preocuparnos?* CORDIS – Comisión Europea. https://cordis.europa.eu/article/id/434332-algorithms-are-reshaping-our-newsreading-habits-should-we-worry/es

Hern, A. (2017, 4 de septiembre). *Elon Musk dice que la IA podría conducir a una tercera guerra mundial*. The Guardian. https://www.theguardian.com/technology/2017/sep/04/elon-musk-ai-third-world-war-vladimir-putin

Hitzler, P., Ebrahimi, M., Sarker, M. K., & Stepanova, D. (2024). Neuro-symbolic AI and the semantic web. *Semantic Web, 15*(11), 1–3. https://doi.org/10.3233/SW-243711

Hobbes, T. (2008). *Leviatán* (JCA Gaskin, Ed.). Oxford University Press.
Horowitz, M. C., Allen, G. C., Saravalle, E., Cho, A., Frederick, K., & Scharre, P. (2018). *Artificial intelligence and international security*. Center for a New American Security (CNAS). https://www.cnas.org/publications/reports/artificial-intelligence-and-international-security
Hussain, S., Sohail, T., Afzaal, R., & Khan, M. A. (2024). The future of artificial intelligence in communication. In *Future communication systems using artificial intelligence, internet of things and data science* (1st ed.). CRC Press. https://doi.org/10.1201/9781032648309
Iacovitti, G. (2022). How technology influences information gathering and information spreading. *Church, Communication and Culture, 7*(1), 76–90. https://doi.org/10.1080/23753234.2022.2032781
von Ingersleben-Seip, N. (2023). Competition and cooperation in artificial intelligence standard setting: Explaining emergent patterns. *Review of Policy Research, 40*(5), 781–810. https://doi.org/10.1111/ropr.12538
Kashefi, P., Kashefi, Y., & Ghafouri Mirsaraei, A. H. (2024). Dando forma al futuro de la IA: Equilibrando la innovación y la ética en la regulación global. *Uniform Law Review, 29*(3), 524–548. https://doi.org/10.1093/ulr/unae040
Khan, K., Khurshid, A., & Cifuentes-Faura, J. (2024). Is artificial intelligence a new battleground for cybersecurity? *Internet of Things, 24*, 101428. https://doi.org/10.1016/j.iot.2024.101428
Kugler, M. (2021). The United States of America's embrace of artificial intelligence for defense purposes. In A. Visvizi & M. Bodziany (Eds.), *Artificial intelligence and its contexts* (pp. 183–199). Springer. https://doi.org/10.1007/978-3-030-88972-2_12
Kwet, M. (2019). Digital colonialism: US empire and the new imperialism in the Global South. *Race & Class, 60*(4), 3–26. https://doi.org/10.1177/0306396818823172
Kwet, M. (2021). *Digital colonialism: The evolution of US empire*. Transnational Institute. https://www.tni.org/en/publication/digital-colonialism
Li, B. (2023). AI governance in China: Building a responsible AI ecosystem. *AI and Ethics, 3*(2), 205–218. https://doi.org/10.1007/s43681-023-00159-7
Mansell, R. (2010). The life and times of the Information Society. *Prometheus, 28*(2), 165–186. https://doi.org/10.1080/08109028.2010.503120
Mastrini, G., & De Charras, D. (2005). Twenty years mean nothing: From NWICO to WSIS. *Global Media and Communication, 1*(3), 273–288. https://doi.org/10.1177/1742766505058124
Matic. (2023, 27 de diciembre). *AI in 2023 review: A timeline of artificial intelligence advancements*. Autogpt. https://autogpt.net/ai-in-2023-review-a-timeline-of-artificial-intelligence-advancements/
McChesney, R. W. (2008). *The political economy of media: Enduring issues, emerging dilemmas*. Monthly Review Press.
Menon, S. (2024). El Sur Global: De objeto a sujeto del orden internacional. In *Anuario Internacional CIDOB 2025* (Ed. 2024), 19–29. CIDOB. https://www.cidob.org/publicaciones/anuario_internacional_cidob_2025
Mohamed, S., Png, M.-T., & Isaac, W. (2020). Decolonial AI: Decolonial theory as sociotechnical foresight in artificial intelligence. *Philosophy & Technology, 33*, 9–56. https://doi.org/10.1007/s13347-020-00405-8
Monje, D., & Sierra Caballero, F. (2023). Artificial intelligence: The blind spot of info-communication platform policy-making and regulation in Latin America. *Journal of Digital Media & Policy, 14*(2), 149–167. https://doi.org/10.1386/jdmp_00119_1
Morozov, E. (2022). Critique of techno-feudal reason. *New Left Review, 133/134*, 89–116. https://newleftreview.org/issues/ii133/articles/evgeny-morozov-critique-of-techno-feudal-reason
Muldoon, J. P., & Wu, B. A. (2023). Artificial intelligence in the colonial matrix of power. *Philosophy & Technology, 36*(80). https://doi.org/10.1007/s13347-023-00687-8
Natale, S. (2020). Communicating through or communicating with: Approaching artificial intelligence from a communication and media studies perspective. *Communication Theory, 0*(0000), 1–6. https://doi.org/10.1093/ct/qtaa022

Polygraph.info VOA. (2025, marzo 11). *Cómo China ha utilizado modelos de IA en vigilancia y desinformación contra EEUU*. Voz de América. https://www.vozdeamerica.com/a/china-modelos-ia-vigilancia-desinformacion-contra-eeuu-/8006914.html

Quijano, A. (2014). Colonialidad del poder, eurocentrismo y América Latina. In *Cuestiones y horizontes: De la dependencia histórico-estructural a la colonialidad/descolonialidad del poder* (pp. 778–802). CLACSO. https://biblioteca.clacso.edu.ar/clacso/se/20140507042402/eje3-8.pdf

Renkhoff, J., Feng, K., Meier-Doernberg, M., Velasquez, A., & Song, H. H. (2024). A survey on verification and validation, testing and evaluations of neurosymbolic artificial intelligence. *IEEE Transactions on Artificial Intelligence, 5*(8), 3765–3779. https://doi.org/10.1109/TAI.2024.3351798

Reuters Institute. (2021). *Digital News Report 2021*. Instituto Reuters. https://www.mercadonegro.pe/publicidad/social-media/estudio-facebook-es-la-red-social-que-mas-usan-los-peruanos-para-consumir-noticias/

Ricaurte, P. (2019). Data epistemologies, the coloniality of power, and resistance. *Television & New Media, 20*(4). https://doi.org/10.1177/1527476419831640

Rivas, T. (2025, enero 28). *The end of American exceptionalism? How DeepSeek could shatter the US stock market*. Barron's. https://www.barrons.com/articles/stock-market-deepseek-american-exeptionalism-e9363527?utm_source=chatgpt.com

Salami, A. O. (2024). Artificial intelligence, digital colonialism, and the implications for Africa's future development. *Data & Policy, 6*, e67. https://doi.org/10.1017/dap.2024.75

Samala, A. D., & Rawas, S. (2025). Bias in artificial intelligence: Smart solutions for detection, mitigation, and ethical strategies in real-world applications. *IAES International Journal of Artificial Intelligence (IJ-AI), 14*(1), 32–43. https://doi.org/10.11591/ijai.v14.i1.pp32-43

Sarkin, J. J., & Sotoudehfar, S. (2024). Artificial intelligence and arms races in the Middle East: The evolution of technology and its implications for regional and international security. *Defense and Security Analysis, 40*(1), 97–119. https://doi.org/10.1080/14751798.2024.2302699

Schiller, H. I. (1976). *Communication and cultural domination*. International Arts and Sciences Press.

Schmid, S., Lambach, D., Diehl, C., & Reuter, C. (2025). Arms race or innovation race? Geopolitical AI development. *Geopolitics*. 1–30. https://doi.org/10.1080/14650045.2025.2456019

Shahabuddin, M. (2021). *Minorities and the making of postcolonial states in international law*. Cambridge University Press. https://doi.org/10.1017/9781108678773

Sheth, A., Roy, K., & Gaur, M. (2023). Neurosymbolic AI – Why, What, and How. *arXiv preprint arXiv:2305.00813*. https://arxiv.org/abs/2305.00813

Tallberg, J., Erman, E., Furendal, M., Geith, J., Klamberg, M., & Lundgren, M. (2023). *The global governance of artificial intelligence: next steps for empirical and normative research*. Stockholm University. SSRN. https://ssrn.com/abstract=4424123

Thatcher, J., O'Sullivan, D., & Mahmoudi, D. (2016). Data colonialism through accumulation by dispossession: New metaphors for daily data. *Environment and Planning D: Society and Space, 34*(6), 990–1006. https://doi.org/10.1177/0263775816633195

The Alan Turing Institute. (2025). *Neuro-symbolic AI: Integrating deep learning and symbolic structures*. The Alan Turing Institute. https://www.turing.ac.uk

Thomas, C. A., & Wu, X. (2021, February 25). *How global tech executives view U.S.–China tech competition*. Brookings Institution. https://www.brookings.edu/articles/how-global-tech-executives-view-u-s-china-tech-competition/

Tinnirello, M. (Ed.). (2022). *The global politics of artificial intelligence*. Chapman & Hall/CRC. https://doi.org/10.1201/9780429446726

Vacarelu, M. (2021). Artificial intelligence: To strengthen or to replace traditional diplomacy. In F. Roumate (Ed.), *Artificial intelligence and digital diplomacy*. Springer. https://doi.org/10.1007/978-3-030-68647-5_1

Vincent, J. (2017, September 4). *Putin says the nation that leads in AI "will be the ruler of the world"*. The Verge. https://www.theverge.com/2017/9/4/16251226/russia-ai-putin-rule-the-world

Walter, Y. (2024). Managing the race to the moon: Global policy and governance in artificial intelligence regulation—A contemporary overview and an analysis of socioeconomic consequences. *Discover Artificial Intelligence, 4*(14). https://doi.org/10.1007/s44163-024-00109-4

Weller, T., & Lock, I. (2025). Automated communication's impact on strategic communication: Implications from a systematic review. *International Journal of Strategic Communication, 19*(1), 13–34. https://doi.org/10.1080/1553118X.2024.2379501

Zhu, Q., & Long, K. (2019). How will artificial intelligence impact Sino–US relations? *China International Strategy Review, 1*, 139–151. https://doi.org/10.1007/s42533-019-00008-9

Zhu, R., Feng, Z., & Chen, Q. (2022). Competition of artificial intelligence in big countries: The mystery of power and security. In *2022 8th Annual International Conference on Network and Information Systems for Computers (ICNISC)* (pp. 209–216). https://doi.org/10.1109/ICNISC57059.2022.00051

Chapter 5
Behind the Screen: Exploring the Influence of Artificial Intelligence on Established Media and *Its Implications for* International Security

Ouiam Chafik and Oualid Rais

Abstract The contemporary security landscape has become increasingly shaped by the intersection of artificial intelligence (AI) and media narratives. As AI is rapidly evolving, it is transforming how information is created, shared, and perceived. While these advancements offer significant opportunities, they also raise serious concerns, particularly regarding the spread of propaganda, misinformation, and deliberate falsehoods.

The rapid development of AI has given rise to advanced systems capable of gathering information, applying logical reasoning, and refining their own processes. These advances have made the security environment more complex, sparking discussions about the strategic advantages and related perils of AI-driven media. In a world where international security is already uncertain, the influence of AI on information flows further complicates this landscape.

Amid these developments, this chapter investigates one crucial question: How can we manage the risks of AI-powered media while ensuring international peace and security? Addressing this challenge requires well-defined strategies to counter misinformation, uphold information integrity, and harness AI responsibly. As AI continues to reshape media narratives, a proactive and balanced approach is essential to maintaining trust and security in an increasingly complex world.

Keywords Artificial intelligence · AI-driven media narratives · Strategic advantages · International security considerations · Global stability

---

O. Chafik · O. Rais (✉)
Faculty of Law, Economic and Social Sciences Agdal, Mohammed V University, Rabat, Morocco

Faculty of Legal and Political Sciences, Ibn Tofail University, Kenitra, Morocco

F. Roumate, A. La Rosa (eds.), *Artificial Intelligence, Media and International Security*, Contributions to Security and Defence Studies,
https://doi.org/10.1007/978-3-031-95757-4_5

1 Introduction

The world today is undergoing a crucial transition marked by a new industrial revolution that has and will continue to transform the way in which information is produced, disseminated, and consumed. The term "Fourth Industrial Revolution" was first coined at the 2016 World Economic Forum in Davos, Switzerland, to reveal the stage set by emerging technologies, such as gene editing, smart city technologies, and blockchain, and their expected impact on people's lives—particularly machine learning technologies and new forms of artificial intelligence. Such technologies wield far-reaching influence across a range of sectors and fields, including media and journalism.

With rapid technological and conceptual progress, the technological revolution in artificial intelligence (AI) and robotics has become increasingly evident. These technologies have reached a level of such precision and expertise that machines have become producers of culture and knowledge. This is reflected in the technologies that blend the natural with the artificial and that are now being passed on to us—AI, machine learning, algorithmic bias, language technology, neural technology, and so on. This sample indicates that technology has indeed invaded the human world from within, since it has become accessible through these advancements. It can be asserted that the evolution of humanity in the era of information depends on the interaction between human thought output and the artificial processing of these machines.

Today, in a world where digital transformation defines everything we do, the influence of AI is becoming ever more profound. However, how exactly does AI fit in with evolving media trends? What dual role is it playing in shaping the media landscape and influencing the complex field of international security? Unlike past technological revolutions, AI systems are deeply interconnected and rely on mutual dependencies across different domains. AI is not simply an addition to the existing media production ecosystem; it is a driving force that enhances and reshapes the industry, equipping it with the necessary tools to evolve and adapt to the changing digital landscape. New industries and infrastructures based on AI are arising rapidly, reshaping not only the media sector but also its organisational structures, operating models, and strategic approaches. Much like the revolutionary impact of steam and electricity in their time, these advances are not just boosting productivity; they are redefining the ethical standards of journalism and information sharing. Matters including conflict of interest, transparency of sources, fairness, misinformation, and accuracy of content have all come under scrutiny within this shifting environment.

There is no doubt that the relentless pace of technological advancement, particularly in the area of AI, has profoundly altered the global media industry. As AI becomes increasingly integrated into storytelling, content creation, and audience interaction, its influence extends far beyond how information is disseminated to shape the core of how narratives are constructed and consumed.

This chapter attempts to explore the interplay between AI and the media, focusing on how AI shapes public perception and influences international security. The aim is to dissect the nuanced interplay between smart technology and geopolitical tensions and, by extension, international security, with a specific focus on the corrosion of trust. By navigating through the complexities of misinformation, shadow information, and strategically crafted narratives, we seek to unravel the intricate ways in which the media, operating within the contours of smart technology, contribute to the fragility of trust between nations. Through this examination, we endeavour to shed light on the challenges posed by these dynamics and explore potential trends and avenues for mitigating their adverse effects on international relations.

The challenges of AI-driven media are outlined, particularly in the context of international security, where the dissemination of information, whether accurate or misleading, can have far-reaching consequences. Its impact can be more deeply understood by examining practical cases in which AI is involved, where electoral campaigns and the manipulation of information in times of war and conflict serve as compelling examples. In reviewing these cases, the complexities of AI's ongoing effect on media content are uncovered, revealing its transformative power and ability to undermine the conventional norms within the media landscape.

2 Method

Studying and exploring the influence of artificial intelligence on established media and its implications for international security are based on a blend of systemic and analytic methods. This combination is essential due to the complexity of intersection between AI, media, and international security. Identifying this complexity and examining how AI and media influence international security, as well as how this technology and media shape the global dynamics landscape, require the use of both methods. In addition, technological, societal, and political approaches are used to achieve the aim of this chapter. The technological approach plays a crucial role in explaining the impact, challenges, solutions, and trends related to AI and media.

Societal approach helps to explain how individuals interact with AI—generated media content and how the use of generative AI in media influences public opinion and drives political changes and democratic process, particularly during elections. The political approach is used to explore how AI's implications on media are reshaping international security considering the tensions between states increased by fake news, deepfakes, and other negative consequences of AI in media.

3 Literature Review

A series of studies focus on AI and media, such as the research on "How Generative AI Is Boosting the Spread of Disinformation and Propaganda" By Ryan-Mosley, T. (2023, October 4) in *MIT Technology Review*. Other studies examine media and international security such as the research by Puddephatt, A., et al., on conflict and the role of the media published in *Mediasupport* in 2006.

However, few studies combine the interactions between AI, media, and international security. On such example is the article "Artificial Intelligence, Geopolitics, and Information Integrity, The Global Race for Technological Superiority," by John Villasenor, edited by Fabio Rugge (first edition: November 2019). The analysis presented in this chapter offers a perspective from the field of political science and based on various approaches.

4 AI-Driven Transformations in the Media Landscape

The transition of contemporary society towards an information and services-based economy reflects a form of historical determinism, suggesting that this shift is an inevitable outcome of past technological and economic developments. Academic research into the dynamic processes of nations has shown that human history is marked by disruption and progress. The belief that today's environment mirrors that of the seventeenth and eighteenth centuries is misplaced. While the conditions and developments on which past societies were based have continued to shape the present, technology and its modern capabilities have played an integral role in the social, economic, and political development of humankind from its earliest days.

The ongoing information revolution is a crucial stage in historical development, on par with the first and second industrial revolutions. Although some societies have fallen behind in previous revolutions, today they have the opportunity to participate actively in the information revolution and to benefit from it. However, there is no single path for the transition of countries to an information and knowledge-based society. On the contrary, each country is unique in its experience, moulded by its specific political, economic, cultural, and scientific characteristics, as well as its demographic and social structures and the associated challenges.

While the information revolution has brought about changes in the media industry and the ways in which information is consumed in the increasingly globalised context of the economy, knowledge, and the media, it has also raised a number of challenges, particularly those relating to technology, content production, and the use of modern technologies. In addition, this revolution has given rise to new media and cultural content, evolving publishing methods, new public space and media freedom, and a growing gap between the countries of the North and South, particularly in terms of content and technology production. These challenges have been further exacerbated through the convergence of leading multinational corporations in areas such as communication networks and broadcasting.

Scholarly reflection on these shifts and related issues has expanded from a technical approach and a discourse of astonishment and glorification to a focus on the sovereignty of these advancements as a determining factor. This research demonstrates a communicative approach to societal change and a discourse on social uses and expected benefits. There have been many approaches and attempts to establish new foundations and theoretical frameworks for the media scene in light of the constant development of technology, its widespread use, and the diversity of its applications. However, the complex nature of these matters requires comprehensive consideration at different levels, including social, cultural, economic, political, and international aspects.

Throughout the second half of the twentieth century, media experts and policymakers largely focused on attempting to find a balance between the North and the South and, more broadly, between capitalist and socialist media systems. At the same time, an intellectual and technological evolution was underway, probing the relationship between human cognition and computing. Throughout the developed world, the concept of human–computer interaction has become a defining marker of technological progress.

The rapid rise of digitisation, accelerated by the widespread use of smartphones and social media platforms, has marked a turning point in the global landscape. This ongoing transformation, fuelled by the relentless pursuit of scientific innovation, continues to reshape societies and redefine communication. At the juncture of technology and media, AI has emerged as a transformative force that fundamentally alters traditional media practices in the digital age (Broussard et al., 2018).

Artificial intelligence refers to a set of concepts, techniques, and methodologies that allow computer systems to perform tasks generally associated with human intelligence (Zaragoza, 2023, p. 5). Among its most important breakthroughs is machine learning, which enables systems to continuously refine and improve their analytical capabilities by means of advanced calculation algorithms. It is this capability that has made AI a key driver of digital transformation, particularly in the media sector.

The media industry, which stands at the intersection of human creativity and technological progress, is undergoing profound changes as AI becomes deeply integrated into its landscape. It is not just a question of adopting new tools but of bridging the gap between conventional media models and emerging digital technologies. However, this transition comes with significant challenges, including the dominance of digital platforms, the competition coming from social networks, the spread of misinformation, and the loss of public trust.

This means that the focus must now be on sustainable solutions that enhance the credibility and relevance of the media. Investing in advanced digital tools, developing high-quality content, and adopting innovative approaches to storytelling and analysis are crucial steps. Above all, harnessing AI advances in communication and media technologies is essential to meet the evolving expectations of different audiences and to ensure that the media remains a reliable pillar of the information ecosystem (Global Media Congress, 2024).

These rapid developments have resulted in the hybridisation of media, combining "old" and "new" journalistic standards and practices within advanced digital models. As the media industry continues to adapt to the accelerating waves of digitisation, the intersection of AI and journalism has become an important area of transformation (Bentivegna & Marchetti, 2017). In fact, the launch of ChatGPT in November 2022 marked a turning point in this evolution. By bringing this revolutionary technology into the mainstream, ChatGPT democratised access to AI-driven tools, making certain professional features—such as image, sound, and text generation—more automated and widely accessible.

In response, news outlets have rapidly embraced AI technologies, using them to analyse large datasets, verify information, streamline journalistic workflows, generate news content and visuals, and improve publishing processes through automated sorting and selection. The benefits of these systems are significant, particularly in their ability to execute complex tasks at a remarkable speed by processing large volumes of data. AI has also improved journalistic routines by generating real-time alerts on breaking news and priority issues, allowing for more large-scale media coverage, including in previously underreported areas. Moreover, AI-driven personalisation enables media outlets to provide audiences with tailored news content based on their interests and geographic location.

While AI has and continues to reshape numerous sectors, its direct impact on media is particularly evident in photography, editing, proofreading, translation, and big data management (Boulaghron & Boukhenfer, 2023). The integration of AI applications has revolutionised the news industry by leveraging data-driven algorithms to analyse, generate, and structure news content dynamically. This capability has ushered in an era of interactive journalism, in which information is continuously evolving based on real-time inputs and contextual changes. The role of AI in journalism spans seven key subfields: machine learning, computer vision, speech recognition, natural language processing, planning, scheduling, and optimisation, specialised expert systems, and robotics. However, studies indicate that only three of these—machine learning, computer vision, and planning, scheduling, and optimisation—are currently undergoing further development within the news media sector (Kotenidis & Veglis, 2021).

4.1 AI Techniques in Newsrooms: Automated Content Production

The term "algorithm" primarily refers to automated decision-making. Algorithms can be coded or self-taught by humans through machine learning. Cultural goods and news increasingly pass through information intermediaries known as platforms that rely on algorithms to filter, classify, sort, and promote the information they circulate.

Algorithms have become indispensable in newsrooms and are now a reality in many American and European newspapers that use this technology. The technology is characterised by its ability to produce content faster, in multiple languages, and with fewer errors and biases. As a result, it is thought to improve news quality and accuracy, helping to solve the problem of fake news (Noain-Sánchez, 2022). A notable example is the "Quakebot" programme, created on behalf of the *Los Angeles Times* in 2014. It was one of the first automatic content production applications. Its aim was to monitor US Geological Survey data, identify instances of seismic activity, and generate and publish simple reports about them (Hunt & McKelvey, 2019). Since then, automated content production has become widespread in mainstream media. For instance, *Forbes* and *The New York Times* rely on automated content production tools to generate their media content, achieving results that are almost indistinguishable from human writing (Kotenidis & Veglis, 2021).

Despite these advances, numerous controversies have arisen over the nature of the recommended content, ranging from disturbing videos to conspiracies and political misinformation. These issues have undermined confidence in the impartiality of AI-based systems. Amid this, algorithmic accountability has emerged as a focal point for regulatory innovation, seeking to elucidate automated decision-making processes, assign responsibility, and enhance the overall system (Hunt & McKelvey, 2019).

Many researchers agree that the advances seen in automated content production are mainly attributable to natural language generation (NLG) technology. Over the past decade, this technology has been adopted, developed, and commercialised by various companies, including Arria, Applied Semantics, Automated Insights, and Narrative Science (Caswell & Dörr, 2017). The origins of the latter date back to the 1950s as part of machine translation efforts, and its use has broadened considerably in recent years. These technologies are increasingly used to automate certain routine writing tasks within news outlets, a practice commonly referred to as "automated journalism", a manifestation of quantitative journalism, and sometimes referred to as "algorithmic journalism" or "robotic journalism" (Caswell & Dörr, 2017).

The dominant trend in media circles involves the integration of machine learning algorithms into initiatives intended to decipher readers' complex interests and meet their inclinations. Leading media outlets, such as *The New York Times* and *New Zealand Media and Entertainment*, as well as *Toutiao* in China, have adopted AI-based news applications that use content recommendation engines to offer media content suggestions tailored to recipients' preferences.

Another significant trend in the media industry is the widespread adoption of paywalls, as illustrated by the *Wall Street Journal*'s innovative approach. By deploying machine learning models, non-subscribers to the newspaper are offered a tempting preview of certain publications, encouraging the development of an adaptive paywall that adjusts according to readers' individual preferences. In addition to niche initiatives, third-party companies, such as Piano in the USA and Deep.BI in the UK, have entered the arena, offering machine learning–based solutions for newsrooms (Simon, 2024). This confirms a model of cooperation and the emergence of a whole new set of contributors to the media industry (De-Lima-Santos & Ceron, 2021).

Within artificial intelligence, machine learning plays a crucial role, not only as a distinct domain but also as a key component that seamlessly integrates with other branches of AI. These interconnected fields are shaping the challenging landscape of AI in news media, where the technology is used to interpret text, analyse images and videos using computer vision, and coordinate content delivery using planning and optimisation techniques (De-Lima-Santos & Ceron, 2021).

By bringing these AI capabilities together, news organisations can better understand their audience, strategically plan their content, and optimise the way it is published, thus improving efficiency and engagement.

The growing reliance on machine learning in the news media represents a fundamental shift in the industry. This transformation is evident in everything from personalised content recommendations to the use of paywalls and subscriber retention strategies. In addition, collaborations between leading media organisations and external technology partners highlight an industry that actively embraces innovation. As technology continues to advance, it is clear that the future of news media is deeply linked to the evolution of AI.

4.2 *Data Mining and Automated News Publishing in an Evolving Media Landscape*

Data mining, an interdisciplinary field that encompasses techniques from statistics, machine learning, and database management, plays a pivotal role in the contemporary media landscape. It achieves this by uncovering patterns, relationships, and valuable insights within the vast expanse of big data. At its core, the extraction of this data aims to derive practical insights that contribute to informed decision-making and predictive analysis.

This intricate process unfolds with the meticulous collection of data from diverse sources, including databases, data warehouses, and text documents. Once collected, the data undergoes a sorting and processing phase to rectify anomalies, ensuring the accuracy and suitability of the data for subsequent analysis. Subsequently, an exploratory data analysis phase (EDA) follows, where it explores the characteristics of the dataset, visualises its distribution, and lays the groundwork for identifying initial patterns that guide further investigation.

The essence of data mining lies in the application of sophisticated algorithms to discover patterns, relationships, and trends within the data. This phase encompasses the deployment of various techniques, such as clustering, classification, and regression. The validation and evaluation of data extraction models are therefore crucial in the media field, enabling the testing of complex ideas and hypotheses and ensuring their robustness, reliability, publication suitability, and generalisability.

Moreover, data mining plays a pivotal role in fraud detection, exemplified by the utilisation of techniques such as fake news detection. This application aids in mitigating fraudulent behaviour and contributes to upholding the integrity of information in the media landscape.

While data mining presents significant opportunities in the media landscape, ethical considerations and privacy concerns emphasise the importance of responsible data handling. Extracting knowledge from big data demands a meticulous approach that aligns with ethical standards and complies with relevant regulatory laws. Ensuring privacy protection and maintaining transparency in the data mining process are also crucial aspects of enhancing public trust and addressing the ethical implications of extracting insights from comprehensive datasets (Okorie et al., 2024).

Furthermore, data mining, as a dynamic and influential process in the media landscape, reflects previously raised concerns regarding the replacement of human workers. Similar to the impact of algorithmic news production, the introduction of big data and analysis procedures has not only transformed the news industry in terms of productivity but has also led to the development of journalistic skills. The increasing presence of automation has necessitated a more specialised role for workers to remain competitive. However, contrary to concerns about automated content production replacing human works, algorithmic data mining may expand the capabilities of journalists in terms of analysing massive datasets to allow for meaningful analysis.

The evolution of technology and its complexity, particularly in the realm of social media, have impacted the news industry. A substantial proportion of daily media consumption is ascribed to the Internet, underscoring the pivotal role played by the mechanisms governing news dissemination. These mechanisms rely heavily on algorithms and automated systems to distribute content efficiently.

The increasing reliance of media organisations on online news has given rise to the prominence of automated news dissemination technologies as influential drivers of journalism. News outlets are progressively integrating these innovations into their operations (De-Lima-Santos & Ceron, 2021), thereby ushering in changes in the news system that introduce novel concepts to journalistic practice. This redefinition broadens the term "journalist" to encompass ordinary citizens, exemplified by the phenomenon of citizen journalism (Orellana-Rodriguez & Keane, 2018).

Concurrently, in the pursuit of applying technology to journalism, the utilisation of algorithms has streamlined the process of automated and systematic news dissemination on social media platforms. This has empowered media agencies to effectively reach wider audiences by deploying software agents, colloquially known as "news robots", within the domain now recognised as bot journalism. This method involves the generation of news articles using computer programmes rather than human reporters (Oh et al., 2020).

These technical advancements have not unfolded without vigorous debates regarding their social and cultural implications, including concerns about authorship, labour displacement, and the influence of algorithms. Questions surrounding the accountability, neutrality, and moral transparency of these programs have also been raised. These developments have prompted considerable scrutiny from researchers, highlighting the absence of globally agreed-upon standards for human news gatekeepers. The redirection of news circulation poses challenges and raises pertinent questions about the future of journalism, encompassing potential declines in news quality, censorship issues, and their impact on a significant portion of individuals. This, in turn, intensifies the complexity of evaluating the performance of algorithms in this field (Oh et al., 2020).

4.3 *AI-Powered Media Impact on Public Opinion on Political Affairs*

Artificial intelligence (AI) can no longer be considered an isolated corner of part of news generation; rather, it is swiftly evolving into an integral component of the contemporary news process, impacting every facet from news gathering and production to distribution. (Rinehart & Kung, 2022). The proliferation of algorithms, robots, and AI has promoted public discourse on the associated opportunities, risks, and responsibilities. This discussion extends to the media's role in shaping socio-technical imaginaries (Shin et al., 2022). In addition to its pivotal role in framing the social construction of responsibility and its influence on individual perceptions and opinions, AI integration into the media has profound societal implications (Saurwein et al., 2023).

The integration of AI-supported media into contemporary society has led to profound societal impacts, particularly in shaping perceptions, beliefs, and public behaviours within communities and influencing narratives extending to the international sphere. The customisation of content through AI algorithms has given rise to the phenomenon known as "filter bubbles", a concept first identified by Eli Pariser, the CEO of Upworthy and author of *The Filter Bubble* (2011). Pariser highlighted how Google search operations generate significantly different results based on the user's history. In his work, he emphasised that an individual's computer screen acts as a one-way mirror, reflecting the user's interests while being subject to algorithmic scrutiny with each click, view, share, or comment (Pariser, 2011). In this context, while automated personalisation is often beneficial, it leads to the isolation of individuals from alternative information, sometimes referred to as an "echo chamber". This term encapsulates widespread concern that social media use may limit users' exposure to, or consumption of, diverse information online. This online filtered bubble can restrict recipients from encountering different perspectives, thus encouraging the adoption of more extreme ideological positions. It may also weaken their ability to avoid fake news and bias, potentially contributing to polarisation within society (Kitchens et al., 2020).

Simultaneously, concerns associated with algorithmic bias and justice have surfaced, as AI algorithms may inadvertently perpetuate biases present in training data. This can result in biased content recommendations and the reinforcement of stereotypical images, thereby impacting societal perceptions while contributing to social inequality. The use of AI techniques, including deepfakes and generative algorithms, also raises fears of manipulating public opinion by creating realistic yet fabricated media content, posing challenges to information credibility and the potential for malicious actors to influence public sentiments (Kitchens et al., 2020).

While there is a belief that algorithms can be blind to sensitive features, this is not necessarily the case. Numerous studies have revealed that models trained on incomplete or biased datasets can produce discriminatory outputs (George, 2023). Human biases can intertwine with task accuracy, as classification algorithms may yield false positive and negative results, while filtering algorithms are likely to amplify bias (Dierickx & Lindén, 2023).

The role of AI is evident in shaping political discourse, exemplified by its ability to prioritise specific topics, frame issues, magnify certain voices, and influence public opinion on political matters. Additionally, the automated production of news content through AI raises concerns about the lack of human oversight, potential biases in automated content, and its impact on journalistic standards, potentially altering the nature of information dissemination (Dierickx & Lindén, 2023).

In terms of the influence of AI-supported media on cross-cultural communication, while AI-based translation tools facilitate global interactions, they may also contribute to misunderstandings due to subtle linguistic differences and cultural contexts, impacting international relations and diplomatic commitments.

Narratives shaped by AI-supported media also have repercussions on international stances, as misleading campaigns driven by AI can escalate tensions between nations, shape public opinion on global issues, and contribute to the spread of geopolitical narratives that may not align with reality. Additionally, ethical concerns surrounding AI in media, including issues of privacy, consent for data usage, and responsible information handling, warrant regulation and oversight to address potential risks and ensure adherence to ethical standards. Moreover, variations in regulatory approaches among countries contribute to the disparate impact of AI-powered media on societies (European Parliament, Directorate-General for External Policies, 2024).

The rapid evolution of AI in media demands attention to media literacy to equip the public with the necessary skills to critically evaluate information sources, discern between genuine and manipulated content, and navigate the complexities of narratives mediated by AI. Insufficient media literacy levels can exacerbate the dissemination of false narratives and misleading information, underscoring the importance of educational initiatives to enhance societal resilience against the challenges posed by AI-supported media (Tiernan et al., 2023).

If reliance on technology is intended to overcome political and societal challenges and their associated complexities, the persisting issues accompanying this complexity cannot be resolved solely by outsourcing decision-making processes to AI. While many of the mentioned concerns are not exclusive to AI, its use amplifies existing threats to freedom of expression and media freedom. Effectively addressing these challenges requires careful consideration of the socio-technical context in which AI is deployed, who is using it, and for what purposes. While there can be no one-size-fits-all solution, evaluating and addressing the impact of AI are not meaningful without transparency and accountability (Haas, 2020) .

4.4 AI-Based Narrative Construction and International Security: Case Study of Africa

Generative AI has enabled the automated construction of media content, fundamentally reshaping the way in which information is disseminated. At the core of AI's transformative power lies its capacity to analyse extensive datasets and discern subtle patterns, enabling media outlets to tailor content to the characteristics of individual audiences. However, personalisation, driven by machine learning and algorithms, appears to shape the media landscape where content not only caters to audience preferences but also possesses the potential to influence, or manipulate, perceptions. To understand how AI is impacting the media, it is necessary to investigate the ongoing discourse on the interplay between technological innovation, media dynamics, and public perception. Thus, this section rigorously explores examples illustrating the transformative potential inherent in these narratives, with a specific focus on key areas within the realm of international relations and international security.

As AI tools advance in sophistication, political entities are increasingly harnessing this technology in elections and political campaigns. While informational warfare is not a new phenomenon, the nature and scale of propaganda powered by AI present unprecedented challenges to the stability of political systems around the world.

The integration of big data into political election campaigns has transformed the political landscape. For example, in the 2008 presidential election in the United States, a large-scale analysis of social media data was utilised to enhance fundraising efforts and coordinate volunteers (Larcinese & Miner, 2018). This digital transformation has progressed further to involve the careful integration of AI systems into election campaigns and various aspects related to politics. In the run-up to the 2016 US presidential election, media platforms served as conduits for misinformation, as false information was disseminated by far-right activists, foreign influence campaigns, and fake news sites, thereby intensifying societal divisions. In the subsequent 2020 election, conspiracy theories and baseless claims were amplified on a massive scale, fuelling anti-democratic movements, and as for the 2024 presidential election, the progression of AI technology seemed to have the capacity to rejuvenate disinformation strategies employed in previous instances. AI-generated disinformation not only has the potential to mislead audiences but also poses a significant risk of exacerbating the challenges faced by an already embattled information ecosystem flooded with inaccuracies and deceptive content.

The use of AI in manipulating public opinion can also be exemplified by the deployment of massive swarms of bots spreading propaganda and fake news. These autonomous accounts are programmed to disseminate one-sided messages in the media, creating the illusion of widespread public support. The instances illustrate the utilisation of new media technologies for propagating specific narratives, such as Venezuelan state media employing AI-generated videos to disseminate pro-government messages (Ryan-Mosley, 2023). Similarly, within the United States, incidents have arisen wherein AI-manipulated videos and images of political leaders have circulated widely on social media platforms.

The transition to visual storytelling has significantly impacted the portrayal and perception of conflicts. Relevant parties, cognisant of the profound influence exercised by social media and fuelled by AI, have swiftly adapted to these platforms, utilising them for a spectrum of objectives ranging from disseminating propaganda to recruitment and engaging in psychological warfare (Sarkar & Ghosh, 2024). The escalating power of the media in shaping public opinion has become increasingly apparent, and its significance cannot be overstated.

For example, in the Middle East and North African regions, a significant transformation unfolded in the information landscape, marked by the proliferation of region-wide broadcasters. The latter, alongside their print and online counterparts, wielded considerable influence that could be harnessed to champion resolutions and foster democratic actions or, conversely, could be exploited to reinforce prejudices and solidify the positions of conflicting parties. This recognition of the media's power was grounded in the understanding that in authoritarian regimes, control over media outlets resides with the state. This dynamic makes it nearly impossible to disseminate negative information about the government or to express dissenting viewpoints. This control mechanism serves as a barrier to the free flow of information, shaping public discourse in favour of the ruling regime.

The influence of new information technology is exemplified in movements such as the Arab Spring, where technology played a catalytic role by facilitating organisational efforts, ultimately leading to the overthrow of regimes in various countries (Rosen, 2011). However, the role of technological advancement in the media has also come under scrutiny. For example, in the Israel–Palestine conflict, although a majority of media outlets aspired to communicate the truth, a noticeable gap arose in which not all dimensions of reality were fully revealed. Specific instances include reports concentrating on the demolition of a Palestinian houses without exploring broader implications, such as the displacement of 12 children vulnerable to radicalisation. The act of presenting only partial truths amounted to a betrayal of media integrity (Zahoor & Sadiq, 2021), particularly the impact on the Israeli readership, whose political perspectives were steered towards a narrative centred on terrorism and fear. This influence perpetuated a dehumanising portrayal of Palestinians—a serious transgression attributed to the Israeli media. The intersection of technology and media thus posed challenges, not only in shaping political movements but also in the ethical responsibility of providing comprehensive and truthful information to the public.

Indeed, the narrative surrounding these technologies shifted within a brief span, as the tools initially perceived as emancipators from state-controlled media and enablers of political dissent became instruments wielded by those seeking to undermine democracy in the Western world, notably the strategic and systematic deployment of information manipulation and disinformation emerging as a potent operational tool in the Russia–Ukraine war (Council of the European Union, 2022).

In addition to generative AI tools, governments persist in using older tactics, employing a combination of human and bot campaigns to manipulate online discussions, with at least 47 governments deploying commentators for propaganda spread in 2023—double the number from a decade ago (Funk et al., n.d.).

Moreover, the rapid integration of AI in warfare has become increasingly prevalent. AI has been applied in strategic decision-making, military systems, propaganda, and deception—integral components of warfare throughout history. This utilisation introduces a new dimension to Clausewitz's theory of war, as AI-regulated "principles of war" can be strategically employed to sow confusion among adversaries (Simpson, 2017).

While AI excels in tasks such as image recognition, recommendation systems, and language translation, it falls short in areas requiring human-level adaptability. Current AI systems are often specialised, struggling with novel scenarios, understanding contextual nuances, and multitasking effectively.

In the realm of media, AI's influence extends beyond warfare to include its role in shaping narratives during crises. Governments and political entities worldwide, irrespective of political systems, leverage AI to generate manipulative content—texts, images, and videos—tailored to sway public opinion. This includes automatic censorship of dissenting online content.

In conflict-affected regions such as sub-Saharan Africa, the propagation of disinformation through AI-driven means exacerbates existing tensions (Albrecht et al., 2024). False narratives, attributed violence, and inflammatory accusations circulate rapidly, reaching even those without Internet access through traditional mediums. Instances of misattributed images and videos, coupled with misleading captions, contribute to the escalation of conflicts and the reinforcement of stereotypes.

The media, encompassing traditional outlets and social platforms, may function as a conduit for circulating inaccurate and provocative messages and ideologies that fail to foster a climate of respect or reasoned discourse. Adverse messages possess the potential to sow division within communities and contribute to the perpetuation of stereotypes that fuel instances of violence. Media depictions, on occasion, have the capacity to intensify the narrative of opposing forces and seemingly insurmountable value-based disparities. Frequently, media outlets prioritise the coverage of conflicts, as such content tends to enhance sales and attract a broader audience. In addition, AI plays a critical role in disseminating information about AI's applications in counterterrorism and crisis management. In Nigeria, for instance, the use of cell phones for alerts has saved lives during attacks by groups like Boko Haram. The media's surveillance function, despite concerns about privacy violations, becomes paramount in crisis situations, providing timely information for public awareness and emergency response (Fournier-Tombs et al., 2023).

The integration of AI into warfare and media practices signifies a paradigm shift with both transformative potential and ethical considerations. The interplay between AI, military strategies, and media dynamics shapes not only the nature of conflicts but also public perceptions and responses on a global scale.

As such, this exploration of the case studies in AI-based narrative construction provides a glimpse into the profound transformative influence wielded by AI-driven media narratives. These case studies, ranging from deceptive electoral campaigns to periods of war and conflict, underscore the capacity of AI to shape and manipulate public discourse. As technology continues to evolve, the ethical considerations and societal implications of AI-generated narratives become increasingly pertinent. The manifold impact on geopolitical landscapes, public opinion, and even the dynamics of warfare highlights the need for vigilant oversight and ethical guidelines in the development and deployment of AI-driven media narratives. The lessons gleaned from these case studies serve as a crucial foundation for informed discussions and strategic considerations as societies navigate the intricate intersection of technology and narrative construction.

5 Trends in AI-Driven Media Content and Their Impacts on International Security

In a landscape defined by the pervasive integration of smart technology, the global geopolitical stage has undergone a profound transformation marked by multifaceted implications for international relations. The advent of smart technology, characterised by interconnected digital systems, AI, and data-driven processes, has ushered in an era where information dissemination and connectivity occur at unprecedented speeds and scales. This paradigm shift holds ramifications for the dynamics of diplomatic interactions and geopolitical discourse, necessitating a comprehensive examination of its impact.

The terms "disinformation" and "misinformation" play a crucial role in understanding the dynamics at play. Disinformation, characterised by deliberate and often orchestrated attempts to manipulate people through the delivery of dishonest information, poses a significant threat due to its organised nature, substantial resources, and reinforcement by automated technology. In contrast, misinformation refers to misleading information created or disseminated without manipulative or malicious intent.

In 2016, the Oxford English Dictionary selected "post-truth" as the Word of the Year, intending to encapsulate the prevailing ethos, mood, and concerns of that year with lasting cultural significance (Rocha-Cunha & Vasques, 2022). Initially, a peripheral term, "post-truth", rapidly gained recognition, notably following the Brexit referendum in the United Kingdom and the 2016 US presidential elections. Its most prominent association emerged in the realm of "post-truth politics", where the prefix "post" signifies a conceptual shift, suggesting the diminishing importance, obsolescence, or irrelevance of truth in contemporary political discourse.

This perspective aligns with cultivation theory, proposed by Gerbner et al. (1980), which posits that the media wields significant influence in shaping our worldview. According to this theory, the media is "primarily responsible for our perceptions of day-to-day norms and reality". Consequently, understanding the media's role in shaping public perception becomes essential in comprehending the dynamics of information dissemination and its impact on societal perspectives (Gripsrud, 2015).

5.1 *Rethinking Geopolitics in the Era of AI: Technology, Media, and Trust in International Relations*

The integration of smart technology into the geopolitical arena is not merely a technical evolution; it fundamentally alters the nature of how nations engage with one another. The rapid exchange of information, the omnipresence of digital platforms, and the influence of emerging technologies on decision-making processes contribute to a redefined geopolitical landscape. This transformation brings both opportunities and challenges as the digital realm becomes an integral component of international affairs.

Central to this analysis is the recognition of the paramount importance of trust within the intricate web of international relations (Hoffman, 2002). Trust serves as the bedrock upon which diplomatic engagements are constructed and sustained. In an era where the velocity and volume of information exchange are unprecedented, the erosion of trust poses profound implications for cooperation, negotiation, and conflict resolution.

The media wields a formidable influence over the dynamics of trust between nations, a power that is particularly accentuated in the contemporary era. The pervasive integration of smart technology in the dissemination of information has exponentially expanded the reach and impact of media narratives, offering a platform that can either foster understanding and cooperation or contribute to the erosion of trust and diplomatic relations.

In the intricacy of international affairs, the media plays a crucial role in shaping narratives and influencing public perception, thereby significantly impacting the trust dynamics between nations. As societies become increasingly interconnected, the media becomes a central player in defining the narrative surrounding diplomatic engagements, geopolitical events, and global issues. Its role extends beyond reporting facts to encompassing the interpretation, framing, and contextualisation of information, ultimately shaping the lens through which nations view one another (Berliner & Biddle, 1995).

A nuanced examination reveals that the media's impact on trust dynamics is not a unidirectional process but rather a complex interplay of various factors. The content, tone, and framing of news stories contribute to the construction of national narratives, shaping public opinion and, consequently, the perceptions that nations hold about each other. The choice of language, imagery, and emphasis in media reporting can either build bridges of understanding or reinforce existing stereotypes and biases, thereby influencing the levels of trust between nations.

Moreover, the immediacy and accessibility of information in the digital age amplify the media's influence on trust dynamics. News cycles move rapidly, and the constant flow of information demands swift reactions from governments and the public alike. This accelerated pace not only necessitates a careful and responsible approach to reporting but also underscores the potential for misinformation and misinterpretation, which can be detrimental to trust-building efforts between nations.

The escalating levels of ideological extremity and polarisation pose a potential threat to the credibility of the media, fostering an environment conducive to distrust. Individuals with strong partisan affiliations, marked by heightened engagement, often interpret ostensibly neutral news stories as biased against their own perspectives—a phenomenon known as the hostile media effect (Feldman, 2014). Consequently, those with ideologically extreme positions are likely to perceive mainstream media as biased, favouring the opposing faction, and, as a result, find it challenging to trust the media.

This perceived bias and the assumed impact of the media can, in turn, undermine overall confidence in the fairness of news media, as argued by Tsfati and Cohen (2005). Jones (2004) further demonstrated a correlation between partisanship and media trust, with Cook and Gronke (2001) highlighting a decline in media trust (Jones, 2004, as cited in Hanitzsch et al., 2017). Media trust is intricately linked to public perceptions of various institutions and does not exist in isolation. The erosion of trust in the media reflects a larger sense of disillusionment and global dissatisfaction. This connection highlights the importance of considering the wider context of public trust between nations.

Accordingly, in the contemporary world, conflict stands as a defining characteristic, persisting in various forms since the conclusion of the Cold War. Despite the multitude of conflicts, the sway of media coverage and the consequential impact on public opinion have proven to be a force that transcends governmental intentions. Indeed, the twenty-first century has witnessed the unprecedented weaponisation of information, facilitated by powerful new technology that simplifies the manipulation and fabrication of content. Social networks further amplify falsehoods disseminated by states, as these messages find a receptive audience within uncritical publics (Puddephatt et al., 2006).

The media's role in influencing trust dynamics extends beyond the national level, encompassing global perceptions of nations and their diplomatic engagements. Diplomacy, once conducted primarily behind closed doors, now unfolds in the public eye, with media coverage shaping how nations are perceived on the world stage. Positive and constructive media narratives can enhance a nation's soft power, fostering goodwill and cooperation, while negative or distorted portrayals can sow seeds of mistrust and animosity.

The intensifying global competition has led to the formation of international media alliances, amplifying their pursuit of exclusivity in reporting. This shift in dynamics has profound implications for international relations, as media entities wield considerable influence in shaping perceptions of conflicts.

However, the involvement of the international media can introduce complexities into conflict resolution efforts, as their actions may breed resentment among local populations due to perceived editorial biases. Modern communities exhibit a heightened awareness of the media's power, making it challenging for individuals to comprehend abrupt shifts in media attention. The inherent need for editors and producers to continually captivate domestic audiences can inadvertently foster negative sentiments and suspicion and give rise to conspiracy theories.

Oxford University's recent study underscores the global impact of media dynamics on international relations. The study revealed a significant rise in the number of countries engaging in political disinformation campaigns, more than doubling to 70 in the last 2 years (Oxford Internet Institute, 2020). In each of these nations, evidence indicates the involvement of at least one political party or government entity in manipulating social media platforms. While the majority of these disinformation efforts have been directed domestically, a noteworthy revelation is the strategic attempts by at least seven countries to influence international perspectives, accentuating the interconnected nature of media, politics, and global affairs (Bradshaw, 2019). This underscores the intricate relationship between media dynamics and international relations, emphasising the need for a nuanced understanding of the role media plays in shaping the narratives surrounding conflicts on the global stage.

5.2 Trends in AI's Influence on Information and Geopolitical Dynamics

The highly complex media landscape is currently undergoing a pivotal period characterised by torrents of information and news from diverse sources, making it difficult for media creators to maintain control. This is due to the multitude of actors involved in shaping the media scene. With rapid advancements in AI within the media sector, numerous issues and challenges have emerged related to the transmission and dissemination of knowledge, as well as concerns about the quality and accuracy of information. These challenges, among others, raise important questions about the extent to which media democratisation is possible in light of the current information flows, especially considering the right to freedom of opinion and expression, as enshrined in Article 19 of the Universal Declaration of Human Rights. Alternatively, it raises the question of whether the focus of the media should be on the fleeting nature of events, regardless of their impact on the emotions of the audience and their implications for the stability and security of national and international institutions. This situation necessitates the intervention of the state as an active and responsible entity in maintaining public order and international security.

In light of the increasing influence of AI technologies on the media landscape, this has placed the latter at a crossroads. On the one hand, these technologies enhance the role of the media in keeping up with international events and interactions in a complex environment. On the other hand, they can be misused to mislead public opinion and distort facts and information, potentially affecting the security and stability of society.

While the smooth flow of information is considered a crucial factor in making strategic decisions related to defence, national security, and economic growth, any positive or negative impact of AI on the integrity and accuracy of information is expected to influence the geopolitical dimensions that shape the balance and stability of states' security systems, both domestically and internationally.

In his study titled "Artificial Intelligence, Geopolitics, and Information Integrity", John Villasenor explores the dimensions of the relationship between three key variables: AI, its impact on the integrity and safety of information, and its reflection on the geopolitical context. One of his main conclusions is that the global race to adopt the latest contemporary technologies necessarily affects the stability of nations and their overall security (Villasenor, 2019).

Building on this, three principal ways in which AI shapes the media landscape—and its broader security implications—can be identified. First, AI's analytical capabilities enable media organisations to process vast amounts of data, improve their ability to understand complex issues, clarify uncertainties, and develop more effective strategies to achieve their objectives. Second, AI's predictive power allows for the use of algorithms and big data to anticipate potential conflicts, forecast climate shifts, and detect political instability. By providing early warnings, AI can enhance the media's role in supporting human security. Finally, AI's operational function involves the use of autonomous or semi-autonomous robots, a trend seen across the economic, military, and civilian sectors. However, despite advances in machine learning, these systems have not yet entirely replaced human decision-making, as accountability and ethical responsibility remain firmly in human hands.

The impact of AI on the media industry raises numerous theoretical and practical issues that the existing theoretical literature must address. While major media companies have moved towards "automating" their industry using AI to support their operations and update their mechanisms, this shift has concurrently sparked questions about the extent of change in the future of impartial media industries globally. These industries increasingly rely on attracting talented software developers, significant technological investments, and the capacity to acquire and process big data.

As the sources of these technologies evolve, associated concepts, such as the security of individuals and communities, are also affected. Concerns are growing over the use of AI algorithms to influence and manipulate public opinion, especially amid intense competition among major media-controlling companies. These algorithms determine what information reaches the public through Internet search platforms, mobile phone browsing, facial recognition technology, and other human-related fields. Consequently, some studies indicate that while algorithms may offer opportunities to enhance human security, they can also foster phenomena such as extremism and violence. This occurs because search engines can generate similar results that help form homogeneous communities of extremists or promote certain tendencies, ideas, and values that reflect the perspectives of major tech companies. The programmers of these technical systems are humans with their own interests, biases, and worldviews, thus wielding immense, yet often unseen, influence on public opinion. To explore the technologies influencing the media landscape that may pose a threat to the security of states, we summarise some examples below: - Impact of Deepfakes:

It is important to clarify that "information security" in this chapter refers to the accuracy and integrity of information, considering it to be the cornerstone of ensuring information safety and honesty. Recently, AI has been prominently featured in discussions about information security, particularly concerning the potential negative impacts of its applications.

Deepfake videos have been identified. These videos are produced using deep learning techniques that depict individuals engaging in actions they did not commit or making statements they did not utter. This has become a source of concern for observers and those interested in these technologies. A well-crafted deepfake targeting a politician, for example, if disseminated online at the right time and in the right manner, could potentially undermine their credibility in electoral contests. Moreover, this technology could further compromise information security in various other ways, affecting the entities and security of states (Villasenor, 2019). - Influence via automated accounts(Bots): Bot accounts are programmed accounts managed by software that are linked through social networks and social media platforms to appear as individual accounts. These bots have played a significant role in amplifying misinformation on the Internet. A study by Shao et al. (2018) found evidence of bots on Twitter spreading over 400,000 articles from uncredible sources between 2016 and 2017. The authors reported that these bots played a "disproportionate role in disseminating [...] fake news, conspiracy theories, and junk science". This phenomenon is not limited to Twitter but also extends to other social media platforms like Facebook. - Influence via information control:

Bots have reached influential positions, with their impact observed in the context of the American electoral process in 2016. This has led many researchers to question the extent to which these bots can influence the flow of political information through social media. In this regard, a field study conducted by Woolley and Guilbeault (2017) analysed the election campaigns of candidates in the United States, supported by bots that dominated the periphery and core of political discussions on Twitter. The study concluded that these bots influence the flow of information in two main ways. Firstly, through "manufacturing consensus" or creating the illusion of widespread online popularity to build genuine political support, and secondly, through democratising propaganda, empowering any candidate, and amplifying online interactions to achieve partisan goals.

The field study concluded that robots indeed influenced the flow of information during the 2016 US presidential election (Woolley & Guilbeault, 2017). It can be stated in this context that while numerous studies have demonstrated the extent to which political activists, institutions, and individuals in general have embraced AI-supported technologies, these technologies can also impact the media landscape and operations directly.

Thus, media influence in the age of AI has begun to multiply, affecting international security and various geopolitical dimensions. Notably, this influence can be observed in the institutional security of states during elections, legislative preparations, the promotion of authoritarian regimes, or the suppression of their opponents, leading to crises related to human rights and democracy. Many instances of such media usage to influence opponents have been recorded. Woolley and Guilbeault (2017) pointed out that the "increasing use of bots in political campaigns to interact with users, attack candidates, or focus their subconscious on specific candidates, as if they were human, [...] may threaten political transparency". Such effects directly and indirectly impact the security and stability of state institutions and their democracy and can even lead to complex geopolitical repercussions. For instance, during the 2016 US presidential election, hundreds of millions of Americans were exposed to fake news. A study by the Computational Propaganda Project at the University of Oxford revealed that during that election, "the sharing of professional news content and junk news was equal, meaning the amount of junk news shared on Twitter matched the amount of professional news" (Gallacher et al., 2017). Consequently, media supported by unsecured AI technologies poses a significant challenge to democratic governance and state security.

6 Conclusion

In today's fast-evolving media landscape, artificial intelligence is not merely a tool for technological progress; it is reshaping the very foundation of how media content is created, shared, and consumed. From sophisticated algorithms to advanced machine learning models, AI is transforming conventional media practices in profound ways.

Yet, alongside its vast potential, the integration of AI into the media brings forth a set of complex challenges. The rapid intersection of AI and the media industry presents hurdles at multiple levels, namely, human expertise, technological infrastructure, and the broader regulatory framework governing their interaction. One of the most pressing concerns lies in the nature of the information itself. AI-driven predictions and decisions are only as reliable as the data on which they are trained. Incomplete, biased, or low-quality data can distort AI's analytical capabilities, leading to misinformation, politicisation, or even threats to individual and collective security.

As AI continues to shape the media landscape, it is imperative to establish clear guidelines that uphold the principles of truth and transparency. A well-structured media strategy should account for these challenges, ensuring that AI serves as a force for progress while safeguarding integrity, accountability, and, ultimately, international security.

References

Albrecht, E., Fournier-Tombs, E., & Brubaker, R. (2024). *Disinformation and peacebuilding in Sub-Saharan Africa: Security implications of AI-altered information environments*. United Nations University. https://collections.unu.edu/eserv/UNU:9419/disinformation_peacebuilding_subsaharan_africa.pdf

Bentivegna, S., & Marchetti, R. (2017). Journalists at a crossroads: Are traditional norms and practices challenged by Twitter? *Journalism: Theory, Practice and Criticism, 19*(2), 270–290. https://doi.org/10.1177/1464884917716594

Berliner, D., & Biddle, B. (1995). *The manufactured crisis*. Addison Wesley.
Boulaghron, S., & Boukhenfer, Z. (2023, June 27). *Artificial intelligence and robot journalism: The duality of human and machine - A critical review of new practices in digital media*. ASJP.
Bradshaw, S. (2019). *The global disinformation order 2019 global inventory of organised social media manipulation*. Retrieved from https://demtech.oii.ox.ac.uk/wp-content/uploads/sites/12/2019/09/CyberTroop-Report19.pdf
Broussard, M. (2018). Artificial intelligence. In The MIT Press eBooks. https://doi.org/10.7551/mitpress/11022.001.0001
Caswell, D., & Dörr, K. (2017). Automated journalism 2.0: Event-driven narratives. *Journalism Practice, 12*(4), 477–496. https://doi.org/10.1080/17512786.2017.1320773
Cook, T. E., & Gronke, P. (2001, April). The dimensions of institutional trust: How distinct is public confidence in the media? Paper presented at the 59th Annual Conference of the Midwest Political Science Association, Chicago, IL, United States. https://people.reed.edu/~gronkep/docs/MIDW2001.pdf
Council of the European Union. (2022). *EU Imposes Sanctions on State-Owned Outlets RT/Russia Today and Sputnik's Broadcasting in the EU*. Retrieved from https://www.consilium.europa.eu/en/press/press-releases/2022/03/02/eu-imposes-sanctions-on-state-owned-outlets-rt-russia-today-and-sputnik-s-broadcasting-in-the-eu/
De-Lima-Santos, M., & Ceron, W. (2021). Artificial intelligence in news media: Current perceptions and future outlook. *Journalism and Media, 3*(1), 13–26. https://doi.org/10.3390/journalmedia3010002
Dierickx, L., & Lindén, C. G. (2023, June). Fine-tuning languages: Epistemological foundations for ethical AI in journalism. *2023 10th IEEE Swiss Conference on Data Science (SDS)*. https://doi.org/10.1109/sds57534.2023.00013.
European Parliament, Directorate-General for External Policies. (2024). *Artificial intelligence and international trade: Impact and implications*. https://www.europarl.europa.eu/RegData/etudes/IDAN/2024/754450/EXPO_IDA(2024)754450_EN.pdf
Feldman, L. (2014). In K. Kenski & K. H. Jamieson (Eds.), *The hostile media effect*. Oxford University Press.
Fournier-Tombs, E., Brubaker, R., & Albrecht, E. (n.d.). *Exploring recent developments in artificial intelligence and their impact on disinformation-fuelled conflict*. Unu.Edu. Retrieved December 13, 2023., from https://collections.unu.edu/eserv/UNU:9217/artificial_Intelligence_powered_disinformation.pdf
Funk, A., Shahbaz, A., Vesteinsson, K. (n.d.). *The repressive power of artificial intelligence*. Freedom House. Retrieved December 13, 2023, from https://freedomhouse.org/report/freedom-net/2023/repressive-power-artificial-intelligence
Gallacher, J. D., Kaminska, M., Kollanyi, B., & Howard, P. N. (2017). *Junk news and bots during the 2017 UK General Election: What are UK voters sharing over Twitter?* Computational Propaganda Project. https://demtech.oii.ox.ac.uk/publications/junk-news-and-bots-during-the-2017-uk-general-election/.
Gerbner, G., Gross, L., Signorielli, N., & Morgan, M. (1980). Aging with Television: Images on Television Drama and Conceptions of Social Reality. *Journal of Communication, 30*(1), 37–47. https://doi.org/10.1111/j.1460-2466.1980.tb01766.x
George, C. (2023). Blind spots and biases in media freedom advocacy. *SSRN Electronic Journal*. https://doi.org/10.2139/ssrn.4663244
Global Media Congress. (2024, 29 février). *Global Media Congress - by Capital Events.P4*. https://www.globalmediacongress.ae/en/
Gripsrud, J. (2015). Television: General. In *International encyclopedia of the social & behavioral sciences* (pp. 163–168). Elsevier.
Haas, J. (2020). *Freedom of the media and artificial intelligence*. Office of the OSCE Representative on Freedom of the Media. https://www.osce.org/files/f/documents/4/5/472488.pdf.

Hanitzsch, T., Van Dalen, A., & Steindl, N. (2017). Caught in the Nexus: A comparative and longitudinal analysis of public trust in the press. *The International Journal of Press/Politics, 23*(1), 3–23. https://doi.org/10.1177/1940161217740695

Hoffman, A. M. (2002). A conceptualization of trust in international relations. *European Journal of International Relations, 8*(3), 375–401. https://doi.org/10.1177/1354066102008003003. https://www.asjp.cerist.dz/en/article/227756

Hunt & McKelvey. (2019). Algorithmic regulation in media and cultural policy: A framework to evaluate barriers to accountability. *Journal of Information Policy, 9*, 307–335. https://doi.org/10.5325/jinfopoli.9.2019.0307

Jones, D. A. (2004). Why Americans don't trust the media. *Harvard International Journal of Press/Politics, 9*(2), 60–75. https://doi.org/10.1177/1081180x04263461

Kitchens, B., Johnson, S. L., & Gray, P. (2020, December 1). Understanding Echo Chambers and Filter Bubbles: The Impact of Social Media on Diversification and Partisan Shifts in News Consumption. *MIS Quarterly, 44*(4), 1619–1649. https://doi.org/10.25300/misq/2020/16371

Kotenidis, E., & Veglis, A. (2021). Algorithmic journalism—Current applications and future perspectives. *Journalism and Media, 2*(2), 244–257. https://doi.org/10.3390/journalmedia2020014

Larcinese, V., & Miner, L. (2018). The political impact of the internet in US presidential elections (STICERD Economic Organisation and Public Policy Discussion Paper No. 63). *London School of Economics and Political Science*. https://sticerd.lse.ac.uk/dps/eopp/eopp63.pdf

Noain-Sánchez, A. (2022). Addressing the impact of artificial intelligence on journalism: The perception of experts, journalists and academics. *Comunicación y Sociedad, 35*(3), 105–121. https://doi.org/10.15581/003.35.3.105-121

Oh, C., Choi, J., Lee, S., Park, S., Kim, D., Song, J., Kim, D., Lee, J., & Suh, B. (2020, April 21). Understanding user perception of automated news generation system. *Proceedings of the 2020 CHI conference on human factors in computing systems*. https://doi.org/10.1145/3313831.3376811.

Okorie, G. N., Udeh, C. A., Adaga, E. M., DaraOjimba, O. D., & Oriekhoe, O. I. (2024). Ethical considerations in data collection and analysis: A review: Investigating ethical practices and challenges in modern data collection and analysis. *International Journal of Applied Research in Social Sciences, 6*(1), 1–22. https://doi.org/10.51594/ijarss.v6i1.688

Orellana-Rodriguez, C., & Keane, M. T. (2018). Attention to news and its dissemination on Twitter: A survey. *Computer Science Review, 29*, 74–94. https://doi.org/10.1016/j.cosrev.2018.07.001

Oxford Internet Institute. (2020, December 15). *Spread of disinformation the biggest concern for internet and social media users globally finds new Oxford study*. https://www.oii.ox.ac.uk/news-events/spread-of-disinformation-the-biggest-concern-for-internet-and-social-media-users-globally-finds-new-oxford-study/.

Pariser, E. (2011). The filter bubble: What the Internet is hiding from you. Penguin Books. https://hci.stanford.edu/courses/cs047n/readings/The_Filter_Bubble.pdf

Puddephatt, A., Krogh, T., De Jong, S., Koirala, B., Karikari, K., Møller, L., Pieper, H., Breum, M., Haselock, S., Novicki, M., Byers, E., Westphal, F., Dahlman, C., & Thompson, M. (2006). *Conflict and the role of the media*. Mediasupport.Org. Retrieved from https://www.mediasupport.org/wp-content/uploads/2012/11/ims-voices-of-war-2006.pdf.

Rinehart, A., & Kung, E. (2022). *Artificial intelligence in local news A survey of US newsrooms' AI readiness*. The Associated Press. Retrieved March 11, 2024, from https://www.researchgate.net/publication/363475725_Artificial_Intelligence_in_Local_News_A_survey_of_US_newsrooms"_AI_readiness

Rocha-Cunha, S., & Vasques, R. (2022). Post-truth and post-democracy: The dark side of the democratic planet. In *Global politics in a post-truth age* (pp. 148–161).

Rosen, Rebecca J. (2011, September 3). *So, was Facebook responsible for the Arab spring after all?* The Atlantic. Retrieved from https://www.theatlantic.com

Ryan-Mosley, T. (2023, October 4). How generative AI is boosting the spread of disinformation and propaganda. *MIT Technology Review*.

Retrieved from https://www.technologyreview.com/2023/10/04/1080801/generative-ai-boosting-disinformation-and-propaganda-freedom-house/

Sarkar, S., & Ghosh, A. (2024). Leveraging artificial intelligence to enhance media literacy and combat misinformation. *Journal of Novel Research and Innovative Development, 2*(9), a163–a187. https://doi.org/10.1729/Journal.41684

Saurwein, F., Brantner, C., & Möck, L. (2023, October 21). Responsibility networks in media discourses on automation: A comparative analysis of social media algorithms and social companions. *New Media & Society*. https://doi.org/10.1177/14614448231203310

Shao, C., Ciampaglia, G. L., Varol, O., et al. (2018). The spread of low-credibility content by social bots. *Nature Communications, 9*, 4787. https://doi.org/10.1038/s41467-018-06930-7

Shin, D., Hameleers, M., Park, Y. J., Kim, J. N., Trielli, D., Diakopoulos, N., Helberger, N., Lewis, S. C., Westlund, O., & Baumann, S. (2022, November 17). Countering algorithmic bias and disinformation and effectively harnessing the power of AI in media. *Journalism & Mass, Communication Quarterly, 99*(4), 887–907. https://doi.org/10.1177/10776990221129245

Simon, F. M. (2024). Artificial intelligence in the news: How AI retools, rationalizes, and reshapes journalism and the public arena. *Columbia Journalism Review*. https://www.cjr.org/tow_center_reports/artificial-intelligence-in-the-news.php

Simpson, E. (2017). Clausewitz's theory of war and victory in contemporary conflict. *Parameters: Journal of the US Army War College, 47*(4), 7–18. https://doi.org/10.55540/0031-1723.3100

Tiernan, P., Costello, E., Donlon, E., Parysz, M., & Scriney, M. (2023). Information and media literacy in the age of AI: Options for the future. *Education Sciences, 13*(9), 906. https://doi.org/10.3390/educsci13090906

Tsfati, Y., & Cohen, J. (2005). The influence of presumed media influence on democratic legitimacy. *Communication Research, 32*(6), 794–821. https://doi.org/10.1177/0093650205281057

Villasenor, J. (2019). Artificial intelligence, geopolitics, and information integrity, *The global race for technological superiority* Edited by Fabio Rugge 1, November, p131.

Samuel C. Woolley & Douglas Guilbeault, Computational propaganda in the United States of America: Manufacturing consensus online. Samuel Woolley and Philip N. Howard, Eds. *Working Paper* 2017.5. : Project on Computational Propaganda. comprop.oii.ox.ac.uk. 27 p.

Zahoor, M., & Sadiq, N. (2021). Digital public sphere and Palestine-Israel conflict: A conceptual analysis of news coverage. *Liberal Arts and Social Sciences International Journal (LASSIJ), 5*(1), 168–181. https://doi.org/10.47264/idea.lassij/5.1.12

Zaragoza, P. (2023). *Artificial intelligence and journalism: A multimodal critical discourse analysis of the Instagram page @brut_ia*. DIVA. https://mau.diva-portal.org/smash/record.jsf?pid=diva2%3A1815699&dswid=9913

Chapter 6
Media Diplomacy in the Age of AI: Transformative Potential and Ethical Challenges

Said Hajji

Abstract This chapter lays out a framework through which to examine the intersection of artificial intelligence (AI) and media diplomacy. It aims to uncover the transformative potential of AI in the revolutionization of key aspects of media diplomacy by highlighting the tools and techniques that practitioners can leverage. The study takes a descriptive and analytical approach to outlining and illustrating the manifestations of this transformation through concrete examples. The analysis demonstrates that the integration of AI into media diplomacy, as a component of public diplomacy, is poised to significantly alter daily practices, including through enhanced real-time monitoring and analysis of media coverage and trends; the development of predictive diplomacy tools; expanded opportunities for promoting dialogue, resolving conflicts, and detecting disinformation; and increased reliance by policymakers on data-driven decision-making. However, this integration is also likely to give way to ethical challenges that demand careful consideration and resolution.

This chapter's findings and subsequent discussion constitute a preliminary foundation for future studies working to keep pace with the rapid advancements in AI and its applications in media and media diplomacy. Ultimately, this research encourages academics, policymakers, and practitioners in these emerging fields to engage in meaningful and critical discourse.

Keywords Media diplomacy · Artificial intelligence (AI) · Transformative impacts · Ethical implications

S. Hajji (✉)
Faculty of Law, Economic and Social Sciences Agdal, Mohammed V University, Rabat, Morocco

F. Roumate, A. La Rosa (eds.), *Artificial Intelligence, Media and International Security*, Contributions to Security and Defence Studies,
https://doi.org/10.1007/978-3-031-95757-4_6

1 Introduction

Generative AI has dramatically broadened the general public's interest in AI. This surge of attention has prompted many individuals, including high-ranking officials, to consider the technological and ethical implications of AI for their respective fields. In a recent speech in New York, former Secretary of State Antony Blinken said: "As we work to manage risks, we can and we must also maximize the use of AI for the greater good" (Nkralev, 2023). The digital age in which we live is expected to present all industries and societal activities with surprises in both the near and distant future due to the tremendous recent breakthroughs in AI.

On the one hand, while the public is intensely interested in AI's remarkable achievements—particularly in medicine, engineering, military technology, and other areas of science and technology—few people truly understand the consequences of recent AI developments in fields related to the human, social, and legal sciences. We are undoubtedly facing impending transformations across all levels and sectors, including diplomacy: "Today's emerging technologies will offer new tools and techniques for peacemaking that could impact every step of the process, from the earliest days of negotiations all the way to monitoring and enforcing agreements" (Moore, 2023). Moreover, the intersection of quantum and artificial intelligence (QAI) may have significant geopolitical implications. These two groundbreaking technologies "could reshape existing geopolitical dynamics. Quantum computing's superior cryptography-breaking abilities could disrupt global cybersecurity and intelligence operations, prompting shifts in defense strategies".

On the other hand, diplomacy is undergoing dramatic changes in its forms, agendas, and tools. Media diplomacy has emerged as one of the most influential forms of international relations due to modern media's central role in enhancing and carrying out functions historically fulfilled by traditional diplomatic institutions, especially those of information and negotiation.

While public diplomacy, digital diplomacy, and media diplomacy certainly overlap in several respects, the latter—fueled by both old and new media—has evolved into a powerful tool capable of influencing public perceptions and decision-makers. Media diplomacy facilitates innovative and unconventional means of negotiation by structuring narratives and generating persuasive arguments in support of national interests, positioning itself as a major factor in international interactions.

Notably, AI continues to undergo significant advances, becoming a driver of innovation and renewal across manifold industries. It has effected significant change at every stage in the production process, "enabling new opportunities for value creation along the life cycle from conception to production" (De Silva & Alahakoon, 2022). This includes everything from automating tasks and predicting outcomes to tailoring experiences.

Despite these advancements and successes, however, the literature on the relationship between AI and media diplomacy remains underdeveloped.

This study works to reconcile the perspectives of diplomats and AI experts. Furthermore, it underscores the need to establish a connection between diplomacy—traditionally categorized under law and political science—and AI, which is typically considered an applied science. This discrepancy, among other obstacles, motivated me to conduct this research.

This article's purpose is twofold. First, it investigates the convergence and overlap between AI and media diplomacy. Second, it demonstrates AI's revolutionary potential in the practice of media diplomacy. I place particular emphasis on the following essential question: What effects could AI have on media diplomacy? This effort entails exploring related sub-questions regarding the depth and ethical implications of these effects. The answer to this question may seem straightforward at first glance. However, many difficulties emerge once the question is deconstructed, including difficulties that are inherent in both diplomacy and AI. Consequently, the convergence of these two concepts presents noteworthy difficulties.

Despite the apparent distinction between them as "two different types of communication that run along different paths" (Cohen, 1986, p. 6), AI and diplomacy share several similarities and points of mutual interaction. AI in diplomacy functions as a topic of diplomatic debate, a tool for diplomatic activities, and a factor that shapes the diplomatic environment (Artificial Intelligence and Diplomacy: A New Tool for Diplomats? Diplo Event, 2018). This interdependence, while enhancing understanding, can sometimes cloud our vision. In traditional and digital contexts alike—and in any context pertaining to AI or big data—it may be difficult to distinguish between mutual influences and the constants and variables underlying media diplomacy.

From this perspective, we can compare conventional diplomacy with a new form of diplomacy, just as we may compare traditional media with new media that incorporates AI.

The emergence of AI and its mounting popularity among decision-makers, particularly diplomats, showcases its utility as a tool. It is useful for informing and communicating with stakeholders, making predictions, analyzing data, detecting fake information, and facilitating negotiations. Given the valuable information that it can provide to mediator diplomats about both parties in a conflict, AI may also be valuable as a mediation tool (DiploFoundation, 2022). However, there are risks associated with such functions. The potential for malicious use and the subsequent ethical challenges can disrupt the media's deontological message, compelling stakeholders "to rethink international law and to include ethical concerns in AI development, which is the only way to ensure security and to face the tension between states" (Roumate, 2021). Still, in today's increasingly interconnected digital age, AI can bolster the confidence of policymakers, diplomats, and academics, enabling them to make more informed decisions.

By highlighting this relatively unexplored field, I hope to achieve two goals: first, to shed light on a facet of diplomacy that I have not previously studied, that being media diplomacy, and second, to make a worthwhile contribution to the literature and encourage further academic research on the role of AI in media diplomacy.

2 Methodology

This preliminary research assesses the growing impact of artificial intelligence, aiming to understand the links within a multifaceted, complex, and evolving conceptual triangle involving diplomacy, the media, and artificial intelligence. It adopts a descriptive and analytical approach to identify developments in the interrelationship between media and diplomacy in the modern AI era. Moreover, the study looks at the expanding influence of AI as a new international and multi-sectoral force, examining its impact on the media as a diplomatic communication tool, as a routine practice in international relations, and as a potential guiding force underpinning foreign policies.

3 Literature Review

A basic Google search for the phrase "impact of artificial intelligence on media diplomacy review" reveals that, while there is substantial academic research on both AI and media diplomacy independently, relatively little research has been conducted specifically on AI's impact on media diplomacy despite the recent uptick in academic studies on how AI influences diplomacy more broadly.

Three significant works are pertinent to the topic of this chapter. The first is "Diplomacy in the Media Age: Three Models of Uses and Effects" (Gilboa, 2001), in which Eytan Gilboa argues that the media has evolved into a crucial diplomatic tool capable of influencing public opinion and altering the outcomes of diplomatic discussions. This chapter also addresses the ethical and professional repercussions for the three primary actors behind diplomacy: officials, the media, and the public (in the form of public opinion). Ultimately, it concludes that the media has a dual nature and that its use in diplomacy must be properly regulated. Widely regarded as a point of reference within the field of media diplomacy, this work is pioneering in that it elucidates how the media can offer new possibilities for diplomacy and reshape its practice in the twenty-first century.

The second is Parama Sinha Palit's book, *New Media and Public Diplomacy: Political Communication in India, the United States, and China-Routledge* (De Silva & Alahakoon, 2022), which examines the use of digital technologies and new media in public diplomacy and political communication with a particular focus on their use in the United States, China, and India. The book highlights fundamental changes to public diplomacy that have been prompted by emerging technologies, using specific examples to show how new media has transformed public engagement and influenced perceptions.

The third is Alex Connock's *Media Management and Artificial Intelligence: Understanding Media Business Models in the Digital Age* (Connock, 2022), which explores how AI is changing media business models from creation to distribution, presenting several case studies that highlight AI's potential to foster innovative entrepreneurship, generate new revenue streams, and raise profits. It also extensively demonstrates how new AI tools are impacting the media sector.

Despite the importance of these sources for their perspectives on the dynamics among AI, new media, and media diplomacy, there is still a dearth of comprehensive research on how AI will revolutionize media diplomacy.

Based on its literature review, this chapter aims to fill the gap in the literature by delineating how AI, with its enormous collection, analysis, and prediction capabilities as well as emerging software and robotic assistants, is likely to revolutionize the practice of media diplomacy, enhance cooperation between diplomats, and reshape international relations.

4 Media, Diplomacy, and Artificial Intelligence: A Brief Review of Concepts and Trajectories

Before discussing the overlap between media diplomacy and artificial intelligence, it is crucial to separately define each of the two terms. Doing so will enable us to understand their respective trajectories and the shifts in meaning when they are combined.

4.1 Media, Diplomacy, and Artificial Intelligence: A Conceptual Overview

Different scholars have defined the terms "media," "diplomacy," and "artificial intelligence" in various ways depending on their backgrounds, perspectives, and research contexts. Nevertheless, a common thread runs through these definitions: They all recognize that these concepts are continually evolving.

For instance, "media" traditionally denoted mass communication channels such as newspapers, magazines, radio, and television. However, with the advent of new technologies like the Internet and social media, the definition of media has broadened to encompass these novel platforms. Generally, media may be categorized into three primary types: traditional media, which includes print, broadcast, and outdoor media; digital or new media, which comprises online, social, and mobile media; and hybrid media, which combines elements of both traditional and digital media, such as newspapers with print and online editions. In a broader sense, particularly in the context of international relations—where media serves "as an instrument of foreign policy and international negotiations" (Gilboa, 2001, p. 4)—Marshall McLuhan famously suggests that "the medium is the message" (Medium Is the Message | Encyclopedia.com, n.d.), emphasizing that the way in which we communicate something often carries more significance than the content itself. In a slightly different context, Chomsky and Herman argue that mass communication media shape public opinion by serving the interests of the societal elite. Therefore, the media is not an independent institution but rather a tool used by powerful groups to promote their interests (Herman & Chomsky, 1989, p. 55). They explain that mass communication media "are effective and powerful ideological institutions that carry out a system-supportive propaganda function, by reliance on market forces, internalized assumptions, and self-censorship, and without overt coercion" (Herman & Chomsky, 1989, p. 306), using the propaganda model of communication described in the author's aforementioned work.

As for diplomacy, it has long been defined as formal relations between countries (Berridge, 2001, p. 1). However, with the rising significance of non-state actors (e.g., multinational corporations, nongovernmental organizations), the definition of diplomacy has expanded to encompass these new actors and the tools that they use (Sharp, 2019, p. 4). Paul Sharp's definition of diplomacy "as a synonym for statecraft, foreign policy, and international relations, as well as the making of foreign policy by practitioners" (Hart & Siniver, 2020) thus better reflects the contemporary realities and transformations of diplomatic practice. This evolution is evident in the emergence of public diplomacy in the early twentieth century, that of digital diplomacy in the late twentieth century, that of data diplomacy (Smith & Doe, 2018) at the beginning of the twenty-first century, and that of AI diplomacy (Diplo, 2023) in the second decade of the twenty-first century—all of which reflect the changing nature of diplomacy and the increasingly prominent role of technology. Moreover, alongside major forms of diplomacy like media diplomacy, cultural diplomacy, scientific diplomacy, and sports diplomacy, there are numerous other specialized forms, including disaster diplomacy, funeral diplomacy, and dollar diplomacy.

Similarly, the term "artificial intelligence" traditionally referred to technology that enables machines to simulate human intelligence and, in turn, perform tasks that have long required human cognitive abilities, such as learning, problem-solving, and decision-making. However, through rapid advancements in AI research, the definition of artificial intelligence is ever expanding. As many scholars assert, "Defining AI is not easy; in fact, there is no universally accepted definition of the concept" (Russell & Norvig, 1995). In my view, the definition proposed by the High-Level Expert Group on Artificial Intelligence (AI HLEG) of the European Commission—"Systems that display intelligent behavior by analyzing their environment and taking actions with some degree of autonomy" (Sheikh et al., 2023)—most effectively encapsulates what artificial intelligence has become.

Therefore, media diplomacy is a fusion of media and diplomacy. It refers to the strategic use of mass media and digital platforms to influence public opinion, shape diplomatic narratives, and foster international relations. This description encompasses governments, nongovernmental organizations (NGOs), and other actors leveraging traditional and digital media in pursuit of diplomatic goals. Ebo defines media diplomacy straightforwardly as "the use of the media to articulate and promote foreign policy" (Ebo, 1996, p. 44), while Gilboa asserts that "media diplomacy refers to officials' uses of the media to communicate with state and non-state actors, to build confidence and advance negotiations, and to mobilize public support for agreements" (Gilboa, 2001, p. 10). It also refers, according to Gilboa, to "media-broker diplomacy," through which journalists serve as temporary mediators in international negotiations (Archetti, 2012). Unlike public diplomacy, where state and non-state actors use the media and other communication channels to influence public opinion in foreign societies, media diplomacy involves officials using the media to communicate with actors and promote conflict resolution (Gilboa, 2001, p. 10).

In fact, there are clear differences between the two despite media diplomacy often being mistakenly equated with public diplomacy. While some scholars consider the latter a form of propaganda, Cohen clarifies the distinction between media diplomacy and public diplomacy as follows: "Media diplomacy includes all those aspects of public diplomacy where the media are involved as well as others not associated with public diplomacy including the sending of signals by governments through the media, and the use of the media as a source of information" (Freifeld & Cohen, 1988). For Gilboa, public diplomacy houses a broader scope than media diplomacy; the former "is pursued in the context of conflict resolution, while public diplomacy is conducted in the context of confrontation; media diplomacy usually aims at short-term results while public diplomacy aims at long-range outcomes" (Gilboa, p. 22).

One recent example of media diplomacy occurred when President Emmanuel Macron used X (the social media platform formerly known as Twitter) to address the Moroccan population in the aftermath of the Al-Haouz earthquake in central Morocco. His message was widely rebroadcast by French TV channels to express his support and dispel certain "controversies." However, many observers felt that a more appropriate approach would have been to utilize official diplomatic channels or Moroccan media (Redondo, 2023). Macron's speech came soon after Morocco had declined French aid. Some political and media analysts saw this as an unprecedented diplomatic strategy aimed at swaying Moroccan public opinion in order to pressure the state to accept French aid, which Morocco had refused for logistical and political reasons.

Another illustrative case of media diplomacy, alongside the manifold historical and practical cases discussed by Hasan (2022), involves Ukrainian President Volodymyr Zelenskyy's speeches addressing worldwide and European audiences following the Russian invasion of Ukraine. Throughout the war that followed, President Zelenskyy utilized digital media to directly address and request military aid from Western parliaments. This example showcases a novel use of communication channels (e.g., live broadcasts) to achieve immediate political objectives: "Zelensky's communications with the parliaments of Western democracies during the ongoing conflict … seek to protect Ukraine from Russian aggression" (Saliu, 2022, p. 5).

A more recent example of media diplomacy occurred during the Israel–Hamas conflict in 2023, when Israel's Ministry of Foreign Affairs, led by Israel Katz, launched bold social media campaigns targeting countries that recognized Palestine. Katz shared videos combining Hamas attack footage with cultural symbols from Spain, Norway, and Ireland alongside the following message: "Hamas thanks you for your service." This strategy, intended to influence public opinion and challenge these nations' positions, garnered intense criticism, especially from Ireland, for its provocative tone (McTaggart 2024). Additional examples highlight the contributions that media professionals, news agencies, and other actors in this realm—including "prominent journalists that have even occasionally assumed the role of diplomats, both in crises and peacemaking situations" (Gilboa, p. 23)—have made by conducting covert and overt press coverage through arranged interviews that facilitate hard negotiations, enable the signing of significant treaties, or rally popular support for a cause. Before World War II, Great Britain conducted a discreet campaign to gain public support in the United States, though it was careful to avoid accusations of propaganda given the lingering skepticism from World War I. British diplomats built relationships with US journalists, leveraging their credibility to influence public opinion, "To do so, they built relationships with members of the U.S. press corps, who had more credibility with American audiences. They also restricted direct broadcasts from the British Broadcasting Corporation into the United States" (The Editors of Encyclopaedia Britannica).

Another common practice of media diplomacy among politicians is to travel with journalists so that they may convey their perspectives on a given matter to the public: "Today, significant visits abroad are usually extensively covered by global television and the local media. An American president visiting foreign countries is accompanied by hundreds of correspondents who follow every step of his schedule" (Gilboa, p. 13). Numerous heads of state and heads of government employ journalists as one strategy in the overarching game of diplomacy. This kind of cooperation between journalists and diplomats can be highly beneficial in the pursuit of peace. If one of the parties harbors malicious intent, however, the situation can deteriorate. Here, we may recall the role of Judith Miller, a former journalist for *The New York Times*, who is often associated with the expression "triggering a war"; her work has been heavily criticized for justifying the 2003 invasion of Iraq (Huang, 2023).

Many more cases can be classified under the category of media diplomacy (Mamchii, 2023), although there may not be a universal consensus among analysts on some of them. Regardless, the role played by both technology and media in diplomacy simply cannot be ignored or denied because "the Internet and other information technologies are no longer a peripheral force in the conduct of world affairs but a powerful engine for change" (Bollier, 2003, p. 38). Robinson expresses the pressure of the media as follows: "The new technologies appeared to reduce the scope for calm deliberation over policy, forcing policymakers to respond to whatever issue journalists focused on" (Robinson, 1999). In other words, policymakers often have little time to engage in calm deliberation. "The media's involvement in diplomacy is becoming increasingly important as heads of state and non-state actors make increasing use of the media as a major instrument for communication and negotiation" (Gilboa, p. 23). This explains why many countries resort to using emerging technologies, especially AI systems, to improve their image, defend their strategic interests, and garner public opinion in favor of their foreign policy.

However, when discussing the impact of AI on media diplomacy, we must consider its dual influence. On the one hand, AI significantly affects the media industry, altering the ways in which news is produced, disseminated, and consumed. On the other hand, AI is employed by diplomats to enhance communication, information analysis, and task automation. Thus, the impact of AI on media diplomacy is transitive and inherently transferable, as AI's influence on the media industry eventually extends to diplomatic practices themselves.

4.2 Media, Diplomacy, and Artificial Intelligence: A Multifaceted Evolutionary Journey.

As noted by Nimcj (2019), "Mass media and its evolution came into being as a necessity for people to stay informed and connected in a way that was beyond the capability of humane physical senses." Consequently, the invention of the printing press, the emergence of the radio, the advent of television, and the arrival of the Internet have profoundly impacted the growth of media. These developments have enabled the mass production and distribution of information and ideas across vast distances, effectively uniting individuals on a global scale. As a result, the media has played a crucial role in increasing literacy and knowledge, broadcasting news and world events, providing entertainment, and fostering social relations.

In addition, it is essential to highlight the transformative influence of the online revolution. More specifically, "the commercialization of 5G has greatly accelerated the mobile Internet and has led to disruptive changes in the new concepts, models, and practices of communication and media" (Duan et al., 2020). This shift has also reshaped the structure and functions of diplomacy. To illustrate this relationship, academics often draw direct comparisons between the phases of digital diplomacy and the technological advancements that have shaped the World Wide Web. Terms like Diplomacy 1.0, Diplomacy 2.0, and Diplomacy 3.0 correspond to Web 1.0, Web 2.0, and Web 3.0, and so forth, respectively (Manor, 2017).

Before examining the consequences of AI on media diplomacy, it is important to acknowledge that, despite their distinct origins, artificial intelligence, media, and diplomacy have converged. Artificial intelligence has emerged as an indispensable tool in both the media and diplomatic spheres. This convergence prompts a fundamental question: How will AI revolutionize the landscape of media diplomacy?

5 Discussion

5.1 The Intersection of AI and Media Diplomacy

AI represents one of the most rapid—yet one of the most significant—paradigm shifts in human history; in fact, it is frequently characterized as the fastest-evolving technology. It is a powerful tool that enhances productivity and has the potential to help professionals across a diverse range of fields—including writers, artists, musicians, architects, programmers, doctors, military personnel, and politicians. At the same time, cutting-edge AI technologies (e.g., natural language generation, speech recognition, virtual agents, decision management, biometrics, machine learning, robotic process automation, cloud computing, peer-to-peer networks, deep learning platforms, quantum computing) are driving an exponential transformation that has already far surpassed expectations. Thus, virtually every profession in every field is susceptible to AI-driven changes—"not even diplomacy, one of the world's oldest professions, can resist the tide of innovation" (Moore, 2023).

In the media and entertainment sectors, "AI has dramatically impacted media production and distribution, from recommendation engines to synthetic humans, from video-to-text tools to natural language models" (Connock, p. 2). AI grants real-time insights, uncovers complex correlations, and automates tasks that previously needed to be performed by humans. It can bolster editing systems, music production software, real-time translation, visual effects, dynamic optimization, virtual studios, bandwidth management algorithms, and videogame engines, among countless other applications (Connock, p. 22). These advances have had an immediate impact on the media, which has in turn led to many second-order changes and may ultimately transform the way media interacts with diplomacy.

Before exploring the implications of integrating AI into diplomatic practices—both its broader applications and its specific functions in media diplomacy—it is important to highlight AI's unique capabilities and revolutionary advancements over earlier digital technologies, particularly in data processing, predictive analysis, and decision-making. Before delving into some of the more creative applications of AI, it is worth describing how AI generally operates when tasked with evaluating a situation and making decisions, especially in the context of international relations.

AI functions within a five-stage framework, which is illustrated below in the context of diplomatic negotiations:

- **Input Data Phase:** This phase refers to "any information that is entered into a computer or software program" (Ad-Ins, 2022). During this phase, data is gathered from various sources and provided to the AI system in order to define a problem, condition, or request. In the context of diplomatic negotiations, the first step involves collecting previous negotiation reports, intentions, interests, strengths, weaknesses, historical context, status, relevant statistics, and other significant details pertaining to the involved parties. In addition to traditional sources, data may also come from intelligence reports, diplomatic cables, and media coverage.
- **Processing Phase:** This phase involves "the transformation of the input data into a more meaningful form (information) in the CPU" Data Processing in Computer (2018). In this step, AI algorithms, machine learning, and natural language processing serve to identify patterns, establish rules, and generate human-readable outputs. Once input data is collected, the AI system analyzes it to identify trends, patterns, and models. Various machine learning techniques, including natural language processing and supervised learning, may be employed to achieve this goal.

- **Decision-Making Phase:** This phase refers to the process by which "after processing the incoming data, the AI model must decide or provide a recommendation. Several methods, including rule-based systems and decision trees, can accomplish this" (Hunt, 1992, pp. 306–311). In diplomatic discussions, this phase may lead to various outcomes, such as escalating tensions, finalizing trade agreements, or deciding on military actions.
- **Output Phase:** This phase entails the dissemination of the decisions or predictions generated by the AI system in one of various formats. The output may take the form of reports, recommendations, or a list of options tailored to the specific needs of the diplomats that deployed the AI tool. For instance, "IBM's Cognitive Trade Advisor has already assisted negotiators by responding to questions about trade treaties that might otherwise require days or weeks to answer" (Moore, 2023). Around the world, laboratories are already working on AI chatbots to enhance diplomatic negotiations: "There has been plenty of talk over the years about employing chatbots to serve as negotiating agents. Now, it appears that chatbots, powered by artificial intelligence, may be entering mainstream usage" (McKendrick, 2023).
- **Feedback Loop:** This is "an algorithm that allows an AI model to become more accurate over time. It does this by identifying when an error has been made in the output created by the bot, and feeding this back into the AI model as input, allowing it to avoid similar errors in the future" (Loft, 2023). This phase helps to refine, enhance, and adapt the AI system's performance over time, giving way to alternative—potentially superior—scenarios in similar political situations moving forward, such as peace treaties, declarations of war, and trade agreements.

Evidently, the party with superior data, tools, and AI expertise has a significant advantage. Such a party is better equipped to manage negotiations efficiently and secure the most favorable outcomes, be it in political, commercial, or other arenas.

5.2 Immediate and Potential Impacts of AI on Media Diplomacy

One of the great paradoxes of AI and media diplomacy is that they appear to be at odds with each other. Diplomacy traditionally involves private negotiations and official declarations between countries, while the media's role is to inform the public about global events. Manor explains this inconsistency as follows: "Diplomacy is a profession shrouded by an aura of secrecy and discretion and is thus incompatible with the norm of transparency embedded in digital platforms" (International Affairs, 2023). However, in the information age, these two fields are becoming increasingly intertwined.

What is indisputable is the fact that "today's technologies could assist diplomats with real-time translation of open-source material across languages, enabling them to understand sentiment in foreign societies faster and better, thereby amplifying the impact of their programs" (Nkralev, 2023b). At the same time, the malicious use of AI introduces new challenges for international actors, particularly at the psychological level. These actors "are using AI to achieve their specific beneficial goals while investing greater efforts to limit their vulnerabilities. Consequently, international society faces the psychological impact of non-trusted information, which influences policymaker decisions and drives political changes in global affairs" (Roumate, 2021).

Beyond the various existing indicators that demonstrate the effects of AI on contemporary diplomatic practice, the rapidly evolving technology is poised to revolutionize the field of media diplomacy through the provision of new tools, techniques, and insights. This evolution will undoubtedly give way to both substantial opportunities and grave risks such as *monitoring and analyzing media coverage because* "The new communication technologies, pose challenges; they appear to accelerate the pace at which diplomats are expected to react and deliver their analyses to their respective governments" (Archetti, 2012, p. 9). In an increasingly interconnected world, AI is revolutionizing media diplomacy and has become a powerful tool with which to enhance the effectiveness of diplomacy. By equipping diplomats with advanced tools and real-time information, AI enables them to constantly stay informed, communicate effectively, and assess the impact of their efforts. AI supports diplomats by monitoring media outlets, social platforms, and online forums across multiple languages and regions in real time. This capability keeps them up to date on evolving narratives, debates, shifts in public opinion, and potential perception-related challenges or opportunities. Furthermore, AI can instantly translate media content and diplomatic communications into most languages while accounting for social nuances, religious beliefs, and political or cultural sensitivities. Finally, it can measure the effectiveness of media diplomacy by tracking and "measuring engagement metrics" (Trunfio & Rossi, 2021), such as media coverage and social media interactions. "Diplomacy now faces an unfamiliar digital challenge—that of ChatGPT. Launched in November of 2022, this generative AI chatbot has been the subject of intense media coverage and debates" (Manor, 2023). ChatGPT presents diplomats with significant potential benefits. For one, it can provide diplomats with concise, up-to-date briefings on key issues, historical context, and pertinent international agreements prior to starting negotiations. Moreover, its ability to deliver accurate translations facilitates communication among delegates who speak different languages. ChatGPT can also manage multiple channels of communication, ensuring precise and prompt responses. In addition to streamlining communication, it can automate menial tasks, such as generating meeting summaries and clarifying statements made by negotiation counterparts to ensure there is a mutual understanding. In other words, ChatGPT means the end of diplomacy as we know it (Bjola & Manor, 2023). Recognizing its growing importance, numerous professional websites and specialized institutions now offer training in the diplomatic applications of ChatGPT. This training focuses on mastering AI-driven communication techniques, addressing the ethical implications of AI in diplomacy, and gaining a deeper understanding of ChatGPT's capabilities and potential applications in diplomatic settings (Global Diplomacy Forum n.d.). However, it is essential to acknowledge the challenges and risks associated with using ChatGPT in diplomatic contexts, including its tendency to generate biased or inaccurate content, its limited understanding of complex issues, and the potential for misuse, which could result in the spread of misinformation.

AI-powered predictive analytics are transforming industries like healthcare by identifying trends in patient imaging data and improving treatment outcomes (Docles, 2023). They boast similar potential when it comes to revolutionizing international relations and conflict resolution. AI can play a pivotal role in preventing wars by developing models that analyze historical conflict data, social media trends, TV and radio broadcasts, and geopolitical interactions. These AI-driven models can be utilized to develop advanced early warning systems capable of detecting potential crises and conflicts. Additionally, they can recommend tailored conflict-resolution strategies to decision-makers, including media professionals, to avoid escalation and support successful diplomatic negotiations. In this context, Alexander Hunt—section chief at the US Embassy in Guinea—highlights how embassy staff can benefit from AI tools: "It can help identify potential sources of conflict and instability before problems escalate. By analyzing historical data, social media sentiment, and other relevant factors, AI can provide early warnings, allowing diplomats to take proactive measures to prevent and resolve conflicts more effectively" (United States Department of State, 2023).

The proliferation of disinformation presents a multifaceted challenge for diplomats that encompasses security concerns as well as political, societal, and ideological dimensions. As highlighted by the European Parliament, "Disinformation—AI-enabled or not—is guaranteed to play a role in any future conflicts. Propaganda and disinformation predate AI by centuries, if not millennia, but appear particularly relevant at the moment" (Franke, 2021). However, AI algorithms also have the potential to play a critical role in detecting instances of disinformation and fake news, providing diplomats with the tools necessary to combat false narratives and protect their country's international reputation. In this regard, "even if automatic detection of fake news and disinformation is not fully achievable at the moment and not the primary intent of the authors, machine learning technologies and big data analysis can strongly support journalists and media professionals in identifying disinformation in their daily work." (Nucci et al., 2020). Projects like FANDANGO—whose aim to detect fake news and provide a more efficient and verified communication for all European citizens—are among the most promising efforts in this field (European Science-Media Hub, 2019). AI algorithms can also efficiently trace the origins of misleading information, automating the complex task of mapping foreign media landscapes and identifying the most influential outlets and individuals.

Media diplomacy faces new risks and challenges imposed by data-driven decision-making which refers to "the practice of basing decisions on the analysis of data rather than purely on intuition" (Provost & Fawcett, 2013). Incorporating data-driven approaches can significantly reshape media diplomacy. Extensive research has looked at the AI tools' potential when it comes to diplomatic negotiations, UN peacebuilding and security initiatives, computer-assisted strategic reasoning, and generative pretrained strategy development models (Pokhriyal & Koebe, 2023). AI enhances diplomatic decision-making by analyzing global public perceptions, enabling the formulation of intricate international proposals in line with societal norms. These insights improve the effectiveness of diplomatic communication by enabling diplomats to customize their media responses and optimize their outreach strategies. Furthermore, historical data on media engagement can inform strategic media communication, enabling media diplomacy to foster precise, fact-based international relations.

AI systems not only support diplomats in their tasks but also play a critical role in evaluating Foreign Service candidates' essays and qualifications (both educational and professional). As noted by Keohan and Kravlev (2022), "Software now scores Foreign Service candidates' essays and assesses their educational and professional qualifications" before candidates can proceed to the next stage of the selection process. Diplomats' responsibilities have broadened dramatically alongside the evolving nature of diplomacy itself, which now encompasses the areas of economics, ecology, science, and media, among others. This expansion has led to an increased number of diplomats and rising costs associated with managing the necessary infrastructure. To address these challenges, virtual diplomatic assistants have emerged as valuable tools. Advanced algorithms and robotic systems now enable these assistants to perform tasks effectively through synchronized correspondence, translation services, and real-time corrections, greatly boosting their efficiency and that of diplomatic work overall. Furthermore, as Moore (2023) suggests, "Sophisticated AI systems may even one day reach a level of artificial general intelligence. Such systems could upend our understanding of technology, allowing AI to become an independent agent in international engagements rather than a mere tool."

Recent developments in AI have made it possible to teach people essential conflict resolution skills in new ways. So it is reasonable to assert that "The ability to communicate in a way that transforms conflict and interpersonal differences into opportunities for connection and understanding is a skill that everyone can learn" (Hsu & Chaudhary, 2023). AI offers promising solutions on a global scale by providing tools and methods for crisis management and conflict prevention. Through its vast data collection and processing capabilities, AI can track public narratives and discussions about global tension hotspots across various media channels and suggest corresponding diplomatic strategies and techniques to prevent escalation and bolster crisis management efforts. AI's predictive capabilities benefit diplomats as well as media professionals involved in diplomatic work by transforming the media into a channel for diplomacy. By promoting dialogue and fostering international collaboration on security and peace, AI creates an environment that is conducive to resolving conflicts and sustaining global harmony.

5.3 Ethical Concerns

While AI offers numerous benefits, such as enhanced efficiency and personalization, it also presents an array of significant moral challenges that must be addressed. As Roumate (2021) observes, "In the age of AI, new reforms are needed at different levels considering the changing identity of international society with the emergence of new actors, particularly transnational corporations who have invested in AI more than some States." This is particularly relevant given the growing influence of large media corporations and the ways in which the global media is reshaping international politics—including diplomacy (Seib, 2011).

AI-driven media diplomacy holds great promise, yet it also introduces significant ethical challenges. On the one hand, AI empowers diplomats to tailor their messages to specific audiences with precision, respond swiftly to emergent crises, and utilize data-driven insights to sharpen their diplomatic efforts. For instance, governments already use AI to analyze social media trends, tailor crisis communication, and optimize media strategies, thereby improving the overall efficiency of diplomatic initiatives. Hence, some experts argue that "building the capacity of personnel (diplomats, aid organizations, government offices, etc.) who are central during crises to understand the promises and limitations of AI models and their outputs is an urgent priority" (Pokhriyal & Koebe, 2023).

On the other hand, these advantages present notable ethical concerns. For instance, AI systems can inadvertently perpetuate biases and discrimination, raising concerns about fairness and cultural sensitivity in diplomatic communications. The potential for AI-generated misinformation and the delicate balance necessary between human expertise and AI assistance add further ethical complexities. Moreover, the massive data collection processes necessary to facilitate AI-based analysis heighten security and privacy risks.

Consequently, "given the speed and flexibility of response demanded by the political priority to combat disinformation, it may be that the reform of existing legislation is a more effective and sustainable form of regulation" (European Parliament, 2021). To address these challenges and ensure the responsible and ethical use of AI in media diplomacy, the development of international standards is crucial. These standards must be developed with the aims of preserving human rights, safeguarding privacy, and promoting honesty and equity in diplomatic practices in the digital age.

6 Conclusions

Media diplomacy, whether traditional or modern, integrates seamlessly into the broader framework of public diplomacy. Due to the overlapping communication methods employed, it is challenging to distinguish clear disparities between the two in practice. Consequently, media diplomacy can be regarded as an integral component of public diplomacy. Beyond that, Saliu (2022) argues that "traditional concepts like media diplomacy, public diplomacy, and digital diplomacy no longer fully capture the complexities of modern diplomatic practices. Therefore, a new concept, digital media diplomacy, is proposed to describe these new circumstances more realistically" (p. 16).

Media diplomacy is an established strategy among government officials and international actors seeking to leverage traditional media platforms (e.g., television, radio, newspapers) alongside modern tools (e.g., websites, social media platforms, big data applications). The primary aim of media diplomacy is to advance diplomatic objectives, influence foreign audiences, protect national interests, shape global perceptions, and, in turn, enhance the image of a country or organization on the international stage. We may achieve these goals through a diverse range of media programs, including news broadcasts, series, reports, interviews, investigations, editorial articles, and social media posts. One notable concern for diplomats lies in the evolving impact of internet technologies and AI, as "it is more than predictable that the capabilities of Artificial Intelligence—especially those of Artificial Superintelligence—will further diminish the traditional role of diplomatic missions" (Vacarelu, 2021). This shift is also reflected in traditional media diplomacy, with experiments like a 13-h AI-enabled radio program using "voice clones" and a ChatGPT-written script (Diaz, 2023) demonstrating the transformative potential of AI.

The impact of AI on media diplomacy parallels its effects on other sectors, such as education, which must be safeguarded against external interference and threats to ensure the psychological, cultural, and scientific security of future generations and of the institutions overseeing it (Hajji, 2023). Similarly, sectors like food, health, security, and defense must address the challenges that AI presents. While AI enhances media practitioners' productivity and outcomes, its potential for misuse poses substantial ethical dilemmas, especially in the realm of diplomacy. This domain, often regarded as a "reserved domain" of state activity with high sovereign authority, remains unbound by international law (Jouzier, 2020). The implications of AI misuse extend not only to governments and citizens but also to the public on the receiving end.

The risks associated with the intersection of media diplomacy and AI are steadily mounting. When AI tools become accessible to media practitioners who lack adequate diplomatic knowledge and skills, their potential for misuse rises. Such practitioners, using AI to perform diplomatic functions like mediation and negotiation, may intentionally or unintentionally misuse AI's capabilities. For instance, a columnist or television producer could exploit predictive diplomatic tools or AI-generated analyses to publish content that incites panic or uncertainty, such as exaggerated reports of impending conflicts, economic instability, or environmental threats driven by faulty or biased AI analyses.

The convergence of media diplomacy and advanced AI technology signals a profound and potentially uncontrollable transformation. With the increasingly widespread availability of affordable AI tools through start-ups and even some free online platforms, the risks associated with misuse have escalated. Indeed, "You can now easily and accurately make anyone say anything through AI. Just use an online program to record a sentence and listen to it in a famous person's voice" (Cassauwers, 2019). It is therefore imperative to accelerate the training of media professionals and diplomats to mitigate the risks of AI misuse. Such training should equip them to address emergencies stemming from AI misuse in international relations and ensure ethical practices in the use of AI-enabled tools.

To effectively address the complexities associated with modern diplomacy, especially in light of the significant advancements made in AI in recent years, it is crucial to bridge the gap between academic research, diplomatic practitioners, media professionals, and developers of digital systems and technologies. Collaboration, particularly between academics and diplomats, holds great potential to offer valuable insights into how media narratives shape public opinion and influence the development of international policies. As Riley (2014) emphasizes, "Scholars of public argument and of media thus have an important role to play in this process and should be explicitly looking at how the interaction of media sources and coverage may contribute to the framing and resolution of the conflict." This integration is crucial to the development of strategies that leverage media as a tool for resolving conflicts and fostering constructive international relations.

References

Ad-Ins. (2022, June 10). *Definition of data input*. Advance Innovations. https://www.ad-ins.com/learn-the-definition-of-data-input-and-why-its-so-important/

Archetti, C. (2012). The impact of new media on diplomatic practice: An evolutionary model of change. *The Hague Journal of Diplomacy, 7*(2), 181–206. https://doi.org/10.1163/187119112x625538

Berridge, G. (2001). *Diplomacy theory from Machiavelli to Kissinger*. Palgrave Macmillan.

Bjola, C., & Manor, I. (2023, April 25). ChatGPT: The end of diplomacy as we know it. *Global Policy Journal*. https://www.globalpolicyjournal.com/blog/25/04/2023/chatgpt-end-diplomacy-we-know-it

Bollier, D. (2003). *The rise of netpolitik: How the Internet is changing international politics and diplomacy*. The Aspen Institute.

Cassauwers, T. (2019). Can artificial intelligence help end fake news? *Horizon Magazine*. https://ec.europa.eu/research-and-innovation/en/horizon-magazine/can-artificial-intelligence-help-end-fake-news

Cohen, Y. (1986). *Media diplomacy: The Foreign Office in the mass communications age*. Frank Cass.

Connock, A. (2022). *Media management and artificial intelligence, understanding media business models in the digital age*. Routledge.

Data processing in computer. (2018, August 20). Peda.net. https://peda.net/kenya/ass/subjects2/computerstudies/form-3/data-processing

De Silva, D., & Alahakoon, D. (2022). An artificial intelligence life cycle: From conception to production. *Patterns, 3*(6), 100489. https://doi.org/10.1016/j.patter.2022.100489

Diaz, M. (2023, May 2). *Would you listen to AI-run radio? This station tested it out on listeners*. ZDNET. https://www.zdnet.com/article/would-you-listen-to-ai-run-radio-this-station-tested-it-out-on-listeners/

Diplo. (2023) *AI diplomacy: Geopolitics, topics, and tools in 2023*. https://www.diplomacy.edu/topics/ai-and-diplomacy/

DiploFoundation. (2022, May 17). *AI as a tool for diplomacy and mediation* [Video]. YouTube. https://www.youtube.com/watch?v=6JOEW5zLEZM

Docles, E. (2023). Healthcare artificial intelligence: Transforming the future of medicine. *Health Science Journals, 17*(6), 1033.

Duan, P., Zhang, L., Song, K., & Xiao, H. (2020). The push by 5G. In *Communication of smart media* (pp. 119–135). Springer. https://doi.org/10.1007/978-981-15-9464-9_7

Ebo, B. L. (1996). Media diplomacy and foreign policy: Toward a theoretical framework. In A. Malek (Ed.), *News media and foreign relations: A multifaceted perspective* (pp. 47–64). Greenwood Press.

European Parliament. (2021). *The impact of disinformation on democratic processes and human rights in the world*. https://www.europarl.europa.eu/RegData/etudes/STUD/2021/662926/IPOL_STU(2021)662926_EN.pdf

European Science-Media Hub. (2019, June 26). *EU project FANDANGO*. European Science-Media Hub. https://sciencemediahub.eu/2019/06/26/eu-project-fandango/

Franke, U. (2021). *Artificial intelligence diplomacy: Artificial intelligence governance as a new European Union external policy tool*. Directorate-General for Internal Policies of the Union, European Parliament. https://data.europa.eu/doi/10.2861/745637

Freifeld, S. A., & Cohen, Y. (1988). Media diplomacy: The Foreign Office in the mass communications age. *International Journal, 43*(2), 353. https://doi.org/10.2307/40202541

Gilboa, E. (2001). Diplomacy in the media age: Three models of uses and effects. *Diplomacy & Statecraft, 12*(2), 1–28. https://doi.org/10.1080/09592290108406201

Global Diplomacy Forum. (n.d.). *ChatGPT and diplomacy course*. Retrieved December 2, 2024, from https://www.gdforum.org/chatgpt-and-diplomacy-course

Hajji, S. (2023). Educational sovereignty and artificial intelligence challenges: The case of Morocco. In *Artificial Intelligence in Higher Education and Scientific Research* (pp. 101–116). https://doi.org/10.1007/978-981-19-8641-3_8.

Hart, D., & Siniver, A. (2020). The meaning of diplomacy. *International Negotiation, 26*(2), 159–183. https://doi.org/10.1163/15718069-BJA10003

Hasan, S. (2022). Rethinking media diplomacy and public diplomacy towards a new concept: Digital media diplomacy. *Online Journal Modelling the New Europe, 39*, 4–24. https://doi.org/10.24193/ojmne.2022.39.01

Herman, E. S., & Chomsky, N. (1989). Manufacturing consent: The political economy of the mass media. *Contemporary Sociology, 18*(6), 937. https://doi.org/10.2307/2074220

Hsu, A., & Chaudhary, D. (2023). AI4PCR: Artificial intelligence for practicing conflict resolution. *Computers in Human Behavior Artificial Humans*, 100002. https://doi.org/10.1016/j.chbah.2023.100002

Huang, P. (2023, March 18). *20 years on, remembering the mess of misinformation that propelled the Iraq war*. NPR. https://www.npr.org/2023/03/18/1164565624/20-years-on-remembering-the-mess-of-misinformation-that-propelled-the-iraq-war

Hunt, K. J. (1992). Induction of decision trees for rule-based modelling and control. *Proceedings of the 1992 IEEE international symposium on intelligent control*, Glasgow, pp. 306–311. https://doi.org/10.1109/ISIC.1992.225108.

International Affairs. (2023, May 29). *What ChatGPT means for the future of diplomacy*. Medium. https://medium.com/international-affairs-blog/what-chatgpt-means-for-the-future-of-diplomacy-2ac538caef1e

Jouzier, B. (2020). Déclin et persistance de la théorie du domaine réservé: le constat d'un rôle de « transition » du domaine réservé. *Revue Québécoise de droit international, 33*(2), 53–75. https://doi.org/10.7202/1086441ar

Keohan, C. & Kravlev, N. (2022). *Want to be a diplomat? You must make it past an A.I. 'gateway'*. Washington International Diplomatic Academy. https://diplomaticacademy.us/2022/08/07/foreign-service-exam/

"Medium is the Message ." International Encyclopedia of the Social Sciences. . Retrieved May 05, 2025 from Encyclopedia.com: https://www.encyclopedia.com/social-sciences/applied-and-social-sciences-magazines/medium-message

Loft, G. (2023, October 10). *How AI uses feedback loops to learn from its mistakes*. Ultimate. https://www.ultimate.ai/blog/ai-automation/what-is-a-feedback-loop

Mamchii, O. (2023, May 25). *The role of media in carrying out diplomacy in 2023*. Best Diplomats. https://bestdiplomats.org/role-of-media-in-diplomacy/#:~:text=Media%20events%20serve%20to%20end,for%20the%20process%20of%20peacemaking

Manor, I. (2017, November 23). *Digital diplomacy 3.0: Personalized diplomacy*. Exploring Digital Diplomacy. https://digdipblog.com/2017/11/16/digital-diplomacy-3-0-personalized-diplomacy

Manor, I. (2023). *Opinion – ChatGPT and the threat to diplomacy*. E-International Relations. https://www.e-ir.info/2023/04/07/opinion-chatgpt-and-the-threat-to-diplomacy/

McKendrick, J. (2023, March 17). Your next negotiating partner: Artificial intelligence. *Forbes*. https://www.forbes.com/sites/joemckendrick/2023/03/17/your-next-negotiating-partner-artificial-intelligence/?sh=1df828cb605b

McTaggart, M. (2024, May 23). *Israeli foreign minister accuses Ireland of rewarding terrorism, sharing bizarre video of Irish trad music and Hamas fighters*. Irish Independent. https://www.independent.ie/irish-news/israeli-foreign-minister-accuses-ireland-of-rewarding-terrorism-sharing-bizarre-video-of-irish-trad-music-and-hamas-fighters/a919056806.html

Medium is the Message. International Encyclopedia of the Social Sciences. Retrieved May 05, 2025, from Encyclopedia.com: https://www.encyclopedia.com/social-sciences/applied-and-social-sciencesmagazines/medium-message

Mishra, P. (2020, February 27). The quantum AI revolution. *Observer Research Foundation*. https://www.orfonline.org/expert-speak/the-quantum-ai-revolution/

Moore, A. (2023, March 21). From ChatGPT to quantum computing, the new tech could reshape diplomacy. *Foreign Policy*. https://foreignpolicy.com/2023/03/21/ai-artificial-intelligence-diplomacy-negotiations-chatgpt-quantum-computing/

NIMCJ. (2019). *Timeline of the evolution of mass media*. https://www.nimcj.org/blog-detail/timeline-of-the-evolution-of-mass-media.html

Nkralev. (2023). *How to use artificial intelligence in diplomacy*. Washington International Diplomatic Academy. https://diplomaticacademy.us/2023/10/01/artificial-intelligence-diplomacy/

Nucci, F., Boi, S., & Magaldi, M. (2020). Artificial intelligence against disinformation: The FANDANGO practical case. *International Forum on Digital and Democracy*.

Pokhriyal, N., & Koebe, T. (2023). AI-assisted diplomatic decision-making during crises: Challenges and opportunities. *Frontiers in Big Data, 6*, 1183313. https://doi.org/10.3389/fdata.2023.1183313

Provost, F., & Fawcett, T. (2013). Data science and its relationship to big data and data-driven decision making. *Big Data, 1*(1). https://doi.org/10.1089/big.2013.1508

Redondo, R. (2023, September 13). *Emmanuel Macron addresses the Moroccan population to reaffirm his support after the earthquake and reject certain "controversies"*. Atalayar. https://www.atalayar.com/en/articulo/politics/emmanuel-macron-addresses-the-moroccan-population-to-reaffirm-his-support-after-the-earthquake-and-reject-certain-controversies/20230913113703190848.html

Riley, P. (2014). Media diplomacy: Public diplomacy in a new global media environment. In T. A. Hollihan (Ed.), *The dispute over the Diaoyu/Senkaku islands* (pp. 231–244). Springer. https://doi.org/10.1007/978-3-319-01288-4_9

Robinson, P. (1999). The CNN effect: Can the news media drive foreign policy? *Review of International Studies, 25*(2), 301–309. https://doi.org/10.1017/s0260210599003010

Roumate, F. (2021). Artificial intelligence, ethics, and international human rights law. *International Review of Information Ethics, 29*. https://doi.org/10.29173/irie422

Russell, S., & Norvig, P. (1995). Artificial intelligence: A modern approach. *Choice Reviews Online, 33*(03), 33–1577. https://doi.org/10.5860/choice.33-1577

Saliu, H. (2022). Rethinking media diplomacy and public diplomacy towards a new concept: Digital media diplomacy. *Online Journal Modelling the New Europe, 39*, 1–24. https://doi.org/10.24193/OJMNE.2022.39.01

Seib, P. (2011). *The Al Jazeera effect: How the new global media are reshaping world politics*. Potomac Books. http://muse.jhu.edu/chapter/1592980

Sharp, P. (2019). *Diplomacy in the 21st century: A brief introduction*. Taylor and Francis. https://experts.umn.edu/en/publications/diplomacy-in-the-21st-century-a-brief-introduction.

Sheikh, H., Prins, C., & Schrijvers, E. (2023). Artificial intelligence: Definition and background. In H. Sheikh, C. Prins, & E. Schrijvers (Eds.), *Mission AI: The new system technology* (pp. 15–41). Springer. https://doi.org/10.1007/978-3-031-21448-6_2

Smith, J., & Doe, A. (2018). *Data diplomacy: Updating diplomacy to the big data era*. DiploFoundation. https://issuu.com/diplo/docs/data_diplomacy_report_2018

The Editors of Encyclopaedia Britannica. (2023, October). *Public diplomacy: Definition, types, examples, and propaganda*. Encyclopaedia Britannica. https://www.britannica.com/topic/public-diplomacy

Trunfio, M., & Rossi, S. (2021). Conceptualizing and measuring social media engagement: A systematic literature review. *Italian Journal of Marketing, 2021*(3), 267–292. https://doi.org/10.1007/s43039-021-00035-8

U.S. Department of State. (2023, June 14). *ACPD official meeting minutes – June 14, 2023*. https://2021-2025.state.gov/acpd-official-meeting-minutes-june-14-2023/ (Accessed December 1, 2024).

Vacarelu, M. (2021). Artificial intelligence: To strengthen or to replace traditional diplomacy. In F. Roumate (Ed.), *Artificial intelligence and digital diplomacy* (p. 15). Springer. https://doi.org/10.1007/978-3-030-68647-5_1

Chapter 7
AI and Transnational Data Flows: Challenges and Imperatives of Sovereignty

Ahmed Hafidi

Abstract This chapter addresses the centrality of digital data, especially for AI applications, and explores the complexity surrounding transnational data flows. It examines the crucial role of data capture in the race to appropriate this indispensable and highly coveted resource. By exploring the problems associated with the extraterritorial application of laws in the digital domain and the challenges relating to the territorial localization of data, this chapter contributes to a better understanding of the sovereignty claims surrounding digital data and measures their scope. The inevitable consequence of these initiatives is the fragmentation of cyberspace, synonymous with the fragmentation of data, that fuels legitimate disputes. Attempts at regulation aim to ensure data protection and security, which are essential to the viability of AI and its many applications.

Keywords Data sovereignty · Artificial intelligence · Extraterritoriality · Data fragmentation · Regulation

1 Introduction

It is impossible to discuss the various applications of AI without closely considering digital data. Indeed, AI could not exist without digital data. Digital data is also at the heart of modern communication and journalism. Therefore, we cannot overlook the crucial issue of data sovereignty. Moreover, data ownership is essential for the viability of AI and is a prerequisite for its deployment. Indeed, AI relies on access to massive amounts of appropriate digital data, from which it draws its power.

A. Hafidi (✉)
Faculty of Law, Economic and Social Sciences Agdal, Mohammed V University, Rabat, Morocco
e-mail: ahmed_hafidi@um5.ac.ma

F. Roumate, A. La Rosa (eds.), *Artificial Intelligence, Media and International Security*, Contributions to Security and Defence Studies,
https://doi.org/10.1007/978-3-031-95757-4_7

However, the issue of data collection and processing poses numerous challenges and concerns, particularly access to this data and the control required to ensure its availability and security. This chapter aims to study digital data as a fundamental element of AI and its applications, as well as the complex issues surrounding cross-border data flows.

To this end, this chapter will first address the crucial role of digital data, which constitute the raw material of AI, and the growing interest in capturing this data. Second, it will look at data sovereignty by examining the extraterritorial application of laws to digital data, as well as the issues surrounding data localization and cloud computing. Finally, it will consider the scope of digital data claims, reflected in the fragmentation of information and competition to access it, before discussing attempts to regulate data flows.

2 Method

The research method of this chapter combines an analytical, historic-teleological, conceptual and fundamental, and conclusion endeavor. Given the complexity of the topic, the research method requires a combination of three approaches. The political approach is used to analyze the data sovereignty conditioned by technological sovereignty. The legal approach is posed by the topic to analyze the challenges of AI and data fragmentation which require global AI and Internet governance including AI regulation considering the extraterritorial application of laws. The topic of this chapter and the study focusing on AI, data flows, and data sovereignty require the use of technological approach to explain technical challenges related to data transformation and the complexities surrounding transnational data flows and the challenges related to the territorial localization of data.

3 Literature Overview

As fundamental research, the starting point is the review of previous work discussing a similar topic. The vast dimension of the literature on AI, data fragmentation, and data sovereignty reveals three publications that are particularly relevant to the topic of this chapter.

The first publication, titled "Searching the Clouds: Cloud Act, European Sovereignty and Access to Evidence in the Digital Criminal Space" by Frederick T. Davis and Charlotte Gunka, was published in *Critical Review of Private International Law*, 2021, Issue 1.

The second publication, which focuses on another aspect of the chapter's topic—digital data—is titled "Who Will Capture the 'Gold of the Twenty-First Century'? Battle Over Digital Data" by Cédric Leterme, published in *Monde Diplomatique* in November 2019.

The final publication is an article titled "Game Changer: Structural Transformation of Cyberspace" by Juha Kukkola, Mari Ristolainen, and Juha-Pekka Nikkarila, published by the Finnish Defence Research Agency in 2017.

The first and second articles are published in French. In this chapter, I focus my analysis on the scope of claims regarding sovereignty over digital data and cross-border flows. I explore the impact of data fragmentation and the territorialization of cyberspace, as well as the tensions surrounding AI and the governance model for the Internet that States and their national infrastructures are adopting.

3.1 The Centrality of Digital Data in Communication Processes

Digital data has been described as "the new oil" or "the twenty-first-century's gold." Capturing this data has thus become a major focus globally: we now talk of "big data" as a "great opportunity" (MacGregor, 2018).

Awareness of the importance of digital data is growing. As Leterme (2019) rightly points out, "Every Internet user is an importer-exporter of data who, more often than not, is unaware of it." However, it takes time for governments and organizations to adopt this paradigm shift, and who controls this digital data is a recurring question.

E-commerce is one example that illustrates this shift in the perception of the importance of data and the status that can be attributed to data. E-commerce does not solely involve selling products over telecommunications networks. Indeed, "behind the Trojan horse of e-commerce lies the ownership of data" (Leterme, 2019). This critical question of control and ownership of data represents a major challenge for AI and its various applications.

It is not only the quantity of data that poses concern but how it is used. Relevant and appropriate data are the raw materials for AI applications, including deep learning and social engineering. The ability of AI algorithms to make data "speak," that is, to give it a certain form of intelligence, yields significant predictive power. Cambridge Analytica's alleged role in the 2016 election of former US President Donald Trump and the outcome of the Brexit referendum speaks volumes about the potential stakes involved in data ownership. Capturing citizens' data without their knowledge and using it to profile them made it possible for AI applications to manipulate public opinion through targeted messages based on this data.

Given the perceived importance of digital data, both public and private parties are showing renewed interest in this resource. The management, ownership, transmission, and access to data all present challenges. A significant "battle over digital data" (Leterme, 2019) has been declared. The sheer volume of data in question and its economic, political, security, and societal importance demonstrate the growing interest in digital data. Thus, data is "a resource, the control and commercialization of which are the object of power rivalries between stakeholders" (Gérard, 2018. p.138).

The most powerful States are vying for this fundamental resource and its strategic advantages. They project their influence into cyberspace, thereby reinforcing their soft power. Big Tech, or the Tech Giants (e.g., Alphabet, Amazon, Apple, Meta, and Microsoft), fuel the controversy by insisting on treating data as a mere commodity. International bodies such as the World Trade Organization (WTO) are also entering this debate. Nongovernmental organizations are using this fundamental resource to articulate their political, social, or environmental demands, often in contradiction with the official positions of their parent States.

3.2 Data Sovereignty: The Test of Cross-Border Data Flows

The notion of sovereignty deserves to be revisited in light of current developments in AI and emerging technology. This notion "appeared at the dawn of the modern age, with political theorists such as Jean Bodin in the 16th century, John Locke in the 17th century and Jean-Jacques Rousseau in the 18th century" (Ganascia et al., 2018, p. 5). *Sovereignty* can be defined as "the principle of international law according to which an independent State [...] exercises eminent and exclusive power over its territory" (Lacoste, 2003, p. 357). Transposing this concept into the digital realm poses enormous difficulties. Indeed, digital technology "broadens the paradigm of sovereignty by increasing the number of its bearers" (Ganascia et al., 2018, p. 21), which must be reconciled with the principle of "indivisibility of sovereignty" (Lemaire, 2012).

In this context, the idea of territory persists. While *territory* can be understood as the delimited space over which a state exercises its sovereignty, *digital territory* "transcends state borders and is seen more as a place of *influence* [emphasis added] for sovereign entities" (Martin, 2017, p. 110). However, territorial logics of power are increasingly prominent, fueling claims to digital sovereignty. Attachment to territory remains the current interpretation of state sovereignty, a corollary of state independence.

This corollary means that data sovereignty cannot be properly considered without technological sovereignty: control of the physical layer of cyberspace (Roumate, 2024, p. 61). Even domestic Internet communications may pass through the physical networks in other countries before returning to the country of origin, leading to a potential loss of legal data protections and exposure to mass surveillance. Therefore, data sovereignty must be supported by technological sovereignty. Controlling and protecting such data require access to state-of-the-art technology, including encryption protocols, algorithms, cloud technologies, and sovereign operating systems.

Claims of sovereignty over digital data are becoming increasingly assertive on all fronts, including in developed or developing countries and coalitions such as the Association of Brazil, Russia, India, China, South Africa, Ethiopia, Indonesia, Iran, and the United Arab Emirates (BRICS). These claims have been amplified in the "post-Snowden world."

Edward Snowden's 2013 revelations about the large-scale digital surveillance carried out by US intelligence services marked a turning point in the regulation of data accumulation by large companies, particularly American ones. The General Data Protection Regulation (GDPR), adopted in the European Union (EU) on May 25, 2018, was a direct response to this situation. On the US side, the Clarifying Lawful Overseas Use of Data (CLOUD) Act, enacted on March 23, 2018, has fueled suspicion about data security and use. In connection to the Patriot Act, the CLOUD Act enables US authorities to access data held by major American digital companies, even if based outside the United States.

But what is striking is that, in both cases, we are dealing with *extraterritoriality*, which occurs when a state "claims to apprehend, through its legal order, elements located outside its territory" (Salmon, 2001, p. 211). An example is the Microsoft case from 2014. American judges ordered Microsoft to hand over the data of one of its foreign customers, even though the data was stored in Ireland. The criterion the judges put forward to apply American law was the nationality of the company providing the service, in this case, Microsoft, and not the place where the data is stored. This decision raises suspicions of data capture by American companies in a context marked by the extraterritorial application of American legislation. The issue goes far beyond protecting personal data and concerns "the effects of the implementation of criminal proceedings by one State on the sovereign territory of another State" (Davis & Gunka, 2021, p. 52). As established, criminal proceedings are "the translation of the principle of State sovereignty into law enforcement" (Davis & Gunka, 2021, p. 52). This reflects a key aspect of the impact of extraterritoriality on sovereignty in general and, a fortiori, that of digital data.

The CLOUD Act thus emerges "as a further step in American extraterritorial unilateralism" (Davis & Gunka, 2021, p. 52) by focusing on the simple criterion of data *access* rather than storage. This pragmatism on the part of the American authorities is also a response to the geographical fragmentation of data, especially with the development of cloud computing.

Other legislation, notably in the UK and the EU, has included provisions similar to the CLOUD Act, particularly regarding extraterritorial reach. In the UK, for example, the Crime Overseas Production Orders (COPO) Act was passed in February 2019 and "appears to be even more aggressive than the CLOUD Act when it comes to the extraterritorial scope of computer search seizures" (Davis & Gunka, 2021, p. 60).

In the EU, the extraterritoriality of digital data had been scrutinized even prior to the adoption of the GDPR. The Court of Justice of the European Union (CJEU) examined this issue in the Google vs. Spain case, where the court held that "European data protection law applied to the activities of Google Inc. established abroad" (Thelisson, 2019, p. 503). The GDPR enshrined this extraterritorial perspective by applying both to data controllers *and* processors not established within the EU, when such processing "is aimed at persons in the Union and is linked to offers of goods or services (even free of charge) in the Union, or to the profiling of the behavior of such persons on the territory of the Union" (Thelisson, 2019, p. 504).

Two criteria thus emerge for the geographical application of the GDPR: one, the place of residence of the controller, and two, the location of the persons who are the subject of the processing. This instrument extends even further to the issue of international data transfers, requiring that in any transfer to a third country, the controller or processor must ensure that the country in question "offers an adequate level of protection" (Thelisson, 2019, p. 509) to ensure data security and prevent misuse.

Data *localization*, or the choice of where data is stored, is one of the major levers available in the push for data sovereignty and, by extension, provides the possibility of guaranteed reversibility. The invalidation by the CJEU of the so-called "safe harbor" transatlantic agreement on October 6, 2015, sheds light on this point. In the same vein, several countries impose data location requirements, including in Europe (i.e., Germany, Russia, Greece), Asia (i.e., Taiwan, Vietnam, Malaysia), Latin America (i.e., Brazil), and Australia (Geist, 2018). Similarly, foreign companies operating in China are legally required to store their data there as China believes it to be "a national security issue" (Leterme, 2019).

These legitimate moves toward ensuring local data storage can be hampered by a lack of resources such as data centers, especially in developing countries. Plans for localized data storage are driven by concerns about data availability and security. However, if the physical location of data in a given territory is superseded by the extraterritorial scope of relevant legislation, data localization may not be a practicable solution.

Cloud computing offers flexibility for data localization and, as a result, creates a "fundamentally new paradigm for state evidence gathering" (Davis & Gunka, 2021, p. 50). The geographical fragmentation and dispersion of data pose significant challenges in this context. Of course, such approaches would not be appropriate for storing sensitive information.

The position of the Tech Giants is diametrically opposed to these approaches to data sovereignty: "to defend principles such as the free circulation of data and the refusal of any obligation to localize the storage of personal information […] in order to limit government intervention in their activities" (Leterme, 2019). Significant tensions characterize the relationship between trade agreements on access to digital data and data sovereignty. For example, the Comprehensive and Progressive Agreement for Trans-Pacific Partnership (CPTPP) is currently the standard approach in modern agreements involving e-commerce or digital trade rules. However, this agreement, signed in February 2016, enshrines the supremacy of the position of the Tech Giants. Its chapter on e-commerce "takes up almost word for word the main demands made by lobbies such as the Internet Association and the Computer and Communication Industry Association, which bring together the heavyweights of the sector" (Leterme, 2019).

The major economic and financial stakes surrounding the issue of digital data highlight its importance and explain the race to corner the market, even if it results in stripping digital data of any sovereignty.

4 Discussion

4.1 Data Fragmentation and Sovereignty

Data cannot escape the vagaries of the ecosystems in which they evolve. Though the Internet currently retains its essential characteristic of interoperability, the ongoing trend is toward fragmentation. Driven by national security interests and the desire to control cross-border data flows, this fragmentation inevitably leads to a territorialization of the physical, logical, and semantic layers of cyberspace. The risk is that the global Internet will become fragmented—subdivided into as many Internets as there are States. The examples of China and Russia already corroborate this trend: China's great "digital wall" shows how such a compartmentalization of the Internet contributes to its fragmentation. Similarly, the Russian Internet, "the Runet," can be disconnected from the global Internet yet continue to function autonomously (Kukkola et al., 2017, p. 77).

This desire for autonomy and independence also drives the BRICS countries. Following Edward Snowden's revelations in 2013, BRICS began building an Internet infrastructure that would bypass that of the United States. In September 2013, then-President Dilma Rousseff of Brazil announced the construction of a submarine cable linking the BRICS to Europe. Generally, States prioritize creating their own national infrastructures, such as a sovereign cloud or sovereign operating systems. These demands are likely to fuel the already-existing structural asymmetries within cyberspace, widening the gap between countries that possess resources and power in cyberspace and those that do not.

Private players also drive the fragmentation of Internet content, using methods such as selective algorithms and general terms of use (GTUs), sometimes adapted to local legislation. All these actions contribute to the Balkanization of the Web and starkly contrast the spirit of the early days of the Internet, whose watchwords were freedom and neutrality. This situation must also be considered in the context of the destination, circulation, and protection of data. The fewer obstacles there are to the open circulation of data, the more information will be available for AI to be improved.

4.2 A Contested Model for AI and Internet Governance

In the wake of Edward Snowden's revelations, a number of ethical questions have emerged. The legitimacy of US supremacy in cyberspace also suffered a major blow. Claims to data sovereignty have multiplied, whether concerning State security, the protection of privacy, or corporate information assets. As a result, tensions surrounding the model of governance to adopt in cyberspace have increased.

BRICS has been particularly vocal in its demands to contest Internet governance. The economic dynamism of the BRICS countries, and their regional and global weights, makes them the biggest competitors to the United States in this space. BRICS seems best poised to counterbalance American domination in this field, since they have the most significant means at their disposal. BRICS has also voiced the boldest criticism of the widespread surveillance practiced by US intelligence services. The BRICS undersea cable project to bypass US infrastructures and escape surveillance also attests to the scale of the BRICS reaction. The stakes involved in such surveillance may be political, diplomatic, or economic, especially as concerns commercial transactions, contracts, or industrial secrets.

Wide differences of opinion exist among States and individuals about the best model for AI and Internet governance. In BRICS, Brazil, India, and South Africa favor more open governance, Russia favors a cyberspace governed by international law, and China maintains its national model with all its attendant controls. The basic approach of these countries remains the claim to sovereignty over digital data, which involves, among other things, sovereignty over cyberinfrastructures.

In the countries of the Global South, it would be risky to consider any protest model, for good reason: most of these countries are in a state of technological dependence, making it impossible for them to adopt such an option. The considerable volume of data generated in these countries is exploited elsewhere. This situation has been termed *cyber-colonization*: "The word is very blunt, but technically it is a colonial-type approach: you exploit a local resource by setting up a system that attracts added value to your economy" (Badaoui & Najah, 2021. p. 8). Data mining perpetuates the vulnerability and dependency of these countries.

Another challenge for these countries is influencing negotiations in international forums, for example, during WTO negotiations on e-commerce. These countries need "a form of digital sovereignty enabling these states to acquire their own national sector before considering multilateral negotiations" (Leterme, 2019), to allow them to participate in negotiations and capitalize on the opportunities offered by exploiting their own data.

4.3 Attempts at Regulation and Governance of Cyberspace

It is no exaggeration to speak of a certain degree of anarchy in the governance of cyberspace. This anarchy stems from the absence, whether desired or not, of a supranational regulatory body. Therefore, cooperation between the various public and private players is necessary, rather than compliance with any legislative regime, in order to ensure the optimal functioning and stability of cyberspace. While a number of conventions and regulations have been codified by international bodies, the scope of these initiatives is quite limited.

The question of Internet governance is far from garnering the required consensus, even in principle. Globally, two irreconcilable visions predominate: the multistakeholder model, advocated for by the United States and other countries, and the intergovernmental model, advocated for by China and other countries. These starkly different visions have prevented the formation of any significant agreements, particularly at the World Summit on the Information Society (WSIS). In other multilateral fora, such as the WTO, divergences still surround the subject of e-commerce, which is proving to be a highly complex issue, especially due to the status accorded to digital data. The legal vacuum in this area benefits the most powerful companies in the sector, particularly the Tech Giants, who perpetuate their profits by methodically lobbying decision-makers in the economic and commercial spheres in the United States. They are working toward a regulatory framework aligned with their interests, with a primary objective to enable unrestricted cross-border data flows.

The divergences on e-commerce that emerged at the 11th WTO Ministerial Conference in Buenos Aires speak volumes about the scale of the challenges. Some countries favor deregulating the sector, whereas others do not see e-commerce as a priority. A third group favors deregulation but not in the way that the countries of the Global North envision it. This situation remained unchanged at the most recent ministerial conference, the 12th. The limitations on governance in this sector directly impact data flow, availability, and security.

5 Conclusion

Discussing the viability of AI and its many applications is not productive without considering the digital data resource that constitutes its very essence. Analysis of the context of digital data is essential, given the current state of controversy over the governance of cyberspace. Ensuring sovereignty over data, a corollary of data availability and security, requires ever greater efforts due to the complexity of the issues at stake. In addition to the challenge of defining how data should be treated in international transactions, vulnerabilities arise from the extraterritorial application of laws and localization constraints. The international environment is marked by shortcomings in the global governance of cross-border data flows, exacerbated by the fragmentation of cyberspace.

Efforts to codify and draw up conventions, even if they are only partly effective, are still the best way to reach a consensus on the fate of digital data. Without such a consensus, digital data and, along with it, AI will suffer from the inevitable and ongoing Balkanization of the Internet.

References

Badaoui, S., & Najah, R. (2021). Janvier. In *Intelligence artificielle et cyber-colonisation: implications sur Afrique, Policy paper*. Policy Center for the New South. https://www.policycenter.ma/sites/default/files/2022-08/PP_21-03_Badaoui-Najah.pdf

Davis, F. T., & Gunka, C. (2021). Perquisitionner les nuages - *CLOUD Act,* souveraineté européenne et accès à la preuve dans l'espace pénal numérique. *Revue Critique De Droit International, N°* 1(1), 43–66. https://www.cairn.info/revue-critique-de-droit-international-prive-2021-1-page-43.htm.

Ganascia, J-G., Germain, E., & Kirchner, C. (2018, Mai). *La souveraineté à l'ère du numérique: Rester maîtres de nos choix et de nos valeurs*, CERNA. https://www.allistene.fr/files/2019/05/55708_AvisSouverainete-CERNA-2018.pdf

Geist, M. (2018, April 4). *Data rules in modern trade agreements: Toward reconciling an open internet with privacy and security safeguards*. Centre for International Governance Innovation. https://www.cigionline.org/articles/data-rules-modern-trade-agreements-toward-reconciling-open-internet-privacy-and-security/

Gérard, C. (2018). Les données numériques au cœur de nouveaux conflits géopolitiques. *Regards croisés sur l'économie, 23*, 138–143. https://www.cairn.info/revue-regards-croises-sur-l-economie-2018-2-page-138.htm

Kukkola, J., Ristolainen, M., & Nikkarila, J. (2017). *Game changer: Structural transformation of cyberspace*. https://www.researchgate.net/publication/321767657_GAME_CHANGER_Structural_transformation_of_cyberspace

Lacoste, Y. (2003). *De la géopolitique aux paysages: dictionnaire de la géographie*. Armand Colin.

Lemaire, F. (2012). Propos sur la notion de « souveraineté partagée » ou sur l'apparence de remise en cause du paradigme de la souveraineté. *Revue française de droit constitutionnel, 92*, 821–850. https://www.cairn.info/revue-francaise-de-droit-constitutionnel-2012-4-page-821.htm

Leterme, C. (2019, Novembre). *Qui captera « l'or du XXIème siècle » ?* Bataille autour des données numérique, Monde diplomatique, Novembre 2019. https://www.monde-diplomatique.fr//2019/11/LETERME/60937?id_article=60937

MacGregor, I. (2018, March 5). *Big data: The Canadian opportunity*. Centre for International Governance Innovation. https://www.cigionline.org/articles/big-data-canadian-opportunity/

Martin, V. (2017). La République numérique en débat au Parlement: le projet de commissariat à la souveraineté numérique. *Les Nouveaux Cahiers du Conseil constitutionnel, 57*, 107–120. https://www.cairn.info/revue-les-nouveaux-cahiers-du-conseil-constitutionnel-2017-4-page-107.htm

Roumate, F. (2024). AI and Technological Sovereignty. In *Artificial intelligence and the new world order. Frontiers of artificial intelligence, ethics and multidisciplinary applications*. Springer. https://doi.org/10.1007/978-3-031-50312-2_5

Salmon, J. (2001). *Dictionnaire de droit international public*. Emile Bruylant.

Thelisson, E. (2019). *La portée du caractère extraterritorial du Règlement général sur la protection des données* (pp. 501–533). Revue internationale de droit économique. https://www.cairn.info/revue-internationale-de-droit-economique-2019-4-page-501.htm

Chapter 8
Artificial Intelligence on Journalism: Limits and Risks

Hassan Benouaachane

Abstract Artificial intelligence (AI) has rapidly transformed numerous industries, and journalism is no exception. AI technologies have been harnessed to streamline news production, analyze data, and even create content. While these advancements are promising in terms of enhancing efficiency and aiding in the fact-checking process, they have also introduced a set of inherent risks and limitations that demand careful consideration from journalists, news organizations, and society. This paper conducts a comprehensive review of the relevant literature to explore the potential drawbacks and constraints associated with the integration of AI in journalism. It centers on issues encompassing accuracy, bias, job displacement, ethical concerns, and the enduring role of human judgment. The findings reveal that AI poses a significant threat to the integrity of professional journalism, raising essential questions about its role and responsibilities in a rapidly evolving media landscape. However, despite these fundamental limitations and risks, there is also evidence that AI holds substantial promise within the journalism industry. This study envisages a future where journalism evolves through a unique model of direct human–machine collaboration, redefining the role of journalists and their engagement with AI. In this dynamic environment, the chapter underscores the critical need to strike a delicate balance between AI's potential benefits and the risks to ensure that journalism continues to fulfill its vital function in informing and shaping society.

Keywords Artificial intelligence · Generative AI · Journalism · Algorithms · News · Limitations · Risks

---

H. Benouaachane (✉)
Faculty of Law, Economic and Social Sciences, Mohammed VI University, Rabat, Morocco

International Institute of Scientific Research, Marrakech, Morocco

F. Roumate, A. La Rosa (eds.), *Artificial Intelligence, Media and International Security*, Contributions to Security and Defence Studies,
https://doi.org/10.1007/978-3-031-95757-4_8

1 Introduction

Artificial intelligence (AI) has ushered in a new era in the world of technology, dominating discussions for quite some time due to its ever-expanding influence on modern society. AI has made significant inroads across various industries, such as healthcare, finance, transportation, and media. These changes are particularly apparent in the field of journalism, where AI-powered technologies are reshaping established practices, news production and dissemination, and the general structure and functioning of media organizations. The integration of AI into the news industry is having a significant impact on a broad spectrum of topics.

Due to its rapid development, AI has become an integral part of the business model for news organizations worldwide. Recent reports, surveys, and estimations have highlighted numerous immediate opportunities for journalism. Many scholars argue that AI's role is to support journalistic professionals in their work, assisting with a wide range of activities such as content generation, fact-checking, and audience engagement through personalized content. It has the potential to enhance human efficiency and accuracy and expand the scope of news coverage. AI systems are now handling tasks that were once exclusively within the domain of human journalists, including decision-making, interpretation, and editorial judgment (Bronwyn et al., 2022).

The automation of news production has sparked intense debates about the impact of AI on journalism. These debates revolve around the intersection of AI and journalism, seen both as an opportunity for newsrooms and as a potential threat to the profession's core principles.

Discussions of AI's transformative effect encompass both positive breakthroughs and concerns about issues like misinformation, discrimination, and societal inequalities. These developments have ignited debates about AI-generated news articles and their impact on traditional media; some argue that AI could revolutionize how news is accessed and consumed, while others have raised concerns about the quality and authenticity of AI-generated content. Other studies suggest that readers perceive AI-written news as less accurate than human-generated news, attributing this to the lack of human motives and emotions in AI.

Studies focusing on the opportunities of AI advocate for the use of such systems in news production, citing benefits such as enhanced data analysis and investigative reporting (Stray, 2019). However, others caution that AI tools may have a detrimental impact on the quality of output and may compromise journalistic ethics and values; AI's reliance on predefined rules and constraints, its inability to operate beyond predefined parameters, and the opacity and lack of transparency in AI systems all contribute to these concerns. Nevertheless, one of the most significant challenges of this new context is that, in addition to routine tasks, AI applications are replacing the cognitive aspect of journalistic work (Fieiras-Ceide et al., 2022). These observations highlight the evolving landscape of journalism with the increasing integration of automation and the need for media professionals to adapt to changing skill requirements and technological advancements.

The implementation of automated AI systems in journalism is a topic of significant research interest and raises critical questions concerning the quality of journalism, ethical implications, and the potential impact on the employability of journalists. Investigating these aspects is essential for understanding the evolving landscape of journalism in the age of AI.

AI's practical deployment is a relatively new phenomenon, and academic research on the subject is still developing. There is a lack of emphasis on journalist-facing systems, and, to our awareness, no prior research has aimed to extract requirements, design, or assess AI systems for journalists considering human values. This underscores the need for more comprehensive exploration of how AI tools can be developed and implemented in journalism while upholding the ethical and professional values that are fundamental to those within the industry. This chapter investigates the evolving field of AI in journalism, aiming to contribute to the ongoing discussion about its critical impact. By analyzing the different perspectives and approaches within the existing literature, it aims to understand the current state of AI in journalism, focusing on its limitations and potential risks and providing input for practitioners to expand its applicability. Moreover, this work underscores the need for a balanced approach that combines AI's strengths with human oversight to ensure responsible and beneficial deployment of these novel technologies. To this end, we will address the following questions: How has AI changed the journalism landscape and how can AI tools be leveraged by news organizations? What are the limitations and key roadblocks when bringing AI into the newsroom? Finally, focusing on its potential risks, what are the implications of AI in the field of journalism?

In order to provide context and address these questions, the rest of this chapter is organized as follows. The second section outlines the methodological decisions that have been taken in the context of the subject under consideration. Section 3 explores the extent of AI adoption in newsrooms, exploring the various applications of AI in journalism and considering why news organizations are interested in AI. Section 4 examines the limitations and hurdles that news organizations encounter when implementing AI, discussing the various obstacles and issues that arise during the integration of AI into newsrooms. Finally, Sect. 5 analyzes the potential risks and concerns associated with the use of AI in journalism, including ethical, technical, and social issues. The final section presents the main findings of the study and offers valuable insights for researchers, practitioners, and policymakers.

2 Methodology

The primary goal of this work is to review and consolidate the current body of academic literature related to the use of AI in journalism. This section aims to provide a synthesis of the existing academic literature on the topic of AI usage in journalism, with a specific focus on identifying and understanding the limitations and risks associated with the use of AI in this field. The researcher therefore conducted a literature review to achieve a comprehensive understanding of this particular issue.

A literature review is a common research technique that involves systematically gathering, evaluating, and synthesizing information from previously scholarly works, such as academic papers, books, reports, articles, and other sources. The review includes a significant amount of scientific material published in peer-review journals and scientific conferences and covers the period from 2017 to 2023, prioritizing recent studies and research articles while also including relevant book chapters.

To collect relevant material, the researcher initially selected multiple academic publication databases, including the Web of Science, Google Scholar, and Scopus. These databases are well-known sources of scholarly articles and publications. The selection of materials was based on a search through the titles, abstracts, and keywords of the articles indexed in these databases. Through this process, 65 research publications directly relevant to the topic of AI and journalism were identified.

To properly delimit the literature search, this review only includes relevant sources that pertain to the research questions and excludes papers outside the domain of the purpose of the study. Consequently, 35 studies were included in the literature review. After reviewing these studies and discussing them in relation to the topic of study, this paper answers the research questions and provides a detailed discussion on the limitations and risks of AI in the context of journalism.

3 The Race to Adopt Artificial Intelligence

There have been substantial advancements in AI in recent years, and it is increasingly seen as a transformative force across various industries, including media and news organizations. Integration of AI is considered essential for competitiveness. AI technologies are reshaping journalism by disrupting the traditional landscape of news reporting and dissemination; these technologies have become integral to the news industry, marking a significant shift that started with the digitalization of news and widespread Internet usage. This section outlines the existing limitations and potential negative impacts of AI and highlights how AI cannot be adopted at a scale in the media industry unless more emphasis and resources are put on this issue.

The term AI carries various meanings, including systems that imitate human intelligence to perform tasks typically requiring human intelligence (UK Government, 2017). This definition emphasizes the ability to replicate human intelligence within machines and is associated with theoretical research on simulating human cognition and reasoning. However, this article focuses on the practical, task-oriented aspect of AI, particularly in the context of journalism-related technologies. Here, AI pertains to systems designed to perform specific tasks within journalism traditionally associated with human intelligence.

AI technologies are primarily developed for practical applications, serving as tools to improve various processes such as communication. The integration of AI has brought significant advancements and transformations to the field of journalism. The journalism and media industry has been experiencing a digital transformation for several decades, and this ongoing process has had a profound impact on all aspects of its work processes. AI has the potential to profoundly transform various aspects of the news ecosystem, from content creation and distribution to audience engagement and analysis.

The Internet, digital transformation, and the shift to online platforms have disrupted traditional business models and editorial processes in the journalism industry. This disruption includes reduced advertising revenue, changes in audience behavior, and distribution challenges. Print media, for instance, has suffered from declining readership and advertising revenues, resulting in the closure of numerous newspapers and magazines. AI, once a concept restricted to science fiction, has become a practical tool capable of alleviating some of these pressures (Broussard et al., 2019). In alignment with today's business landscape, its adoption is now a matter of necessity rather than choice. AI, often considered a dual-use technology, holds the potential for both positive and potentially harmful applications. The potential of AI tools to evolve into content-generating agents is a significant shift from their current role as a mediator of human communication (Guzman & Lewis, 2020). This evolution may help to optimize production processes, enhance the media's economic viability, and create novel business models based on personalized content. The impact of AI on the media, journalists, and audiences is indeed intricate and diverse.

Despite journalists' concerns about AI potentially replacing their roles, its integration into newsrooms continues apace. The impact of AI-driven innovation, exemplified by publicly accessible generative AI technologies like ChatGPT, has drawn significant attention in journalism. Consequently, senior leadership teams in nearly every newsroom are now urgently prioritizing AI-driven innovation (Caswell, 2023). Some newsrooms have already introduced AI to streamline operations, enhance the user experience, automatically produce stories, and create more personalized content. A recent Reuters Institute survey (Newman et al., 2021) shows that nearly 70% of media managers view AI as crucial to their organization. As a result, numerous reports and surveys have evaluated AI's use in the media industry and identified potential application areas.

The adoption of AI in newsrooms has gained traction in recent years, with prominent outlets like *The New York Times*, *The Washington Post*, and the *Associated Press* implementing AI projects (Chan-Olmsted, 2019). These projects typically focus on data analysis, automated content generation, and improved recommendation systems. However, given that it is far too expensive for the majority of media companies, the adoption of AI is uneven, and the majority of organizations are in early or experimental stages (Beckett, 2019). The United States and European nations have been at the forefront of AI applications in the news industry (de-Lima-Santos & Ceron, 2021), whereas smaller media houses and those in developing nations have been slower to integrate AI technologies into their workflows (Jamil, 2020). The disparities in AI adoption can be attributed to various factors, including economic and professional constraints, technical expertise, specific organizational goals, and other considerations. There is a consensus that the media industry may face challenges and competition from other actors if it does not rapidly embrace and implement automation (Linden et al., 2019); while many news organizations are aware of AI's potential, the risk they face is falling behind, and even elite news organizations that have embraced AI still have room for improvement in fully realizing its potential. Moreover, they often rely on external funding sources and third-party vendors, such as Google, to support their AI projects and innovations or help them develop AI solutions for their business (Cook et al., 2021).

The diverse applications of AI have captured the interest of journalists themselves, and in some regions, they have enthusiastically adopted AI in news production (Schapals & Porlezza, 2020). At the organizational level, a key motivation is enhancing strategies and potentially increasing revenue streams. AI offers benefits in various areas, including content personalization, targeted advertising, and audience engagement, which can result in higher subscription and advertising income. According to a JournalismAI global survey conducted by the London School of Economics and Political Science (LSE), approximately 73% of surveyed news organizations believe that generative AI applications like Bard or ChatGPT present new opportunities for journalism by improving efficiency, productivity, and creativity (Beckett & Yaseen, 2023). AI-powered algorithms can assist journalists by automating routine tasks such as generating high-quality content, transcribing interviews, and summarizing information from diverse sources, thus enabling them to focus on critical activities and creative aspects of journalism such as investigative reporting, storytelling, and in-depth research and analysis.

Many also see AI as a potential solution to address disruptions in the journalism industry and improve its operations, acting as a valuable tool in enhancing business processes and strengthening audience relationships. Enhancing efficiency in newsrooms, content relevance for audiences, and cost reduction are among the key aims for using AI in journalism. For example, a further JournalismAI report (Beckett, 2019), which surveyed 71 news organizations across 32 countries, underscores that efficiency is the primary motivation behind the adoption of AI in the industry. Due to its impact on a wide range of areas including newsgathering, production, and distribution, practical applications of AI cover various aspects of the news industry. These applications include personalization and audience content recommendations, content tagging, automated story writing, text summarization, and text-to-audio conversion using synthetic voices (Newman, 2022).

AI is a valuable tool for various aspects of journalism, impacting different stages of the news production process. It aids in tracking news trends, collecting and organizing information, automatically generating news articles, and distributing content through personalized recommendation systems. The majority of news organizations, roughly 75%, use AI in their operations. Additionally, approximately 80% of these organizations anticipate that AI will play an increasingly important role in their future endeavors (Beckett & Yaseen, 2023). Many have already established or are in the process of developing institutional strategies to leverage AI technologies.

AI is expected to play an increasingly important role in assisting journalists with data extraction and information gathering, enabling newsrooms to gather material from various sources and helping the editorial team gauge an audience's interests as part of a data-driven production cycle (Beckett & Yaseen, 2023). AI tools can swiftly process vast data volumes and efficiently identify relevant information; they can assist in data analysis, uncover trends, and support investigative reporting by detecting patterns and anomalies within datasets, revealing stories and connections that might otherwise be missed. Media organizations have also developed AI chatbots systems to identify all kinds of information, enabling AI to analyze vast data for timely investigations and verify contributions from the crowd for reliability. Under such circumstances, news bots offer an opportunity for many news organizations to adapt and adjust to the social media environment. One example is Reuters' News Tracer, which tracks social media in real time (Opdahl et al., 2023).

A key benefit of AI tools is streamlining and expediting various facets of content creation by automating tasks such as keyword research, topic suggestions, content optimization, and even content generation. These algorithms can swiftly analyze extensive datasets and are therefore invaluable for data-driven journalism and supplying essential information for news articles. Furthermore, AI can assume a pivotal role in fact-checking by cross-referencing data with a wide array of sources and databases, which is traditionally a time-consuming and labor-intensive task for journalists. According to a 2017 Tow Centre Report, numerous media outlets in the United States have already integrated AI into their fact-checking processes (Hansen et al., 2017); errors can be eliminated by quickly verifying claims and statements, thus helping to guarantee the accuracy and integrity of news content. Fact-checking chatbots are now employed in news production to corroborate or debunk claims, and the data amassed can be utilized to identify trends in misinformation and serve as inspiration for feature articles. However, it is important to note that while AI can assist in these aspects, human oversight remains crucial to verify and contextualize the information generated by AI, as well as to maintain ethical standards in journalism.

Given these wide-ranging applications, AI clearly plays a significant role in journalism across various stages of the news production process. Automated content generation is a prominent example. AI-powered content generation relies on algorithms and machine learning models to create news articles, reports, or other textual content without direct human involvement. This process can produce news articles at a significantly faster rate compared to human journalists and is particularly valuable for routine and data-driven stories such as financial reports or sports results, helping to reduce labor costs associated with news production. While it does not replace human journalists, it complements their work by handling repetitive and data-intensive tasks, which can produce significant savings in terms of time and resources. AI can also generate content at a scale that is challenging a human team to match, making it suitable for news agencies with large audiences or those seeking to expand their content output. Additionally, it can be used to create personalized news content for individual readers, tailoring stories based on users' interests and preferences. It can sift through extensive datasets and generate insights or stories based on trends, patterns, and data analysis, which is particularly valuable for fields like financial news, sports statistics, and election coverage.

AI plays a pivotal role in optimizing content distribution strategies, ensuring that stories reach the right audiences across various platforms. Approximately 90% of media organizations utilize AI technologies in news distribution for tasks such as fact-checking, proofreading, natural language processing (NLP) applications, trend analysis, summarization, and generating code (Beckett & Yaseen, 2023). AI-powered systems can curate and recommend news articles and content in accordance with users' interests, reading history, and behavior, thus challenging the traditional editorial role in selecting and presenting news. By tailoring news streams to the individual tastes of each reader, it is possible to enhance reader engagement and retention, particularly in an era of information overload. Media companies are also developing bots and widgets to monitor readers' history and suggest stories. For example, *The Washington Post's* Clavis uses an algorithm to categorize stories with keywords and then matches these keywords with readers' preferences to recommend relevant content (Kim, 2019).

Journalism is undergoing a significant transformation, with AI technologies playing a substantial role. These disruptions can streamline news production, increase efficiency, and offer new ways to engage with readers. However, it is important to note that there are also certain limitations and concerns, such as the lack of human depth, the accuracy of AI tools, and the impact on the role of human journalists. AI is not a silver bullet for journalism but rather a powerful tool that requires a deeper understanding from members of the news industry (Dhiman, 2022). When used appropriately, AI can significantly enhance the capabilities of journalism; successful integration relies on achieving a balance between recognizing AI's potential and understanding its limitations. This understanding is essential to effectively support and enhance AI capabilities within newsrooms.

4 The Limitations and Roadblocks of Artificial Intelligence

AI has demonstrated significant potential in terms of speeding up news collection, improving data analysis, and even generating content. As with any technology, however, it has weaknesses and challenges that can affect accuracy and ethical considerations. Despite its promise, there are constraints and limitations that impact the quality of journalism. Addressing these limitations is crucial to prevent AI from causing harm and to maintain human control. This section examines the boundaries and limitations of AI in journalism, highlighting the areas where human involvement remains indispensable.

Despite the increased prevalence of AI within the industry, it remains difficult for news agencies and journalists in low-income and unstable economies to take advantage of devices, software/or programs, and automation based on AI. Despite active experimentation with AI, many news organizations have encountered significant hurdles in implementing change, primarily related to financial limitations, a lack of expertise, and resistance to change within their culture (Beckett, 2019). Incorporating AI into any news company's workflow and processes can be a challenge that requires a deep understanding of the technology, significant resources, technical expertise, and employee training. Overcoming these barriers is essential for the successful integration of AI in the news industry.

The use of AI technology can offer significant benefits, such as time-saving. However, factors like financial resources, flexibility, worker and firm preferences, and incentives can pose challenges to its adoption. While the cost of creating and implementing AI applications has decreased over the years, projects relying on AI for investigative news often require significant investments in technology infrastructure and skilled personnel (De-Lima-Santos & Ceron, 2021). The cost of deploying AI technology is often a major deterrent, making integration unfeasible for many news organizations. It is therefore accessible to only a few major players in the news industry, such as IBM, Microsoft, Google, and Amazon. For those with the means and foresight, integrating AI can be a valuable opportunity to enhance efficiency and competitiveness. Smaller and local news providers, as well as those in less affluent countries, have expressed concern about being left behind due to these limitations (Beckett, 2019; Jaakkola, 2023). For instance, AI adoption in African newsrooms has been limited (Kothari & Cruikshank, 2022), and integrating AI tools into existing systems may require significant time and process reconfiguration across various news organizations.

According to a study by Tsalakanidou (2022), the lack of relevant expertise is one of the main factors slowing down the adoption of AI in the publishing sector. Alongside the significant financial investment, finding qualified personnel and closing the skills gap are a particular challenge. Journalists often lack the knowledge and skills required to work effectively with AI-driven tools, which can limit the quality of their coverage of AI and algorithm-related topics. This gap also hinders their ability to ensure safe and responsible use of AI in the newsroom. AI is an emerging field attached to science and technology that demands specialized expertise, posing a challenge for many organizations, including those in the media industry, in competing with big tech firms that have extended their power into media content. Utilizing their vast resources and expertise, these companies have strategically reinforced their AI dominance by regularly acquiring start-ups that are developing AI solutions. This practice enables them to further concentrate power and discourage potential competitors (Linden, 2017). Additionally, adapting large-scale AI projects to specific media needs can be challenging as off-the-shelf AI applications may not meet the unique requirements of media corporations. News organizations will have to invest in new skills and adapt their working methods to keep up with the evolving landscape of journalism and technology.

The successful integration of AI algorithms in the journalism sector depends on the attitudes of users toward this technology. While AI tools have already found a place in many newsrooms, there are significant limitations related to awareness, acceptance, and adoption (Lambert et al., 2023). Journalists often express resistance to automation and AI due to concerns about job security, changes in work practices, and skepticism toward new technology (Beckett, 2019). The primary hurdle is the low level of acceptance among journalists, stemming from a lack of understanding of how AI tools can enhance their processes. As well as concerns regarding job losses and disruption to established workflows, a concern for many professionals is a loss of control, exacerbated by a lack of confidence in using AI. Additionally, the journalism industry's reluctance to share data with AI developers has resulted in a scarcity of real-world data to demonstrate AI's true value in media. The hostility among journalists is due also to their limited knowledge about AI, the perceived threat of being replaced by robots, deficiencies in AI-related skills, and the belief that AI tools may erode the essence of journalism (Naoaín, 2022). This deep-seated distrust toward technology presents a significant obstacle. Overcoming this challenge involves both upskilling the workforce with AI-related skills and raising awareness about the benefits and possibilities that AI can offer to journalism professionals and editorial teams.

Although AI-generated news content has gained prominence as a tool for automating the creation of news articles, it has inherent limitations in comparison to human journalism. AI can produce fast, reliable, and objective news content, but it lacks the critical elements of context, analysis, ethics, creativity, adaptability, and human empathy that human journalists bring to the profession. AI algorithms are improving in accomplishing specific tasks but will always fall short in areas like feelings, compassion, and creative and critical thinking. Furthermore, while AI offers efficiency and speed in content creation, it cannot replace human journalists' roles in reporting, creating, and fact-checking articles. To maintain authentic journalism with a deeper understanding of context, empathy, creativity, and communication, it is important not to rely too heavily on AI. The rest of this section highlights the irreplaceable role of human journalists in delivering comprehensive, ethical, and high-quality news coverage.

The main criticism of AI content tools in journalism is the concern that automated content lacks a personal touch and creativity, which are crucial for authentic journalism. Critics argue that AI-generated content lacks the nuanced and creative aspects that human journalists bring to their work. As journalism is fundamentally a creative human practice, creativity is essential for producing high-quality, engaging, and thought-provoking journalism.

While AI has made significant strides in various fields, including journalism, it still falls short in replicating the depth and breadth of human creativity, which is closely tied to our subconscious, intuition, and emotional intelligence. AI operates on algorithms and mathematical models, recognizing patterns and making data-driven predictions; as a result, it is not inherently creative in the way humans are. AI lacks the ability to generate entirely new ideas or concepts because human creativity is linked to subconscious processes, intuition, dreaming, spontaneity, and emotional intelligence. Overreliance on these tools can lead to formulaic or repetitive content that fails to capture the depth and diversity of human experiences and perspectives. Human creativity is also associated with risk-taking and adventure, which is deeply connected to our survival instincts. Programming these complex human traits into AI systems is a formidable challenge as it involves understanding and simulating human consciousness and cognition. This limitation poses challenges in using AI for tasks that demand original thinking and the ability to adapt to the ever-changing and complex nature of journalism.

While a significant advantage of AI systems is speed and the ability to generate news articles and reports from extensive datasets, the effectiveness of these systems relies on the quality of the training data. AI excels when abundant, high-quality data is available. In the context of automated journalism, where structured data is converted into news stories, data quality is paramount. Poor data quality or a lack of available data is a major obstacle to successful adoption and deployment of AI and machine learning projects. A survey by Trifacta (2020) demonstrated that a notable percentage (33–38%) of respondents faced setbacks in their AI and machine learning initiatives due to poor data quality. In journalism, data quality is vital to ensure accurate and reliable AI models and initiatives. AI models draw insights and analytics from their input data; if the training data is biased, inaccurate, or incomplete, the AI's results will reflect these issues. Insufficient training data can lead to AI systems producing content that does not align with user preferences, reducing their usefulness. Additionally, these systems may unintentionally perpetuate existing biases by limiting exposure to diverse content (Ignatidou, 2019). Due to AI's reliance on vast amounts of data, it is crucial to have high-quality, domain-specific data resources. If the data provided contains historical inaccuracies and biases, these will be reflected in AI-generated content. While news automation systems can produce a large volume of articles quickly, they are not immune to errors caused by algorithmic faults or inaccurate data. It is important to recognize that although AI tools can automatically generate news pieces from datasets, their performance and quality are heavily dependent on the quality of the underlying data.

The availability of vast amounts of data in machine-readable formats is a crucial factor in shaping the quality and credibility of media content. This provides an incentive to create efficient procedures to collect, organize, visualize, and model the data in question (Leonelli, 2020). Typically, data and information suitable for AI analysis are in digital form; however, a potential challenge arises when AI-generated content becomes prevalent on the Internet and the automated data sources are updated infrequently. While AI systems can reliably produce high-quality articles, their effectiveness is severely limited by the scarcity of essential data sources. AI technology is excellent at generating readable content, but it cannot replace on-site research, interviews, and in-depth discussions. Stories and events that rely on these traditional journalistic methods remain crucial for quality reporting. Therefore, it is imperative that technical tools do not hinder or restrict the content produced by journalists. This applies to various journalistic contexts, including constructive or legal journalism, where AI can offer assistance but is not capable of fully replacing the nuanced and context-rich texts created through human expertise.

Unlike humans, AI systems lack the judgment, contextual understanding, common sense, and intuition needed for many real-world situations. Their effectiveness relies on the quality of the data used for training and the scenarios considered during training. These systems can identify patterns and make predictions based on available data, but this can lead to errors and inaccuracies, especially in complex or unexpected situations. As it is often impossible to train AI on all potential scenarios, these tools struggle with idiomatic expressions, cultural references, and figurative language. AI also struggles to understand speech that relies on context, culture, language, and politics (Duarte & Llansó, 2017). Additionally, AI is limited in its ability to analyze various types of data, including natural language text, social media posts, sound files, and video recordings. As data complexity increases, AI's ability to automatically make sense of it diminishes. This lack of common sense can lead to errors, especially in new situations. In journalism, the limited ability to understand context, exercise judgment, and employ common sense is a significant limitation that can hinder the performance and application of AI systems. Newsrooms often struggle to provide necessary context from older stories as AI tends to prioritize newer information.

News publications are increasingly using AI systems in their newsrooms for tasks like data gathering, content generation, and distribution, aiming to enhance efficiency and commercialize their operations. AI can generate news stories based on past datasets, which are typically collected from various Internet sources, including written articles, books, images, audio, and code. However, this process frequently occurs without proper compensation, citation, permission, or acknowledgment of the original creators. This practice raises ethical and legal concerns related to copyright infringement and plagiarism. For instance, the *Daily Mail* is considering legal action against Google for scraping a large number of copyrighted articles during the development of Bard without permission (Warrington, 2023).

AI systems like ChatGPT also rely on Internet content for training, which raises concerns regarding copyright and infringement. Legal challenges related to web scraping and data ownership are significant hurdles and include concerns such as violating website terms of service, copyright infringement, data privacy laws, competitive issues, and the misuse of scraped data. A further issue for news organizations is the use of personal data for AI algorithms and new product development, meaning all professionals within the industry have a significant responsibility to design, implement, and use AI tools responsibly. These challenges may limit journalists' ability to effectively use AI systems in news production and hinder responsible reporting on AI's societal impact. To address these concerns, news organizations need to be vigilant and implement safeguards to prevent potential infringements (Gondwe, 2023). For instance, CNET suspended its use of large language models (LLMs) in January 2023 due to numerous factual errors and instances of plagiarism in AI-generated articles that lacked clear disclosures (Christian, 2023).

The technology in question is not perfect and, like other complex systems, carries inherent biases. These imperfections can lead to errors that have significant consequences. Malicious use of AI tools can produce convincing fake content, notably deepfakes, underscoring the need for human oversight and rigorous quality checks. Consequently, it is not advisable to rely on this technology without supervision. Fact-checking and verifying the credibility of sources are foundational building blocks of good journalism, but the sheer volume of AI-generated outputs makes complete oversight challenging. Automated and human identification and correction of errors both have limitations and unintended consequences, while data cleaning, which AI could assist with, is often done manually due to legal restrictions.

This limitation can skew the pool of knowledge, potentially misrepresenting wider trends, as some data may be incidental and not reflective of broader patterns.

Although AI can assist in various journalistic tasks, it cannot fully replace human journalists. Certain aspects of journalism, such as investigative reporting and in-depth analysis, rely on human judgment and experience. AI should be viewed as a tool to support human journalists rather than replace them. While AI technologies might alleviate some of the pressures on journalists, concerns have been raised that they could compromise professional journalistic values like transparency, accountability, and responsibility. Due to the accuracy issues in current AI systems, including LLMs, relying solely on them can be risky and irresponsible. News organizations should refrain from commercial use of these tools without a solid understanding of the risks they pose.

5 The Potential Risks of Artificial Intelligence

News organizations are increasingly turning to AI for various tasks such as automated content tagging, news gathering, news production, and distribution. AI-powered tools offer several advantages to journalism, but they also come with associated risks that can limit their beneficial impact. These potential risks can affect news organizations, journalists, and newsreaders and can stem from different sources, including biases from training data, system errors, workforce reductions, and poor governance. Major risks involve an excessive amount of automated content, reduced human involvement, and the potential for personalized news leading to limited diversity in information. Successful integration of AI into the journalism industry requires careful consideration and management of these risks.

There is a pressing need to safeguard the sustainability, incomes, and job security of journalists, media workers, and other journalism professionals as a result of the rapid spread of AI in newsrooms. At its most extreme, the automation facilitated by AI could jeopardize job security, reduce opportunities for journalists, and challenge the traditional role of journalists by replacing tasks traditionally carried out by humans. The incorporation of AI in newsrooms has resulted in the automation of various journalistic tasks (Jamil, 2020), placing further pressure on journalists to adapt and remain competitive by acquiring programming and digital skills. The implementation of AI in journalism has both promising possibilities and potential pitfalls, making it crucial to find a balance that benefits both the industry and its workforce.

As AI becomes more sophisticated, it can automate various tasks traditionally performed by reporters, such as data analysis, content generation, summarization, and even basic news reporting. Consequently, media companies may become heavily reliant on AI tools to produce content, streamline their operations, and expand their reach, resulting in job losses and a sense of job insecurity among journalists. There is a risk that many jobs may become redundant (Simon, 2022). As a result, there is a real threat of job losses and a devaluation of the unique skills and expertise that journalists bring to the profession. This issue is not limited to the distant future; many writers and journalists are already experiencing job insecurity due to AI's impact (Chin-Rothmann, 2023), and there is a growing risk that automated tools will increasingly replace human professionals. Some news outlets have already taken steps to replace employees with AI, such as Microsoft's layoffs in 2020 (Boulanger, 2020). Furthermore, research has indicated that generative pretrained transformer (GPT) models have the potential to affect the job functions of 80% of the US workforce, with writers, reporters, and journalists being particularly vulnerable (Eloundou et al., 2023).

In addition to concerns about its impact on employment and job security, the rapid deployment of AI in the journalism industry has had significant social and ethical consequences. AI can potentially disrupt traditional journalism practices and business models in a harmful way. As automated systems can generate news articles quickly and at a lower cost, media organizations may become increasingly reliant on them, reducing the need for human journalists. While AI can create new employment opportunities, it also demands a different set of skills and can result in job polarization and income inequality. There is a risk of a significant skills gap, where workers displaced by AI lack the necessary skills to take advantage of new opportunities. The replacement of routine, manual, repetitive tasks may create a divide between high-skilled AI-related jobs and lower-skilled positions that AI cannot easily replace. The broader concern is that AI's impact on the media industry could exacerbate existing societal inequalities. According to Acemoglu and Restrepo (2022), automation technologies, particularly AI, have led to wage inequalities in the United States by causing relative wage declines for workers specializing in routine tasks.

Moreover, media plays a crucial role in shaping public opinion and disseminating information. If AI systems influence content in a way that is not diverse or reflective of various perspectives, it can contribute to social inequality. Furthermore, a shift toward personalization may compromise journalism's traditional role as a public service, reducing it to marketing and eroding editorial autonomy through data-driven tools (Milosavljević & Vobič, 2019). AI solutions can also have cascade effects, such as moving reporters from writing to data management, editing automated stories for clarity and context, and overriding the need for traditional news outlets by providing direct access to automated content, especially in the case of sports reporting (Kunert, 2020). These effects underscore the multifaceted impact of AI on both the labor market and the journalism industry more specifically. The risk lies in potentially reducing the role of human journalists, leading to a decline in their investigative and critical thinking abilities. Overreliance on AI tools might reduce human involvement; consequently, the essential skills that humans bring to the field will be eroded, and the depth and overall quality of journalistic work will be impacted. Overdependence on automation may stifle creativity and innovation, and there is a risk of excessively producing stories that align with predicted engagement figures, possibly sacrificing relevance and suitability for the audience. The danger here is that machines will take over work without human supervision, which is why it is important to develop the requisite editorial skills to shape such systems.

As discussed above, AI technologies can have limitations and errors, which can lead to inaccuracies in news articles due to machine errors, context comprehension limitations, and information misinterpretation. The use of AI-generated tools has significant consequences that require careful consideration, consultation, and regulation. These technologies have introduced unprecedented risks, including algorithmic bias, misinformation, and the creation of filter bubbles. These risks can undermine the integrity and quality of journalism by introducing bias and errors, generating fake news and deepfakes that are difficult to distinguish from reality, diminishing human action and accountability, invading privacy and security, and eroding trust and credibility in news organizations. It is therefore crucial to address and manage these risks when using AI in journalism.

Journalists are increasingly adopting AI-driven tools without thoroughly examining their implications or fully understanding the potential problems associated with them. While AI holds promise, there is a growing debate about the risks it poses. One significant challenge is the risk of algorithms generating errors and bias. According to the aforementioned JournalismAI report, 60% of respondents expressed concerns about issues like algorithmic bias leading to inaccuracies or biased coverage (Beckett, 2019). Algorithmic bias can result from training data that is unrepresentative or incomplete, as well as a reliance on flawed information. This bias can manifest as production bias inherent in the data input, training data, and generated content and applies to both the data used to train AI models and the data collected when developing news stories. Mishandling data can lead to editorial mistakes such as inaccuracies, distortions, and even discrimination against specific social groups or viewpoints.

Algorithms are often seen as rational, neutral, efficient, and reliable tools. However, in the realm of data adoption and news writing, the scope of data considered and how it is used is determined by human-written code. Algorithms inherently carry and reflect human bias because they are created by humans; unsurprisingly, therefore, the resultant AI-generated content may be biased. The two primary forms of bias in this context are data bias and algorithmic discrimination (Strauß, 2021). Poorly trained algorithms can be particularly damaging to journalism as they may exacerbate existing stereotypes or perpetuate discrimination. AI models are typically trained using historical datasets, which can contain biases and ethical complications (Guzman & Lewis, 2020). As a result, AI-generated content can unintentionally perpetuate existing biases and prejudices, posing a significant risk to fairness and impartiality in news reporting. One of the most pressing concerns is the potential to worsen existing societal biases. Some algorithms may inadvertently replicate and amplify gender and racial biases, which are considered unfair, unjust, or harmful, especially to specific groups. Fundamentally, if the data that AI models are trained on contains biases, the content produced is likely to perpetuate inequalities and prejudices, undermining the principles of fair and impartial news reporting.

Biases in AI algorithms can emerge due to a lack of diversity in the training data (van Dalen, 2012) and the inherent influence of human values in algorithm design. AI systems can perpetuate biases present in their training data, especially when they reflect ideological and political biases (Ferrara, 2023). This can result in news stories and content favoring certain perspectives, which is socially, morally, politically, and legally problematic. The media bias can affect all news consumers, potentially influencing, for example, voters and election outcomes. In addition to these concerns regarding algorithms, there are worries about how this technology could exacerbate fraudulent practices within the industry. Despite their complexity, when language processing models are trained with incomplete or biased data, they are likely to generate false or biased stories. The presence of biased or low-quality training data for AI models can, in turn, impact the quality of information disseminated to the audience, affecting their ability to stay informed and their right to accurate information. The risk of poor-quality journalism practices can further erode the audience's respect for the journalism profession and legitimize attacks on news media by those who seek to silence critics (Ireton & Posetti, 2018).

These systems display algorithmic biases that have the potential to substantially influence their recommendation outputs. This can result in preference manipulation or privacy breaches for users (Himeur et al., 2022). Furthermore, AI-driven personalized news content based on users' preferences can create "filter bubbles," where readers are primarily exposed to information that aligns with their existing beliefs. This can limit diversity of perspectives, reinforce biases, and contribute to political and social polarization. There is a danger that automated systems will repeatedly recommend the same trusted informants, reducing diversity and excluding new voices or less-connected informants from the news (Opdahl et al., 2023). Consequently, when it comes to political issues and other sensitive topics, encouraging users to engage with content that only reinforces their own points of view and therefore excludes other perspectives or issues that affect minority groups may clash with the mission of offering a diversity of information to the public (Helberger, 2019).

AI algorithms, which rely on multiple datasets to generate content, are susceptible to biases present in the data they use. Consequently, incorrect stories often stem from inaccuracies in the initial input data. There have been instances of bias in journalism due to the use of AI. For example, in 2015, such software generated a story incorrectly reporting a drop in Netflix's stock value when it had more than doubled (Zhn, 2023). The lack of human supervision in various automated content generation processes can lead to errors, resulting in inaccurate or biased content. Uncontrolled use of AI in content generation can jeopardize the accuracy of information. Therefore, it is crucial to ensure that the data used for automated storytelling is as unbiased, clean, and well sorted as possible to produce accurate stories.

AI algorithms have the capability to cover a wide range of topics and sources, including social media and online content, enabling quick and efficient news article production for real-time news coverage. However, as discussed above, there is a risk of inaccuracy and bias in these AI-generated articles because they rely on algorithms that are only as objective as the data they are trained on. Although current AI models search through a vast wealth of Internet text data to provide responses to questions, they do not distinguish between reliable and unreliable sources. This lack of discrimination can lead to responses based on disinformation or misinformation, potentially resulting in incorrect or biased content and posing a risk to the veracity of information (Pocino, 2021). Accordingly, there are concerns that a lack of human oversight and judgment in AI-generated reporting could lead to biased or misleading content, as well as errors and inaccuracies in news. This may further erode public trust in journalism, and news organizations using machine-written content could face criticism when mistakes occur. Moreover, AI-generated content often fails to disclose its sources, making it difficult to verify the information's accuracy. There is clear evidence for a developing lack of trust, with studies suggesting that readers tend to view news written by AI as less accurate than news written by human journalists (Longoni et al., 2022). These findings emphasize the importance of digital and media literacy skills in using these systems; without careful training and monitoring, AI tools can inadvertently produce or amplify disinformation and misinformation, contributing to the spread of inaccurate information and public confusion.

According to a study conducted by Kim (2019), approximately 60% of news stories produced by different media platforms to achieve political, economic, and social benefits are fake. Thus, disinformation poses a significant threat to journalism by making it challenging to distinguish accurate information, ultimately damaging the industry's credibility. This undermines journalism's role as a trusted source of knowledge in society. However, despite advancements in technology, human oversight remains crucial for identifying untrustworthy sources and false or harmful information. Fact-checking organizations and their experts are facing a growing challenge due to the increasing volume of false information and the sophistication of bots spreading fake news (Demartini et al., 2020). There is genuine concern regarding the lack of supervision of automatically generated content and the possibility of false information bypassing journalistic fact-checking processes. Journalists typically rely on their traditional fact-checking skills, which are effective in many cases; however, due to time pressures or the need for quick publication, they may prioritize their professional experience and judgment over thorough fact-checking and therefore unintentionally publish unchecked or false information (Santos, 2023). The failure of algorithms to filter harmful and inaccurate content raises concerns over newsrooms' ability to protect their users from misleading information. This issue underscores the importance of maintaining high journalistic standards even when working under tight deadlines to ensure the accuracy and reliability of news reporting.

The aspects presented should not be seen as reasons not to use AI; rather, they should be used to formulate requirements to make the use of AI targeted and effective with suitable measures and precautions. The integration of AI technology in news organizations offers promising opportunities for enhancing journalism; however, news outlets must proceed with caution and maintain their core values of accuracy, objectivity, and diversity of perspectives. To harness the benefits of AI in journalism while mitigating its potential risks, responsible development, algorithm transparency, granting user control, and fostering media literacy are essential steps. Striking a balance between technological innovation and the preservation of journalistic integrity is imperative to maintain a healthy and informed information environment for the public.

6 Conclusion

This chapter highlights the importance of AI in journalism and its potential to revolutionize the industry. It constitutes a valuable reference for journalists, practitioners, and academics working on the implications of AI usage within the news industry. Based on our analysis of academic and industry literature, it is evident that AI is becoming increasingly common in journalism and has the potential to bring about transformative changes in various aspects of the field. The data suggests that leading newsrooms have embraced AI technologies to enhance efficiency, reduce expenses, and engage their audiences. However, smaller media outlets and those in developing countries are facing financial and technical constraints that have prevented them from keeping pace with these developments. Although its specific impacts are still uncertain, it is now widely accepted that AI will reshape journalism in an incremental way, albeit in the long term.

The results of this chapter indicate that the existing literature tends to portray AI in a positive light, emphasizing its potential and advantages. Indeed, in the context of journalism, AI offers benefits such as personalized content, targeted advertising, increased audience engagement, and the potential for higher revenue. This optimistic view underscores AI's transformative role in the field. However, it is crucial to remember that AI should complement and enhance human journalists rather than replace them. Human oversight remains vital in verifying and providing context for AI-generated content and maintaining ethical standards. AI, in its present state, has limitations, including its lack of depth and nuance in storytelling and potential accuracy issues. Striking a balance between recognizing the potential of AI and understanding its limitations is essential for its effective integration into newsrooms.

In studies examining the adoption of AI in journalism, researchers have addressed several of the associated risks. The most frequently mentioned risks in the existing literature are technological limitations, potential job losses, the lack of diversity of journalistic reporting, and ethical concerns. Our data analysis demonstrates that discussions about these risks have increased in recent public debates, aligning with previous studies on AI and journalism. This indicates that algorithms have become a major topic of debate, especially the associated issues of bias and transparency. To successfully incorporate AI into journalism, it is crucial to do so responsibly and thoughtfully. This is essential to maintain the quality, credibility, and reliability of the information industry. It is essential to address issues such as bias, resistance to change, and ethical considerations. Journalists and news organizations should consider AI as a tool that can improve their work, with the value of human journalists being reflected in those aspects that are difficult for AI to replicate such as critical thinking, empathy, creativity, and understanding context.

In this rapidly evolving landscape, striking the right balance between technological innovation and upholding journalistic ethics and values is key. By doing so, it is possible to ensure that AI serves the public's need for accurate, diverse, and trustworthy information while upholding the core principles of journalism.

References

Acemoglu, D., & Restrepo, P. (2022). Tasks, automation, and the rise in US wage inequality. *Econometrica, 90*(5), 1973–2016.

Beckett, C. (2019). *New powers, new responsibilities—A global survey of journalism and artificial intelligence.* LSE Polis Report, The International Centre for Journalists (ICFJ). https://drive.google.com/file/d/1utmAMCmd4rfJHrUfLLfSJ-clpFTjyef1/view

Beckett, C., & Yaseen, M. (2023). *Generating change: A global survey of what news organisations are doing with AI.* London School of Economics and Political Science. https://static1.squarespace.com/static/64d60527c01ae7106f2646e9/t/6509b9a39a5ca70df9148eac/1695136164679/Generating+Change+_+The+Journalism+AI+report+_+English.pdf

Boulanger, G. (2020, May 29). Microsoft is cutting dozens of MSN news production workers and replacing them with artificial intelligence. *The Seattle Times.* https://www.seattletimes.com/business/local-business/microsoft-is-cutting-dozens-of-msn-news-production-workers-and-replacing-them-with-artificial-intelligence/

Bronwyn, J., Rhianne, J., & Luger, E. (2022). AI everywhere and nowhere: Addressing the AI intelligibility problem in public service journalism. *Digital Journalism, 10*(10), 1731–1755.

Broussard, M., Diakopoulos, N., Guzman, A. L., Abebe, R., Dupagne, M., & Chuan, C. H. (2019). Artificial intelligence and journalism. *Journalism and Mass Communication Quarterly, 96*(3), 673–695.

Caswell, D. (2023, September 19). *AI and journalism: What's next?* Reuters Institute. https://reutersinstitute.politics.ox.ac.uk/news/ai-and-journalism-whats-next

Chan-Olmsted, S. M. (2019). A review of artificial intelligence adoptions in the media industry. *International Journal on Media Management, 21*, 193–215.

Chin-Rothmann, C. (2023, August 31). *Navigating the risks of artificial intelligence on the digital news landscape.* Center for Strategic and International Studies. https://www.csis.org/analysis/navigating-risks-artificial-intelligence-digital-news-landscape

Christian, J. (2023, January 23). *CNET's AI journalist appears to have committed extensive plagiarism.* Futurism. https://futurism.com/cnet-ai-plagiarism

Cook, C. C., Garcia, E., Gyulnazaryan, H., Melano, J., Parusinski, J., & Sabadan, A. (2021). *The next wave of disruption: Emerging market media use of artificial intelligence and machine learning* (1st ed.). International Media Support (IMS).

De-Lima-Santos, M. F., & Ceron, W. (2021). Artificial intelligence in news media: Current perceptions and future outlook. *Journalism and Media, 3*(1), 13–26.

Demartini, G., Mizzaro, S., & Spina, D. (2020). Human-in-the-loop artificial intelligence for fighting online misinformation: Challenges and opportunities. *IEEE Data Engineering Bulletin, 43*, 65–74.

Dhiman, D. B. (2022, October 18). *Artificial intelligence and voice assistant in media studies: A critical review.* SSRN. https://ssrn.com/abstract=4250795

Duarte, N., & Llansó, E. (2017, November). *Mixed messages? The limits of automated social media content analysis.* Center for Democracy & Technology (CDT). https://cdt.org/wp-content/uploads/2017/11/Mixed-Messages-Paper.pdf

Eloundou, T., Manning, S., Mishkin, P., & Rock, D. (2023, August 22). *GPTs are GPTs: An early look at the labor market impact potential of large language models.* https://arxiv.org/pdf/2303.10130.pdf

Ferrara, E. (2023). Should ChatGPT be biased? Challenges and risks of bias in large language models. *ArXiv.* https://doi.org/10.48550/arXiv.2304.03738

Fieiras-Ceide, C., Vaz-Álvarez, M., & Túñez-López, M. (2022). Artificial intelligence strategies in European public broadcasters: Uses, forecasts and future challenges. *Profesional De La información, 31*(5).

Gondwe, G. (2023). *Exploring the multifaceted nature of generative AI in journalism studies: A typology of scholarly definitions.* SSRN. https://ssrn.com/abstract=4465446 or https://doi.org/10.2139/ssrn.4465446

Guzman, A. L., & Lewis, S. C. (2020). Artificial intelligence and communication: A human–machine communication research agenda. *New Media & Society, 22*(1), 70–86.

Hansen, M., Roca-Sales, M., Keegan, J., & King, G. (2017). *Artificial intelligence: Practice and implications for journalism.* Tow Center for Digital Journalism and the Brown Institute for Media Innovation. https://academiccommons.columbia.edu/doi/10.7916/D8X92PRD

Helberger, N. (2019). On the democratic role of news recommenders. *Digital Journalism, 7*(8), 993–1012.

Himeur, Y., Sohail, S. S., Bensaali, F., Amira, A., & Alazab, M. (2022). Latest trends of security and privacy in recommender systems: A comprehensive review and future perspectives. *Computers & Security, 118*, 1–28.

Ignatidou, S. (2019, December 19). *AI-driven personalization in digital media.* Chatham House. https://www.chathamhouse.org/sites/default/files/021219%20AI-driven%20Personalization%20in%20Digital%20Media%20final%20WEB.pdf

Ireton, C., & Posetti, J. (2018). *Journalism, fake news and disinformation: A handbook for journalism education and training.* UNESCO Series on Journalism Education.

Jaakkola, M. (2023). *Reporting on artificial intelligence: A handbook for journalism educators.* UNESCO Series on Journalism Education.

Jamil, S. (2020). Artificial intelligence and journalistic practice: The crossroads of obstacles and opportunities for the Pakistani journalists. *Journalism Practice, 15*(10), 1400–1422. https://doi.org/10.1080/17512786.2020.1788412

Kim, H. (2019). *AI in Journalism: Creating an ethical framework.* Syracuse University Honors Program Capstone Projects. https://surface.syr.edu/honors_capstone/1083

Kothari, A., & Cruikshank, S. A. (2022). Artificial intelligence and journalism: An Agenda for journalism research in Africa. *African Journalism Studies, 43*(1), 17–33.

Kunert, J. (2020). Automation in sports reporting: Strategies of data providers, software providers, and media outlets. *Media and Communication, 8*(3), 5–15.

Lambert, S. I., Madi, M., Sopka, S., Lenes, A., Stange, H., Buszello, C. P., & Stephan, A. (2023). An integrative review on the acceptance of artificial intelligence among healthcare professionals in hospitals. *NPJ Digital Medicine, 6*(1), 111.

Leonelli, S. (2020). Scientific research and big data. In *The Stanford encyclopedia of philosophy.* https://plato.stanford.edu/archives/sum2020/entries/science-big-data/

Linden, C. G. (2017). Algorithms for journalism: The future of news work. *The Journal of Media Innovations, 4*, 60–76.

Linden, T. C.-G., Tuulonen, H. E., Bäck, A., Diakopoulos, N., Granroth-Wilding, M., Haapanen, L., Leppänen, L. J., Melin, M., Moring, T. A., Munezero, M. D., Siren-Heikel, S. J., Södergård, C., & Toivonen, H. (2019) . News Automation : The rewards, risks and realities of 'machine journalism' . World Association of Newspapers and News Publishers, WAN-IFRA , Frankfurt. https://wan-ifra.org/insight/report-news-automation-the-rewards-risks-and-realities-of-machine-journalism/

Longoni, C., Fradkin, A., Cian, L., & Pennycook, G. (2022, July 21–22). News from generative artificial intelligence is believed less. In *2022 ACM conference on fairness, accountability, and transparency (FAccT '22). Seoul, Republic of Korea.* ACM.

Milosavljević, M., & Vobič, I. (2019). 'Our task is to demystify fears': Analysing newsroom management of automation in journalism. *Journalism, 39.*

Naoaín, A. S. (2022). Addressing the impact of artificial intelligence on journalism: The perception of experts, journalists and academics. *Comunicacion y Sociedad, 35*(3), 105–121.

Newman, N. (2022). *Journalism, media, and technology trends and predictions 2022.* Reuters Institute for the Study of Journalism. https://reutersinstitute.politics.ox.ac.uk/journalism-media-and-technology-trends-and-predictions-2022

Newman, N., Fletcher, R., Schulz, A., Andi, S., Robertson, C. T., & Nielsen, R. K. (2021). *Reuters Institute digital news report 2021.* Reuters Institute for the Study of Journalism.

Opdahl, A. L., Tessem, B., Dang-Nguyen, D. T., Motta, E., Setty, V., Throndsen, E., Tverberg, A., & Trattner, C. (2023). Trustworthy journalism through AI. *Data & Knowledge Engineering, 146.*

Pocino, P. V. (2021, December). *Algorithms in the newsrooms: Challenges and recommendations for artificial intelligence with the ethical values of journalism*. Catalan Press Council. https://fcic.periodistes.cat/wp-content/uploads/2022/03/venglishDIGITAL_ALGORITMES-A-LES-REDACCIONS_ENG-1.pdf

Santos, F. C. C. (2023). Artificial intelligence in automated detection of disinformation: A thematic analysis. *Journalism and Media, 4*(2), 679–687.

Schapals, A. K., & Porlezza, C. (2020). Assistance or resistance? Evaluating the intersection of automated journalism and journalistic role conceptions. *Media and Communication, 8*(3), 16–26.

Simon, C. (2022). As AI advances, will human workers disappear? *Forbes*. https://www.forbes.com/sites/forbestechcouncil/2022/06/28/as-ai-advances-will-human-workers-disappear/?sh=7c4d8b945e68

Strauß, S. (2021). Deep automation bias: How to tackle a wicked problem of AI? *Big Data Cognitive Computing, 5*(2), 2–14.

Stray, J. (2019). Making artificial intelligence work for investigative journalism. *Digital Journalism, 7*, 1076–1097.

Trifacta. (2020). Obstacles to AI and analytics adoption in the cloud. *Inside AI News*. https://insidebigdata.com/white-paper/obstacles-to-ai-analytics-adoption-in-the-cloud/

Tsalakanidou, F. (2022). AI technologies and applications in media: State of play, foresight, and research directions. *AI4Media*. https://www.ai4media.eu/wp-content/uploads/2022/03/AI4Media_D2.3_Roadmap_final.pdf

UK Government. (2017). *Industrial strategy: Building a Britain fit for the future*. https://assets.publishing.service.gov.uk/media/5b5afcc7ed915d0b7d353647/industrial-strategy-white-paper-print-ready-a4-version.pdf

Van Dalen, A. (2012). The algorithms behind the headlines: How machine-written news redefines the core skills of human journalists. *Journalism Practice, 6*(5–6), 648–658.

Warrington, J. (2023, July 14). Daily Mail prepares for legal battle with Google over AI copyright. *Daily Telegraph*. https://www.telegraph.co.uk/business/2023/07/14/daily-mail-prepares-legal-battle-google-ai-copyright/

Zhn, M. (2023, July 22). Netflix subscribers surged but its stock plummeted. Here's why. *ABC News*. https://abcnews.go.com/Business/netflix-subscribers-surged-stock-plummeted/story?id=101518301

Chapter 9
Artificial Intelligence and Media Communications in Russia

Sergey Davydov, Maria Krasheninnikova, Maria Lukina, and Andrey Zamkov

Abstract The introduction of artificial intelligence (AI) technologies in various Russian industries is currently considered a priority direction of development. The field of media and communications is one of the sectors in which AI is in great demand. The results of this study indicate significant differences in the attitudes toward AI held by expert subgroups. In general, representatives of the media and communications industry have positive attitudes toward the prospect of using AI for journalistic practices. News feed personalization and automatic text generation and analysis are considered the most promising areas for such use.

Keywords Russian journalism · Media and communications · Artificial intelligence

1 Introduction

Usually, Russia is not ranked among the leading countries in terms of the elaboration and implementation of AI technologies. The economic sanctions imposed by a number of countries have had a negative impact on the pace of technological development in Russia. Furthermore, the departure of major IT companies from the domestic market has reduced the availability of advanced software and hardware

S. Davydov (✉)
International Laboratory for Social Integration Research, Department of Sociology, Faculty of Social Sciences, HSE University, Moscow, Russia
e-mail: sdavydov@hse.ru

M. Krasheninnikova · M. Lukina
Department of New Media and Communication Theory, Faculty of Journalism, Lomonosov Moscow State University, Moscow, Russia

A. Zamkov
Problem Research Laboratory for the Comprehensive Study of Actual Problems of Journalism, Faculty of Journalism, Lomonosov Moscow State University, Moscow, Russia

F. Roumate, A. La Rosa (eds.), *Artificial Intelligence, Media and International Security*, Contributions to Security and Defence Studies,
https://doi.org/10.1007/978-3-031-95757-4_9

technologies. At the same time, Russian experts are convinced that the country has a significant potential for technological and social innovations, which are supported by public policies (The digital economy from theory to practice: How Russian businesses use artificial intelligence, 2019).

Indeed, Russia is currently implementing a national program called Digital Economy of the Russian Federation, which was approved in 2019 (The digital economy of the RF, 2023). This program identifies AI as one of nine nationally significant projects. The other projects include the regulation of the digital environment, personnel for the digital economy, information infrastructure, information security, digital technologies, digital public administration, development of manpower potential for the IT industry, and ensuring Internet access through the development of satellite communications. Also in 2019, President Vladimir Putin signed the National Strategy for the Development of Artificial Intelligence for the Period until 2030, which contains the following definition of AI: "A set of technological solutions that allows simulating human cognitive functions (including self-learning and searching for solutions without a predetermined algorithm) and obtaining results when performing specific tasks that are at least comparable to the results of human intellectual activity" (Decree of the President of the Russian Federation Dated October 10, 2019, no. 490 "On the development of artificial intelligence in the Russian Federation", 2019).

The public perception of digital technologies, including AI, has repeatedly become the subject of opinion polls in Russia. According to a study published by Russian Public Opinion Research Center WCIOM research company in December 2022, 87% of Russian adults have at least heard something about AI technologies, and 36% believe they are able to explain what AI is. More than half (55%) of the respondents said that they trusted this technology, though 32% said they did not; also, 13% found it difficult to express their opinions on the matter. Among the positive effects of the development of AI, the respondents most often mentioned "freeing up time from routine and monotonous work" (65%), "labor productivity increases" (65%), and "reduced time spent on routines" (65%). Among the possible negative effects, they mentioned that AI "collects data that can be stolen" (62%) and that it "can be used for personal gain" (61%), in addition to "the risk of making decisions for which no one will be held accountable" (58%) (Artificial intelligence: Threat or bright future?, 2022). According to the National Portal for the Field of Artificial Intelligence, as of the summer of 2023, Russian universities "[have] approved 85 master's programs and 21 bachelor's programs in AI" (These technologies have already become a part of our lives, 2023).

The current international context indicates that there is significant interest in the topic of AI implementation, which is confirmed by a large number of studies, scientific articles, industrial reviews, and forecasts published by a wide range of academic, industrial, and government experts, as well as auditing and research institutions. Since 2018, the topic of AI has been included in reviews and forecasts by large professional services companies, both domestic (Sber, Skoltech, and VK) and foreign (Gartner, Deloitte, McKinsey, Accenture, and PwC), as well as in reports published by Stanford University (The AI index report. Measuring trends in artificial intelligence, 2022) and the Reuters Institute for the Study of Journalism (RISJ) (Digital News Report, 2022).

A report by Stanford University examined the number of patents for AI technologies, which is also a sign of technology development. In 2010, the number totaled 2560; in 2021, it increased more than 55 times, reaching 141,241 units (The AI index report. Measuring trends in artificial intelligence, 2022).

A study by the University of Oxford's RISJ, which investigates the impact of technology on journalism and the media and communications sector, found that AI is the next-generation technology. According to this report, in a few years, AI technologies will change the work of the media and media communicators, including journalists, in connection with 5G wireless networks, augmented reality, and smart devices. In this list, experts assigned the most important role to AI.

The RISJ study includes the following successful cases of AI use in media companies:

- The BBC used an AI chatbot to answer questions about COVID-19 based on its trusted sources and official information.
- The Peruvian news agency Ojo Public created a tool to identify potential corruption schemes in public procurement contracts.
- The *South China Morning Post* uses AI to identify new audiences that are similar to its current one and better target new subscribers.
- The news agency Reuters uses speech-to-text technology to transcribe historical videos dating back to 1896, which helps in searching for keywords in different languages.
- The Canadian newspaper *The Globe and Mail* has delegated many editorial functions to the Sophie program, which is based on AI.
- Eight major publications in a joint AIJO (abbreviation for AI + JOurnalism) project are using AI technologies to monitor gender and racial bias.

According to analysts at the RISJ, the introduction of AI into media practices could exacerbate the gap between large media companies and media structures that do not have the funds to invest in long-term research on AI and pay data specialists. Though it may be possible to develop off-the-shelf AI solutions in the future, the cost of doing so is likely to be high. Ultimately, the majority of respondents (65%) in the RISJ report believed that large publishers will benefit the most from AI adoption.

The data analytics company Gartner uses a technological maturity model to determine the trajectories of AI development in different countries. According to its terminology, the state of the Russian AI market is transitioning between the end of the hype cycle and a plateau of productive growth. Furthermore, the innovative behaviors of the Russian media sector can be characterized in terms of E. Rogers's innovation diffusion model, including the main contingent of players in the transitional group of ideal types that range from the "early followers" to the "late majority" (Rogers, 2003).

A report published by Stanford University in March 2022 contains the Global Artificial Intelligence Development Index, which is based on a multifactor quantitative analysis of open data from 2017 to 2021. The index's metrics count the following elements: articles on AI in scientific journals, citations of publications on AI, conference proceedings on AI, citations of conference proceedings on AI, AI databases and their citations, and AI patents. Also assessed are the investment in AI technologies, the opening of new AI-related companies, the hiring index for AI specialists, and the penetration of AI skills in businesses. Based on these measures, the Global Artificial Intelligence Development Index places the Russian Federation in the 23rd position out of 29 measured countries (Global AI vibrancy tool. Who's leading the global AI race?, 2022).

A study jointly conducted by the Russian Association for Electronic Communications (RAEC), HSE University, and Microsoft showed that the Russian IT expert community ranks Russia among the countries with a high potential for the implementation of AI. The main directions of AI development in the federation coincide with global trends. This development refers to "agents (automated support services for banks, medical and telecommunications institutions, chatbots for customer services); algorithms that optimize the decision-making process … ; automation of production processes in general companies, [and] 'smart' devices (pattern recognition systems, cleaning robots)" (The digital economy from theory to practice: How Russian businesses use artificial intelligence, 2019: 6–7). According to these experts, the leaders in the implementation and use of AI in the Russian market are industrial enterprises, banks, telecommunications companies, and retail.

The field of media and communications falls within the leading areas for AI implementation. The budgets are more modest in this sector, and the key activity is related to the processing of information. In this article, we consider the results of a study implemented by the RAEC, HSE University, and the Faculty of Journalism at Lomonosov Moscow State University in 2022. Next, we will briefly describe the study's methodology, after which we will present the findings and discuss them.

2 Methods

When developing the research program for the current survey, we relied on the definition of AI from the national strategy cited above as well as on the expert definition found in the framework of the 2019 survey by the RAEC, HSE University, and Microsoft, which states the following: "[AI] is a set of technologies for processing various types of data and information; in particular, [AI is] capable of interpreting such data, extracting knowledge and using it to achieve certain goals" (The digital economy from theory to practice: How Russian businesses use artificial intelligence, 2019: 16).

The AI technologies used in media and communications solve specific applied cognitive tasks by replacing the routine processes of media practice and by intellectually supporting creative processes. In essence, we are talking about computing systems designed to solve the problem of processing symbolic and numerical information (texts, statistics, graphics, visual data, etc.), which imitate the principles of logical reasoning, speech activity, the functioning of neural networks, and nonverbal forms of human behavior.

Our scope was limited to that segment of the media system that is associated with the mass media, journalism, and media communications. Segments such as computer games, films, music, books, social networks, and digital ecosystems were not considered.

We used multivariate analysis to examine data obtained during desk research and the qualitative and quantitative stages of our project; we also used surveys conducted since 2017, including the longitudinal observation of the introduction of AI technologies into the activities of both domestic and foreign media companies and into the professional practices of journalists and media communicators.

The quantitative part of the project consisted of an online questionnaire aimed at journalists and media communicators. The questionnaire was set up on the EnjoySurvey platform by the research company OMI Russia. A quota sample was used; soft quotas were set by gender, age group, region, and specialization of the employing company. Quotas were necessary to ensure the variability of the sampled population.

A mixed-methods approach to the recruitment of respondents was used. This included the following steps:

- Inviting representatives of the target audience to fill out the questionnaire (based on contacts from public sources)
- Publishing a link to the questionnaire on the website of a partner organization (the Union of Journalists of Russia)
- Inviting participants through the mailing list of a partner nonprofit organization (New Russian Media)

Data was gathered from May 23 to October 29, 2022. The number of collected questionnaires was 176.

The qualitative part of the study included the following steps:

- One focus group interview with five media experts (conducted on April 14, 2021, at the RAEC's office).
- Ten individual focused interviews conducted from March 2021 to October 2022 with experts from the media and academia, as well as with the developers of the implemented systems. These respondents represent three target groups of experts: members of the academic community studying AI, media managers using AI technologies in newsrooms, and developers who create AI products for customers in the media and communications industry.

The average duration of the interviews was 50 min. The interviews were conducted either face-to-face or online via Zoom.

3 Desk and Qualitative Research: Various Discourses of AI

During the preliminary stage of the study and a number of pilot projects, it became clear that AI technologies are actively being used by large companies in the media and communications sector, especially in the field of IT. This is true of both foreign businesses (Google, Amazon, Microsoft, etc.) and Russian ones (Yandex, VK, Sber, etc.).

From a global perspective, the pioneers of the introduction of algorithmic solutions into various editorial operations and processes were the Associated Press, the *New York Times*, and the BBC. In Russia, in addition to the abovementioned IT giants, Interfax, RIA Novosti, RBC, and Sports.ru started using AI in media, journalism, and communications early on. Other media companies also had some experiences of doing so, but they were not always successful.

AI technologies have long been used in editorial practices; they have also partially replaced the functions of many employees of media enterprises, including journalists. The use of AI technologies in the media sector can be categorized based on the different types of data that are processed, which include natural language (written and oral speech), audio information, numerical data, images, and graphic information.

Our interviews with Russian academic experts showed a fairly high level of consistency in their assessments of the current state of research and development in the field of AI, its technical potential, and the risks associated with its application in the social and humanitarian spheres, including the media. At the same time, the wide range of opinions spanning academic and public discourses is noteworthy. Almost all the interviewed experts were unanimous in their critical assessments of the hype and hoaxes linked to AI, which served, in their opinion, to push new technologies on the market.

Experts from different academic schools were very critical of the common understanding of AI. In their opinion, a computer system can be considered "intelligent" only when it actually implements a minimal set of human abilities and when it actually imitates the chains of actions of human intelligence. The computing architecture of this process includes a fact base, a knowledge base, and a reasoning problem solver. This type of AI is best suited to support partnerships with humans.

Our interviews with representatives of IT companies showed a shortage of these experts, which is probably caused by insufficient market maturity. The lack of qualified specialists with engineering degrees has been noted as a factor that hinders the introduction of AI in the media industry. The penetration of AI into business and the media is also hampered by the lack of collaboration between IT specialists, companies, and media outlets, as well as by the inability of the customer to assign tasks to the developer. The experts from this subgroup considered automatic information retrieval, search and classification of information feeds, automatic generation of content adapted to the interests of different target audiences, and recommendation systems as typical tasks. Furthermore, these experts singled out Russia as the leader in the technological modernization of the media, alongside the United States and China.

The experts from the IT companies that develop domestic AI solutions were usually focused on the interests of their customers and media holdings. They characterized the AI technologies used in their companies as something that "makes the lives of editors and users easier—a tool for improving the news's life cycle."

According to the interviewees, the most advanced foreign media companies successfully implementing AI solutions are the Associated Press, the *New York Times*, and the *Financial Times*. In Russia, they listed RBC, Yandex, Interfax, and VK Group/Mail.Ru. The media sector as a whole was identified as the undisputed future leader in the use of AI innovations due to its constantly growing volume of content. The competitive potential of Russia in the field of media robotization was assessed optimistically by the developer community.

The mass implementation of quantum computing was noted as one of the global technological trends that can radically change the landscape of both AI and its media applications. According to the experts, in the near future, AI will be trained to understand what the user wants to read or watch, that is, it will learn to recognize information preferences.

The opinions of foreign technology companies were represented by Microsoft, which has a special technology program that supports the media and fair journalism in general. According to an expert from this corporation, the media industry has seen a significant increase in opportunities driven by the penetration of technology. This is testified by the formation of large amounts of data and analytical tools, which places increased demands on the skills necessary to work with them. In this context, work is greatly simplified, and routine tasks are handed over to technology; hence, journalists have more space to solve creative problems.

The developers identified the ethics of using AI technologies in journalism and the media and communications sector as a special set of problems, especially regarding content manipulation and disinformation. People's attitudes toward abuse and having basic education were identified as important solutions to these problems.

The focus group, as well as the individual in-depth interviews with representatives of the media industry, made it possible to identify the main editorial processes in which AI technologies are currently being used. The main one is the selection of a topic based on the interests of the potential audience. Editorial staff use special algorithms to analyze audience indicators and user preferences in order to determine more accurately the list of priority topics. Searching and verifying information—fundamental journalistic processes—are also being partially entrusted to specialized algorithms.

Perhaps the most controversial and pressing topic discussed in the industry is the generation of news texts and headlines. The survey respondents basically agreed that at the current stage of development of technology and society, the use of algorithms to create such texts can only be limited by quality, topic, complexity, and journalistic sources.

Furthermore, the experts believed that it is necessary to free journalists and editors from working on routine template texts, as they should focus on more creative and nonstandard tasks. AI technologies are already helping journalists in their daily editorial practices by transcribing interviews, translating texts, creating captions, selecting illustrations, and working with big data.

The experts drew attention to the fact that there are no perfect programs yet, for example, for transcribing the speech of different speakers. In this case, a specialist has to manually check and correct the work of "smart assistants." Another important function is tagging (the placement of links to publications related to a topic), which in many editorial offices is now automatically performed by an algorithm.

AI also helps editors work on the texts written by journalists by checking spelling, punctuation, style requirements, and background selection. Today, some editorial offices use software programs to rewrite and copyright texts, that is, to work on secondary media products.

An important task for a journalist and his algorithm assistant is fact-checking. The verification of information cannot be completely automated yet since a very large number of potential sources still require human interaction and communication.

However, certain simple operations, such as checking proper names or geographical names, can be entrusted to an algorithm. Some media outlets also use smart editorial systems that allow them to automatically supplement publications with all sorts of "attachments" in the form of references, supplementary information, videos, and graphics.

The media experts named the tracking of user comments on editorial websites as one of the priority tasks for AI. The algorithm, which groups comments into categories ("100% approved," "100% rejected," and "pending approval"), allows the human moderator to work only on the "pending approval" group, which saves editors money on hiring staff to track user activity.

Another significant common topic that the industry experts spoke about was the distribution of content thanks to the use of AI systems, including its personalization based on audience interests analyzed by algorithms. In this case, the main goal is to expand audience coverage by automating the distribution of journalistic products.

While praising the effectiveness of AI systems in this distribution, the experts also talked about the dangerous side of this process—the creation of an "information bubble" for the consumer. This can be "burst" by strong editorial recommendations of socially significant content.

When discussing content distribution, the experts touched upon the problem of studying the sociodemographic characteristics of their audiences; they compared this process in the media and in social networks, where users willingly provide significant amounts of personal data when registering. Media outlets have to separately collect and analyze this information, including with the help of AI systems, in order to correctly imagine the typical consumers of their content.

The media managers who participated in both the focus group and the individual interviews mentioned the topic of the financial viability of purchasing and supporting AI systems for editorial offices. Today, expensive AI products are available only to major players in the Russian media field. Another problem is finding specialists on the market who are ready to implement and develop these systems in the media products as well as use them in editorial offices.

4 Quantitative Research: The Attitudes of Russian Journalists and Media Professionals Toward AI

Let us turn to the results of the quantitative survey, starting with the general characteristics of the sample.

The respondents lived in all eight federal districts of Russia, with the majority (69.3%) representing cities with a population of over one million. Those living in small and medium-sized settlements accounted for 30.7% of the sample. The approximate gender ratios were 3/5 for women and 2/5 for men. The age of the respondents ranged from 19 to 70 years, the average being 36 years. The distribution by age group was as follows: 18–24 years, 18.2%; 25–34 years, 36.9%; 35–44 years, 21.6%; 45–55 years, 17.0%; and older than 55 years, 6.2%. The vast majority of respondents (87.0%) were studying for or possessed higher education degrees. Furthermore, 57.4% had received specialized education related to journalism, media communications, advertising, and public relations, while 42.6% had been educated in nonspecialist subjects.

We will now examine the professional activities of the survey respondents. When answering the question concerning the area of specialization of their organization/company, the following were most often mentioned: Internet media (35.2%), print press (19.9%), television (17.6%), and radio (9.7%). Also, 55.1% of the respondents worked in state-owned companies, while 44.9% were employed by private firms. The share of qualified specialists in the sample was 56.3%. The share of middle and senior managers was 39.3%. The respondents' work experiences in the media and communications sector ranged from 1 to 30 years, with an average of 13 years. The distribution of these experiences was as follows: 1–2 years, 18.2%; 3–5 years, 13.6%; 6–10 years, 19.9%; 11–20 years, 27.3%; and 21 years or more, 21.0%.

In general, the respondents demonstrated an optimistic attitude toward the implementation of AI technologies in Russia. As Table 9.1 shows, 86.9% of the sample thought that AI is an opportunity rather than a threat for the country; 13.1% held the opposite view. Regarding the media and communications sector, the level of optimism was even higher—91.5% versus 8.5%. However, it is notable that when assessing the prospects of AI for the country as a whole, the respondents more often

Table 9.1 AI: opportunity or threat?

	For Russia, %	For the Russian media and communications sector, %
Definitely an opportunity	50.0	42.6
Possibly an opportunity	36.9	48.9
Possibly a threat	9.7	7.4
Definitely a threat	3.4	1.1

preferred the decisive answer "definitely an opportunity" (50.0%) to the more nuanced one "possibly an opportunity" (36.9%). In contrast, when it came to the sector, a cautious assessment was more popular (48.9% versus 42.6%). The first result can be attributed to a generally positive attitude toward AI. The second may reflect the fact that the respondents were more aware of the possible problems of introducing this technology into their industry; hence, they were more sensitive to them.

The second pair of questions addressed the development of AI technologies, and it revealed a consensus in the industry (see Table 9.2). The majority of respondents believed that the development of AI was lagging behind that of other nations both in Russia as a whole (85.3%) and in the Russian media and communications sector (86.9%). In relation to the country as a whole, most respondents felt that the gap with the leading economies of the world was insignificant (56.3%) rather than significant (29.0%). However, in relation to the media and communications industry, the two assessments were almost equal (44.9% and 42.0%, respectively). This means that the lag was felt more acutely in one's area of professional activity.

Two questions were asked to explore the respondents' opinions regarding the leaders of AI implementation in the field of media and communications. The first question concerned the international context, while the second one looked at the Russian one. For each question, the respondent could indicate up to three organizations or companies.

When interpreting the results (Table 9.3), it is important to consider that the respondents answered based on their ideas of the boundaries of the industry. When asked about the world leaders in AI implementation, 83.5% of respondents gave meaningful answers. A total of 69 companies were named. At the top of the list by a wide margin was Google (including its corporate projects), which was mentioned in 38.1% of the questionnaires. Yandex (with corporate projects; 14.8%) and Apple (11.9%) came in second and third. It is noteworthy that the top ten positions include very different actors that have both direct and indirect relationships with the media communications sector. There are developers of software services (Google, Yandex, and Microsoft), IT equipment manufacturers (Apple), social media businesses (Meta and Facebook), and classic media companies (e.g., the *New York Times*, Bloomberg, the BBC, and *The Times*).

Table 9.2 Current level of AI development

	In Russia, %	In the Russian media and communications sector, %
AI development is significantly ahead compared to the world's leading economies	5.1	4.5
AI development is slightly ahead compared to the world's leading economies	9.7	8.5
AI development slightly lags behind compared to the world's leading economies	56.3	44.9
AI development significantly lags behind compared to the world's leading economies	29.0	42.0

Table 9.3 Media communications organizations/companies that lead in the implementation of AI technologies

In the world			In Russia		
No.	Organization/company	%	No.	Organization/company	%
1	Google (and projects)	38.1	1	Yandex (and projects)	54.5
2	Yandex (and projects)	14.8	2	VK/Mail.ru	30.1
3	Apple	11.9	3	Sber/Sberbank	22.7
4	*The New York Times*	10.8	4	RBC	9.7
5	Bloomberg	10.8	5	RIA Novosti/MIA Russia Today	5.7
6	Microsoft	10.2	6	TASS	5.1
7	Meta	10.2	7	Rambler	4.0
8	Facebook	8.5	8	MTS	3.4
9	BBC	5.1	9	Telegram	2.8
10	*The Times*	4.5	10	Sports.ru	2.8

Concerning the Russian context, the meaningful response rate was slightly lower (79.5%), and the list of Russian organizations/companies was somewhat shorter (58). The top three positions were taken by Yandex (with corporate projects; 54.5%), VK/Mail.ru (30.1%), and Sber (22.7%). The classic media businesses in the top ten list were RBC, MIA Rossiya Segodnya, Rambler, TASS, and Sports.ru. The other five places included large IT firms and even a banking ecosystem (Sber) and a telecommunications operator (MTS).

The results indicated that there was considerable experience of using AI in the field of media communications. Moreover, while some technologies were intended for individual use, others were used at the corporate level, and only a small group of specialists worked with them (see Table 9.4).

Among the technologies found in the first group, voice assistants (41.5%), automatic text translators (27.3%), and transcriptionists of audio recordings (26.7%) were mentioned most often. In the second group, the top three technologies dealt with the personalization of news feeds (27.3%), recommendation services (23.9%), and the transcription of audio recordings (18.8%).

The top three AI technologies that will develop most rapidly in the media and communications sector over the next 5 years are the personalization of news feeds (41.5%), automatic text creation (39.2%), and text analytics (31.8%). Among the proposed options, the respondents assessed the prospects for image recognition technologies in the least favorable way (11.9%).

On average, each respondent listed 2.0 technologies that were used in their company/organization/editorial office as well as 2.2 technologies of which they had user experience. Furthermore, the respondents mentioned an average of 2.8 technologies that will be actively developed in the next 5 years. Among the main barriers/obstacles to the implementation of AI in the field of media communications, the industry representatives most often mentioned a lack of funds (51.1%) and employees' insufficient qualifications and lack of experience (42.0%). The least significant problem was the lack of data (13.6%).

Table 9.4 Uses and perspectives of AI technologies

No.	Technology	The respondent has user experience, %	Used in organization, company, editorial, %	Will develop most rapidly in media communications over the next 5 years, %
1	Automatic text generation	8.0	10.2	39.2
2	Automatic text translation	27.3	17.6	22.2
3	Face recognition in images	20.5	12.5	19.9
4	Image recognition	24.4	17.6	11.9
5	News feed personalization	19.1	27.3	41.5
6	Predictive analytics	4.5	9.1	19.3
7	Recommendation services	15.9	23.9	29.0
8	Sentiment analysis of speech and text	3.4	4.0	13.1
9	Text analytics	11.9	18.2	31.8
10	Text transcription of audio recordings	26.7	18.8	27.3
11	Voice assistants	41.5	17.6	19.3
12	Other	19.3	20.5	2.3

5 Discussion and Conclusions

In the sample, the general opinion was that the use of AI technologies greatly simplifies the job of media workers; routine tasks can be handed over to algorithms, and journalists have more time to solve creative problems. This opinion can be considered a result of the main drivers behind the development of AI technologies in the editorial offices of Russian media. The following drivers explain the positive trends in the transformation of editorial processes that are observed at present.

- Automatic conversion of text to multimedia formats. Editors are experimenting with tools that turn news texts into visual stories. Typically, this function is available for mobile phones (e.g., extracting quotes and using animations).
- Improving automatic translation thanks to neural models. More and more news organizations are taking advantage of these tools, which offer translations of texts as well as audio and video materials into 100 languages at minimal cost. However, supporting AI for the languages spoken in small nations remains an unresolved problem due to the low commercial attractiveness of doing so.
- Simplification and replacement of the routine operations of editorial systems and media workers. These operations include the generation of short newsreels; categorization by topic and geolocation; "body kits" and the selection of backgrounds; the analysis of user comments; the creation of niche news

feeds; recommendation services for content distribution, including its personalization; speech recognition for transcripts, translations, and captions; pattern recognition and computer vision for selecting illustrations; and verification and fact-checking.

However, along with optimistic forecasts of the use of AI in editorial processes, one should also consider the risks associated, among other things, with the uncontrolled spread of this technology. The challenges are becoming increasingly clear.

- Since 2021, even in professional media, more and more deepfake videos have been published, though most of these try to entertain rather than mislead. In the United Kingdom, Channel 4 published a fake video of the Queen conveying an "alternative" Christmas message. In it, the Queen was wearing a brooch in the shape of the COVID-19 virus, and she made jokes about her family members. The AI company Synthesis released a "fake Santa" video in which the legendary figure delivered personalized greetings. Social media, especially YouTube and TikTok, are full of fake videos and audio files created by AI. Regarding Russian examples, in 2021, an advertisement for the mobile operator Megafon was released that used a digital image of the American actor Bruce Willis (Sidorova, 2022).
- One of the main challenges can be considered the abuse of AI technology and the manipulation of content. For example, in the context of journalism and media communications, AI can be used to produce deliberate disinformation based on false data.
- The lack of an established market for IT companies and software developers specializing in AI solutions for the media leads to the development of software products in editorial offices, which has serious financial costs.
- Analysts predict that the use of AI technologies could widen the gap between large media businesses and smaller companies that do not have the money to invest in innovation, including the provision of powerful hardware support.
- The smart approach to regulation proposed by experts is hampered by a number of factors: users' underdeveloped professional skills, lack of user trust in radical innovations due to the opacity of the innovations themselves, fragmentation of regulators, and the lack of a universal language for describing the penetration of new technology, including in the media and communications sector.
- A serious challenge is the development of ethical rules for the use of AI in the media and journalism, as well as their mandatory codification. This problem will be overcome by implementing transparency in the work of editorial offices, preserving the audience's right to information about interactions with AI, establishing a ban on transferring power to AI in matters of moral choice when preparing media content, assuring joint responsibility of the editors and software developers for the consequences of the operation of AI systems, and identifying a range of topics for which the use of AI is ethically unacceptable.

According to the results of this study, the main issue with AI can be seen as the development of ethical rules for the use of new technologies in media and journalism and their mandatory codification. Based on a joint study by the RAEC and Microsoft, which was released in 2021, the use of AI carries tangible risks associated with discrimination, bias, threats to privacy, and possible errors. There are several levels at which these risks can arise, including the development and training of the algorithm, the phase of providing it with data, and implementation (Approaches to developing ethical solutions in the field of artificial intelligence, 2021).

To begin work on understanding the ethical aspects of the use of AI, its regulation, and the formation of responsibility, the largest Russian IT players (Yandex, Sber, Rostelecom, VK, and MTS) signed the national code of ethics proposed by the Alliance for AI in collaboration with the Analytical Center for the Government of the Russian Federation (Code of ethics for artificial intelligence, 2021). The main emphasis was placed on anthropocentricity, precaution, controllability, responsibility, morality, and nondiscrimination. It is worth noting that there are already several dozen ethical codes in the world dedicated to the interactions between AI and humans. Some of these codes have been developed by government organizations, while others belong to commercial entities.

Almost all currently known ethical codes on the use of AI are focused either on IT companies or on organizations with a high degree of digitalization of their work processes. However, as socially responsible and significant public-sphere actors, journalism and the media require a special approach to the regulation of AI use. All the experts and the authors of this study propose the following ethical principles for the implementation of AI technologies in communications, the media, and editorial practices:

- Transparency in the use of AI technologies and the right of the audience to be informed about interactions with AI
- Responsibility of media communicators, editors, journalists, and software developers for the consequences of the use of AI systems
- A ban on transferring power to AI in matters of moral choice when preparing content
- Identifying a range of topics for which the use of AI is ethically unacceptable

References

Approaches to developing ethical solutions in the field of artificial intelligence. (2021). RAEC. Retrieved September 19, 2023, from https://raec.ru/upload/files/ethical-ai.pdf (in Russian).

Artificial intelligence: Threat or bright future? (2022, December 28). WCIOM. Retrieved September 19, 2023, from https://wciom.ru/analytical-reviews/analiticheskii-obzor/iskusstvennyi-intellekt-ugroza-ili-svetloe-budushchee (in Russian).

Code of ethics for artificial intelligence. (2021). Alliance for Artificial Intelligence. Retrieved September 19, 2023, from https://ethics.a-ai.ru/assets/ethics_files/2023/05/12/%D0%9A%D0%BE%D0%B4%D0%B5%D0%BA%D1%81_%D1%8D%D1%82%D0%B8%D0%BA%D0%B8_20_10_1.pdf (in Russian).

Decree of the President of the Russian Federation Dated October 10, 2019, no. 490 "On the development of artificial intelligence in the Russian Federation". (2019). Retrieved September 19, 2023, from http://www.kremlin.ru/acts/bank/44731 (in Russian).

Digital News Report. (2022). Reuters Institute for the Study of Journalism. Oxford University. Retrieved September 19, 2023, from https://reutersinstitute.politics.ox.ac.uk/digital-news-report/2022.

Global AI vibrancy tool. Who's leading the global AI race? (2022). Stanford University. Retrieved September 19, 2023, from https://aiindex.stanford.edu/vibrancy/ (in Russian).

Rogers, E. M. (2003). *Diffusion of innovations* (5th ed.). Free Press.

Sidorova, D. (2022, October 27). Why celebrity deepfakes are increasingly appearing in advertising. rb.ru. Retrieved September 19, 2023, from https://rb.ru/story/deepfakes-in-ads/ (in Russian).

The AI index report. Measuring trends in artificial intelligence. (2022). Stanford University. Retrieved September 19, 2023, from https://aiindex.stanford.edu/ai-index-report-2022/.

The digital economy from theory to practice: How Russian businesses use artificial intelligence. (2019). RAEC. Retrieved September 19, 2023, from https://raec.ru/upload/files/190715-ii.pdf (in Russian).

The digital economy of the RF. (2023). Ministry of Digital Development, Communications, and Mass Media of the Russian Federation. Retrieved September 19, 2023, from https://digital.gov.ru/ru/activity/directions/858 (in Russian).

These technologies have already become a part of our lives. Artificial intelligence is changing the Russian economy. How does it work? (2023, May 14). Lenta.ru. Retrieved September 19, 2023, from https://lenta.ru/articles/2023/06/14/airecr/ (in Russian).

The manufacturer's authorised representative in the EU is Springer Nature Customer Service Centre GmbH, Europaplatz 3, 69115 Heidelberg, Germany. If you have any concerns regarding our products, please contact ProductSafety@springernature.com

Printed and bound by CPI Group (UK) Ltd, Croydon, CR0 4YY
30/09/2026
02225513-0011